Preferences and Decisions
under Incomplete Knowledge

Studies in Fuzziness and Soft Computing

Editor-in-chief

Prof. Janusz Kacprzyk
Systems Research Institute
Polish Academy of Sciences
ul. Newelska 6
01-447 Warsaw, Poland
E-mail: kacprzyk@ibspan.waw.pl
http://www.springer.de/cgi-bin/search_book.pl?series=2941

Vol. 3. A. Geyer-Schulz
*Fuzzy Rule-Based Expert Systems and Genetic
Machine Learning, 2nd ed. 1996*
ISBN 3-7908-0964-0

Vol. 4. T. Onisawa and J. Kacprzyk (Eds.)
*Reliability and Safety Analyses under
Fuzziness, 1995*
ISBN 3-7908-0837-7

Vol. 5. P. Bosc and J. Kacprzyk (Eds.)
Fuzziness in Database Management Systems, 1995
ISBN 3-7908-0858-X

Vol. 6. E. S. Lee and Q. Zhu
Fuzzy and Evidence Reasoning, 1995
ISBN 3-7908-0880-6

Vol. 7. B. A. Juliano and W. Bandler
Tracing Chains-of-Thought, 1996
ISBN 3-7908-0922-5

Vol. 8. F. Herrera and J. L. Verdegay (Eds.)
Genetic Algorithms and Soft Computing, 1996
ISBN 3-7908-0956-X

Vol. 9. M. Sato et al.
Fuzzy Clustering Models and Applications, 1997
ISBN 3-7908-1026-6

Vol. 10. L. C. Jain (Ed.)
*Soft Computing Techniques in Knowledge-based
Intelligent Engineering Systems, 1997*
ISBN 3-7908-1035-5

Vol. 11. W. Mielczarski (Ed.)
Fuzzy Logic Techniques in Power Systems, 1998
ISBN 3-7908-1044-4

Vol. 12. B. Bouchon-Meunier (Ed.)
*Aggregation and Fusion of Imperfect
Information, 1998*
ISBN 3-7908-1048-7

Vol. 13. E. Orłowska (Ed.)
Incomplete Information: Rough Set Analysis, 1998
ISBN 3-7908-1049-5

Vol. 14. E. Hisdal
*Logical Structures for Representation
of Knowledge and Uncertainty, 1998*
ISBN 3-7908-1056-8

Vol. 15. G. J. Klir and M. J. Wierman
Uncertainty-Based Information, 2nd ed., 1999
ISBN 3-7908-1242-0

Vol. 16. D. Driankov and R. Palm (Eds.)
Advances in Fuzzy Control, 1998
ISBN 3-7908-1090-8

Vol. 17. L. Reznik, V. Dimitrov and
J. Kacprzyk (Eds.)
Fuzzy Systems Design, 1998
ISBN 3-7908-1118-1

Vol. 18. L. Polkowski and A. Skowron (Eds.)
Rough Sets in Knowledge Discovery 1, 1998
ISBN 3-7908-1119-X

Vol. 19. L. Polkowski and A. Skowron (Eds.)
Rough Sets in Knowledge Discovery 2, 1998
ISBN 3-7908-1120-3

Vol. 20. J. N. Mordeson and P. S. Nair
Fuzzy Mathematics, 1998
ISBN 3-7908-1121-1

Vol. 21. L. C. Jain and T. Fukuda (Eds.)
*Soft Computing for Intelligent Robotic Systems,
1998*
ISBN 3-7908-1147-5

Vol. 22. J. Cardoso and H. Camargo (Eds.)
Fuzziness in Petri Nets, 1999
ISBN 3-7908-1158-0

Vol. 23. P. S. Szczepaniak (Ed.)
Computational Intelligence and Applications, 1999
ISBN 3-7908-1161-0

Vol. 24. E. Orłowska (Ed.)
Logic at Work, 1999
ISBN 3-7908-1164-5

continued on page 209

János Fodor
Bernard De Baets
Patrice Perny (Editors)

Preferences and Decisions under Incomplete Knowledge

With 13 Figures
and 15 Tables

Physica-Verlag

A Springer-Verlag Company

003
P923

Prof. Dr. János Fodor
Szent István University
Department of Biomathematics and Informatics
Faculty of Veterinary Science
István u. 2
1078 Budapest
Hungary
Email: jfodor@univet.hu

Prof. Dr. Bernard De Baets
University of Gent
Department of Applied Mathematics,
Biometrics and Process Control
Coupure Links 653
9000 Gent
Belgium
Email: Bernard.DeBaets@rug.ac.be

Prof. Dr. Patrice Perny
LIP 6 (Paris 6 University)
Case 169
4 Place Jussieu
75252 Paris Cedex 05
France
Email: Patrice.Perny@lip6.fr

ISSN 1434-9922
ISBN 3-7908-1303-6 Physica-Verlag Heidelberg New York

Cataloging-in-Publication Data applied for
Die Deutsche Bibliothek – CIP-Einheitsaufnahme
Fodor, János; De Baets, Bernard; Perny, Patrice: Preferences and decisions under incomplete knowledge: with 15 tables / János Fodor; Bernard De Baets; Patrice Perny (eds.). – Heidelberg; New York: Physica-Verl., 2000
  (Studies in fuzziness and soft computing; Vol. 51)
  ISBN 3-7908-1303-6

Physica-Verlag is a company in the BertelsmannSpringer publishing group.
© Physica-Verlag Heidelberg 2000
Printed in Germany

The use of general descriptive names, registered names, trademarks, etc. in this publication does not imply, even in the absence of a specific statement, that such names are exempt from the relevant protective laws and regulations and therefore free for general use.

Hardcover Design: Erich Kirchner, Heidelberg

SPIN 10767311   88/2202-5 4 3 2 1 0 – Printed on acid-free paper

This volume is dedicated to Marc Roubens on the occasion of his sixtieth anniversary.

Our distinguished colleague Marc Roubens is 60 this year. He has set high standards in research and teaching, and many colleagues have benefited from his deep and broad knowledge and have been infected by his enthusiastic lecturing style.

His fundamental contributions cover a wide range of fields of applied mathematics, comprising the areas of preference modelling, clustering and control in fuzzy set theory, multicriteria decision aid in operations research, and data analysis in statistics.

Marc Roubens' personal qualities of commitment, integrity, leadership and initiate leave lasting impression on his colleagues, students and friends. This volume is a token of their appreciation and friendship.

Preface

"Knowledge is power", is a phrase taken for granted by many people. In our world, however, we should be aware of several limitations complicating the exploitation of the available information. Different forms of incompleteness (such as uncertainty, imprecision, vagueness, partial truth and the like) pervade our knowledge.

The aim of this volume is to show that incomplete knowledge can indeed be exploited, thereby leading to a more complete power.

Philippe Vincke's paper extends the well-known preference structures consisting of three binary relations: strict preference, indifference and incomparability. Allowing also weak preference, he characterizes those structures which can be represented by numerical functions and thresholds. The resulting preference structures yield a general framework for already known families like complete or partial pseudo-orders, semiorders and interval orders.

Philippe Fortemps and Jacques Teghem propose the Multi-Objective Fuzzy Area Compensation method for solving multi-objective linear programming problems involving imprecision. Fuzzy numbers are understood as imprecise probability distributions for modelling the imprecision present in the available information. The main features of their approach are described and a comparison with well-known methods is presented.

Vincenzo Cutello and Javier Montero introduce a generalization of classical utility theory using rational fuzzy preference relations for modelling basic preferences. In their approach rationality itself is a fuzzy concept. The main contribution consists of a boosting procedure answering a linearization of the alternatives.

Didier Dubois, Endre Pap and Henri Prade present an important extension of probabilistic mixtures, which play a key role in classical utility theory, to the case of decision under non-probabilistic uncertainty. After introducing and investigating pseudo-additive measures and the counterpart of probabilistic independence of events, hybrid mixtures are defined in an axiomatic way. The obtained family is hybrid indeed: it combines probabilistic and possibilistic mixtures by using a threshold. Based on such mixtures, optimistic and pessimistic hybrid utility functions are also studied.

Javier Montero, Ana del Amo and Elisenda Molina study additive recursive rules of aggregation. Recursiveness, from a theoretical point of view, generalizes the associativity property assuring consistency of the aggregation.

At the same time, recursiveness makes it possible to explain key rules at a practical level.

Ronald R. Yager considers the problem of maximizing information contained in fusion of possibly conflicting data. Two approaches are suggested, each based on some type of meta-knowledge. The first type is a measure of credibility assigned to subsets of observations. The credible fused value is calculated from a subset containing not too conflicting information. The second type means prioritization of observations, indicating discount of data if there is conflict with higher priority observations.

Hannu Nurmi and Janusz Kacprzyk's contribution focuses on plausible aggregation methods using fuzzy preference relations in social choice (group decision making). Basic incompatibilities and paradoxes in the classical theory may be avoided by the use of fuzzy preferences. Three approaches are considered. The first is based on the aggregation of individual preference relations and then defining various solutions. The second defines solutions directly from individual fuzzy preferences, while the third uses fuzzy tournaments.

Salvatore Greco, Benedetto Matarazzo and Roman Slowinski's paper contains interesting results on the fuzzy extension of the rough approximation of decision classes in multicriteria decision making. The approach is based on their previous methodological changes of the original rough set theory as well as their earlier fuzzy extension of the rough approximation by using dominance and similarity relations together.

Jean-Luc Marichal presents an important contribution to the aggregation problem in multicriteria decision aid. By using the Choquet integral as an adequate aggregation operator, it is possible to take into account interactions among criteria. For better understanding of the behavioral properties of the aggregation, the author presents and discusses some indices offering a better understanding of the global importance of criteria, the interaction among criteria, the tolerance of the decision maker, etc.

Michel Grabisch and Christophe Labreuche study the problem of being symmetric or asymmetric when using different evaluation scales in the framework of multicriteria decision making and decision under risk and uncertainty. The Choquet and the Šipoš integrals are involved and compared. While the Choquet integral does not allow to differentiate between negative and positive numbers, the Šipoš integral does.

Jean-Pierre Barthélemy investigates the possibility of extending the basic Dempster-Shafer theory to sets of events more general than Boolean algebras. He therefore approaches capacities, belief and necessity functions in an ordinal way, having in mind applications in non-classical logic and artificial intelligence.

February 7, 2000   J. Fodor, B. De Baets, P. Perny
                                       Budapest, Gent, Paris

Table of Contents

$\{P, Q, I, J\}$ - Preference Structures

Philippe Vincke

Université Libre de Bruxelles
Service de mathématiques de la gestion
Boulevard du Triomphe CP 210-01
B-1050 Bruxelles, Belgium
E-mail: pvincke@ulb.ac.be

Summary. This paper is concerned with preference models including four relations: strict preference (P), weak preference (Q), indifference (I) and incomparability (J). The purpose is to establish conditions allowing to represent these four relations by numerical functions and thresholds, in order to generalize previous results concerning complete or partial semiorders and interval orders, pseudo-orders and $\{P, Q, I\}$ - preference structures.

Keywords: Preferences, numerical representations, thresholds.

1 Introduction

Many researches have been devoted, these last years, to the development of preference models which are less restrictive than the traditional weak order (or complete preorder). The cristicism about the transitivity of indifference (Luce, 1956) [4] led to structures such as the semiorder or the interval order which were thoroughly analyzed (see for example Fishburn, 1985 [2], or Pirlot and Vincke, 1997 [5]). The introduction of different degrees of preference led to the definition of pseudo-orders (Roy and Vincke, 1987 [10]), $\{P, Q, I\}$ - preference structures (Vincke, 1988 [14]) and valued (or fuzzy) relations (Roubens and Vincke, 1985 [7], Doignon et al., 1986 [1], Fodor and Roubens, 1994 [3]). The necessity of modeling incomparability led to an increased interest in partial relations (Roubens and Vincke, 1984 [6], Roy, 1985 [8]).

This paper is concerned with preference models including the four relations which are most present in the multicriteria decision-aid tools based on the outranking approach (Roy and Bouyssou, 1993 [9]): strict preference, weak preference, indifference and incomparability. Strict preference and indifference are the usual components of the weak order (preference structure associated to the traditional decision tool used in management, economy or decision theory). The reader is referred to Roy (1985) [8] for the justification and intuitive meanings of weak preference and incomparability. Our purpose is to establish the conditions which allow to represent these four relations by numerical functions and thresholds, in order to generalize the concepts mentioned here above.

2 Definition and notations

Let A denote a finite set of elements $a, b, c, \ldots$ and $|A|$, its number of elements. A *binary relation* S on the set A is a subset of the cartesian product $A \times A$, that is, a set of ordered pairs (a, b) such that a and b belong to A: $S \subset A \times A$. If the ordered pair (a, b) is in S, we denote $(a, b) \in S$ or aSb; if not, $(a, b) \notin S$ or $a \neg Sb$. Let S and T be two relations on the same set A. The following notations will be used.

$$S \subset T \text{ iff } aSb \Rightarrow aTb, \forall a, b \in A \text{ (inclusion)},$$
$$a(S \cup T)b \text{ iff } aSb \text{ or (inclusive) } aTb \text{ (union)},$$
$$a(S \cap T)b \text{ iff } aSb \text{ and } aTb \text{ (intersection)},$$
$$aSTb \text{ iff } \exists c \in A : aSc \text{ and } cTb,$$
$$aS^2b \text{ iff } \exists c \in A : aSc \text{ and } cSb.$$

A binary relation S on the set A is :

- *reflexive* iff $aSa, \forall a \in A$,
- *irreflexive* iff $a \neg Sa, \forall a \in A$,
- *symmetric* iff $aSb \Rightarrow bSa, \forall a, b \in A$,
- *antisymmetric* iff $aSb \Rightarrow b \neg Sa, \forall a, b \in A$ such that $a \neq b$,
- *asymmetric* iff $aSb \Rightarrow b \neg Sa, \forall a, b \in A$,
- *complete* iff aSb or $bSa, \forall a, b \in A$ such that $a \neq b$,
- *transitive* iff $aSb, bSc \Rightarrow aSc, \forall a, b, c \in A$,
- *negatively transitive* iff $a \neg Sb, b \neg Sc \Rightarrow a \neg Sc, \forall a, b, c, \in A$,
- an *equivalence relation* iff it is reflexive, symmetric and transitive,
- a *strict partial order* iff it is asymmetric and transitive,
- a *partial order* iff it is reflexive, antisymmetric and transitive,
- a *partial preorder* or simply a *preorder* iff it is reflexive and transitive,
- a *weak order* iff it is asymmetric and negatively transitive,
- a *complete preorder* iff it is reflexive, transitive and complete,
- a *complete order* iff it is reflexive, transitive, antisymmetric and complete,
- a *strict complete order* iff it is asymmetric, transitive and complete.

The complement S^c, the converse $\overline{S}$ and the dual S^d are respectively defined by

$$\begin{cases} aS^c b & \text{iff} \quad a \neg Sb, \\ a\overline{S}b & \text{iff} \quad bSa, \\ aS^d b & \text{iff} \quad b \neg Sa. \end{cases}$$

Definition 1 $A \{P, Q, I, J\}$ - *preference structure on a set A is a set of four binary relations P (strict preference), Q (weak preference), I (indifference) and J (incomparability), defined on A, such that :*

- $\forall a, b \in A, aPb$ or bPa or aQb or bQa or aIb or aJb (exclusive or);
- P and Q are asymmetric;

- *I is reflexive and symmetric;*
- *J is irreflexive and symmetric.*

Given a $\{P, Q, I, J\}$ - preference structure, we define the four following irreflexive relations:

$$S_1 = P^2 \cup PQ \cup PI \cup P\overline{Q} \cup QP \cup Q^2 \cup QI,$$

$$S_2 = S_1 \cup IP \cup IQ,$$

$$S_3 = S_1 \cup IP \cup \overline{Q}P,$$

$$S_4 = S_2 \cup S_3.$$

The numerical representation we are interested in consists in assigning, to every element a of A, a real value $g(a)$ and thresholds $q(g(a))$ and $p(g(a))$ in such a way that strict preference, weak preference or indifference between a and b can be represented by some inequalities between these numerical quantities. More precisely, we say that a $\{P, Q, I, J\}$ - preference structure is representable by the model M_1 iff there exist a real-valued function g, defined on A, and real-valued functions q and p, defined on $\mathbb{R}$, such that $\forall a, b \in A$,

$$(M_1) \begin{cases} aPb \Rightarrow g(a) > g(b) + p(g(b)), \\ aQb \Rightarrow g(b) + p(g(b)) \geq g(a) > g(b) + q(g(b)), \\ aIb \Rightarrow \begin{cases} g(b) + q(g(b)) \geq g(a), \\ g(a) + q(g(a)) \geq g(b), \end{cases} \\ 0 \leq q \leq p. \end{cases}$$

This model generalizes the traditional two thresholds model (see for instance Vincke, 1992 [15], page 14) were two actions are indifferent when their values differ by less than the small threshold, one action is strictly preferred to the other when its value is much larger (with a difference greater than the large threshold) and one action is weakly preferred to the other when its value is rather larger (with a difference comprised between the small and the large thresholds). Due to the presence of incomparability, the implications, in model (M_1), cannot be reversed.

In model (M_1), the only condition imposed to the threshold functions is the fact that, $\forall a \in A$,

$$0 \leq q(g(a)) \leq p(g(a)).$$

We will also consider some additional conditions which express a sort of coherence between the principal function g and the thresholds; we respectively denote by (M_2), (M_3) and (M_4) the obtained models:

$$(M_2) \begin{cases} M_1 \text{ with} \\ g(a) > g(b) \Leftrightarrow g(a) + q(g(a)) > g(b) + q(g(b)), \end{cases}$$

$$(M_3) \begin{cases} M_1 \text{ with} \\ g(a) > g(b) \Leftrightarrow g(a) + p(g(a)) > g(b) + p(g(b)), \end{cases}$$

$$(M_4) \begin{cases} M_1 \text{ with} \\ g(a) > g(b) \Leftrightarrow g(a) + q(g(a)) > g(b) + q(g(b)) \\ \qquad\qquad \Leftrightarrow g(a) + p(g(a)) > g(b) + p(g(b)). \end{cases}$$

Finally, we denote by (M_1') the model (M_1) where the simple implications are replaced by double implications, and by $(M_2'), (M_3')$ and (M_4') the derived models with the additional conditions.

3   Main result

Theorem 1 *For each $k \in \{1,2,3,4\}$, the following conditions are equivalent*

- *$\{P, Q, I, J\}$ is representable by model (M_k),*
- *the relation S_k is acyclic.*

The proof is given in appendix 1.

Its interest resides in the fact that the possibility of numerically representing the preference structure is very easily testable; moreover the proof of the theorem is constructive, so that it provides an algorithm to build the functions. In the next sections, we will study the algebraic properties which are imposed on P, Q, I and J by the models (M_k) and make the connections with the results existing in the literature.

4   Algebraic conditions on P, Q, I, J.

It is well known that structures like interval orders, semiorders or pseudo-orders can be characterized by algebraic conditions as, for example,

$$PIP \subset P,$$
$$P^2 \cap I^2 = \emptyset,$$
$$QIP \subset P,$$
$$\dots$$

We present in this section algebraic conditions which are implied by the models (M_k) $(k = 1, 2, 3, 4)$ and which generalize the previous ones. Let us denote by (D_k), $k = 1, 2, 3, 4$ the following sets of algebraic conditions.

$$(D_1) \begin{cases} QIQ \subset Q \cup P \cup J, \\ QIP \subset P \cup J, \\ PIP \subset P \cup J, \\ P\overline{Q}P \subset P \cup J; \end{cases}$$

$$(D_2) \begin{cases} (D_1), \\ (P \cup Q)^2 \cap I^2 = \emptyset, \\ P^2 \cap IQ = \emptyset, \\ QP \cap IQ = \emptyset; \end{cases}$$

$$(D_3) \begin{cases} (D_1), \\ P^2 \cap (I \cup Q)^2 = \emptyset, \\ PQ \cap I^2 = \emptyset, \\ PQ \cap QI = \emptyset; \end{cases}$$

$$(D_4) \begin{cases} (D_2), \\ (D_3), \\ PIQ \subset P \cup J. \end{cases}$$

Theorem 2 *For each $k \in \{1, 2, 3, 4\}$, the acyclicity of S_k (which, by Theorem 1, is equivalent to the representability of $\{P, Q, I, J\}$ by model (M_k)), implies conditions (D_k).*

The proof is given in appendix 2.

The interest of these algebraic conditions is that they are not only necessary, but also sufficient, when $J = \emptyset$, to have a numerical representation with two thresholds, as shown in theorem 3.

Theorem 3 *For each $k \in \{1, 2, 3, 4\}$, the following conditions are equivalent when $J = \emptyset$:*

- *$\{P, Q, I, J\}$ is representable by model (M'_k),*
- *the relation S_k is acyclic,*
- *the conditions (D_k) are satisfied.*

This theorem is a consequence of Theorems 1 and 2 and of the results presented in Vincke (1988) [14]. The reader will also find in this last reference some other variants of the model (M'_1) for the case where $J = \emptyset$.

5 Particular cases

When $J = \emptyset$, the model (M_4') is the pseudo-order (see Roy and Vincke, 1987 [10]) and the other models are particular cases of the $\{P, Q, I\}$ - structures studied in Vincke (1988) [14] and in Tsoukias and Vincke (1998) [13]. If $J = P = \emptyset$, the models (M_1') and (M_2') respectively are the usual interval order and semiorder.

When $P = \emptyset$ and $J \neq \emptyset$, we obtain the structures which were presented in Roubens and Vincke (1985 [7], chapter 4) for introducing the concepts of partial interval order and partial semiorder.

6 Outranking relation associated to a $\{P, Q, I, J\}$ - structure

It is usual, in multicriteria decision analysis, to have an outranking relation S and to deduce from S the different preference situations. Given a reflexive relation S and working with the boolean logic, at most three preference situations can be defined: strict preference, indifference and incomparability. They are deduced from S as follows:

$$aPb \text{ iff } aSb \text{ and } bS^c a,$$
$$aIb \text{ iff } aSb \text{ and } bSa,$$
$$aJb \text{ iff } aS^c b \text{ and } bS^c a.$$

It has been proved (see Tsoukias and Vincke, 1995 [11]) that no other situation can be described on basis of S, using the boolean logic. In particular, it is not possible to characterize an hesitation between strict preference and indifference (called weak preference by B. Roy, 1985 [8]) or to make a distinction between an incomparability due to ignorance and an incomparability due to a conflict. In order to be able to model such situations, it is necessary to extend the logic: this was done and illustrated in Tsoukias and Vincke (1995 [11], 1997 [12], 1998 [13]). The obtained formal language, which is based on a four-valued logic, allows to define (at most) ten different preference situations on basis of a given relation S. The $\{P, Q, I, J\}$ - preference structure presented here can be described and characterized, in this language, from a relation S, six of the ten possible situations being absent. We do not develop this aspect here but the interested reader will find all the necessary elements in the previously mentioned references.

7 Appendix 1: proof of Theorem 1

i) If $\{P, Q, I, J\}$ is representable by (M_1), then S_1 is acyclic

Let $aS_1 b : \exists c$ such that either aPc and $c(P \cup Q \cup I \cup \overline{Q})$ or aQc and $c(P \cup Q \cup I)b$; in the first case, we obtain, by model M_1,

$$g(a) > g(c) + p(g(c)) > g(b);$$

in the second case, we have

$$g(a) > g(c) + q(g(c)) > g(b).$$

In conclusion, aS_1b implies $g(a) > g(b)$, so that S_1 cannot contain a cycle.

ii) If S_1 is acyclic, then $\{P, Q, I, J\}$ is representable by (M_1)

As S_1 is acyclic, there exists an element a such that $aS^c b, \forall b \neq a$: take $g(a) = 0$. In $A \setminus \{a\}$, there exists an element b such that $bP^c c, \forall c \neq b$: take $g(b) = 1$. Continue this procedure and you obtain a function g such that, $\forall a, b \in A$,

$$aS_1b \Rightarrow g(a) > g(b).$$

Now, $\forall a \in A$, define $p(g(a))$ and $q(g(a))$ in such a way that

$$\begin{cases} g(a) + p(g(a)) < g(x), \forall x : xPa, \\ g(a) + p(g(a)) > g(y), \forall y : a(P \cup Q \cup I \cup \overline{Q})y, \\ g(a) + q(g(a)) < g(z), \forall z : z(P \cup Q)a, \\ g(a) + q(g(a)) > g(t), \forall t : a(P \cup Q \cup I)t, \\ q(g(a)) < p(g(a)). \end{cases}$$

This is always possible because

$$\begin{aligned} xPa(P \cup Q \cup I \cup \overline{Q})y &\Rightarrow xS_1y \Rightarrow g(x) > g(y), \\ z(P \cup Q)a(P \cup Q \cup I)t &\Rightarrow zS_1t \Rightarrow g(z) > g(t), \\ xPa(P \cup Q \cup I)t &\Rightarrow xS_1t \Rightarrow g(x) > g(t). \end{aligned}$$

iii) If $\{P, Q, I, J\}$ is representable by (M_2), then S_2 is acyclic

Let aS_2b, so that aS_1b or $a(IP \cup IQ)b$. If aS_1b, then $g(a) > g(b)$ by i). If $\exists c$ such that aIc and $c(P \cup Q)b$, then, by model M_2,

$$g(a) + q(g(a)) > g(c) > g(b) + q(g(b)),$$

so that

$$g(a) > g(b).$$

In conclusion, aS_2b implies $g(a) > g(b)$, so that S_2 cannot contain a cycle.

iv) If S_2 is acyclic, then $\{P, Q, I, J\}$ is representable by (M_2)

As S_2 is acyclic, there exists a function g such that, $\forall a, b \in A$,

$$aS_2b \Rightarrow g(a) > g(b)$$

(by a similar reasoning as in ii).

Now, $\forall a \in A$, define $p(g(a))$ and $q(g(a))$ in the same way as in ii) but with the additional condition that

$$g(a) + q(g(a)) > g(b) + q(g(b)) \text{ when } g(a) > g(b).$$

This is always possible for the same reasons as in ii) and because the existence of an element c such that

$$a(P \cup Q \cup I)c \text{ and } c(P \cup Q)b,$$

which imposes

$$g(a) + q(g(a)) > g(c) > g(b) + q(g(b)),$$

also implies aS_2b and thus $g(a) > g(b)$.

v) If $\{P, Q, I, J\}$ is representable by (M_3) then S_3 is acyclic

Let aS_3b, so that aS_1b or $a(IP \cup \overline{Q}P)b$. If aS_1b, then $g(a) > g(b)$ by i). If $\exists c$ such that $a(I \cup \overline{Q})c$ and cPb, then, by model M_3,

$$g(a) + p(g(a)) > g(c) > g(b) + q(g(b)),$$

so that

$$g(a) > g(b).$$

In conclusion, aS_3b implies $g(a) > g(b)$, so that S_3 cannot contain a cycle.

vi) If S_3 is acyclic, then $\{P, Q, I, J\}$ is representable by model (M_3)

As S_3 is acyclic, there exists a function g such that, $\forall a, b \in A$,

$$aS_3b \Rightarrow g(a) > g(b)$$

(by a similar reasoning as in ii).

Now, $\forall a \in A$, define $p(g(a))$ and $q(g(a))$ (in the same way as in ii) but with the additional condition that

$$g(a) + p(g(a)) > g(b) + p(g(b)) \text{ when } g(a) > g(b).$$

This is always possible for the same reasons as in ii) and because the existence of an element c such that

$$a(P \cup Q \cup I \cup \overline{Q})c \text{ and } cPb,$$

which imposes

$$g(a) + p(g(a)) > g(c) > g(b) + p(g(b)),$$

also implies aS_3b and thus $g(a) > g(b)$.

vii) If $\{P, Q, I, J\}$ is representable by (M_4), then S_4 is acyclic

Immediate consequence of iii) and v).

viii) If S_4 is acyclic, then $\{P, Q, I, J\}$ is representable by model (M_4)

The proof is obtained in combining the reasonings made in iv) and vi). Remark that the simultaneous existence of c and d such that

$$\begin{cases} a(P \cup Q \cup I)c \text{ and } c(P \cup Q)b, \\ b(P \cup Q \cup I \cup \overline{Q})d \text{ and } dPa, \end{cases}$$

which would impose the non-desirable properties

$$\begin{cases} g(a) + q(g(a)) > g(b) + q(g(b)), \\ g(b) + p(g(b)) > g(a) + p(g(a)), \end{cases}$$

is impossible because of the asymmetry of S_4.

8 Appendix 2 : proof of Theorem 2

i) The acyclicity of S_1 implies conditions (D_1)

If $a(QIQ)b$, there exists c such that $a(QI)c$ and cQb; in this case, $b(P \cup Q \cup I)a$ would imply aS_1c and cS_1a, which is impossible, so that $a(P \cup Q \cup J)b$.

If $a(QIP \cup PIP \cup P\overline{Q}P)b$, there exists c such that $a(QI \cup PI \cup P\overline{Q})c$ and cPb; in this case, $b(P \cup Q \cup I \cup \overline{Q})a$ would imply aS_1c and cS_1b, which is impossible, so that $a(P \cup J)b$.

ii) The acyclicity of S_2 implies conditions (D_2)

As $S_2 \supset S_1$, the proof of conditions (D_1) have been established in i). If $(P \cup Q)^2 \cap I^2 \neq \emptyset$, there exist a, b, c, d such that $a(P \cup Q)c$, $c(P \cup Q)b$, aId and dIb, so that $d(IP \cup IQ)c$ and $c(QI \cup PI)d$, giving dS_2c and cS_2d, which is impossible. If $(P^2 \cup QP) \cap IQ \neq \emptyset$, there exist a, b, c, d such that $a(P \cup Q)c, cPb, aId$ and dQb, so that $d(IP \cup IQ)c$ and $cP\overline{Q}d$, giving dS_2c and cS_2d, which is impossible.

iii) The acyclicity of S_3 implies conditions (D_3)

As $S_3 \supset S_1$, the proof of conditions (D_1) have been established in (i). If $P^2 \cap (I \cup Q^2) \neq \emptyset$, there exist a, b, c, d such that $aPc, cPb, a(I \cup Q)d$ and $d(I \cup Q)b$, so that $d(IP \cup \overline{Q}P)c$ and $c(PI \cup P\overline{Q})d$, giving dS_3c and cS_3d, which is impossible.

If $PQ \cap (I^2 \cup QI) \neq \emptyset$, there exist a, b, c, d such that $aPc, cQb, a(I \cup Q)d$ and dIb, so that $d(IP \cup \overline{Q}P)c$ and $cQId$, giving dS_3c and cS_3d, which is impossible.

iv) The acyclicity of S_4 implies conditions (D_4)

As $S_4 = S_2 \cup S_3$, the proof of conditions (D_2) and (D_3) have been established in (ii) and (iii). If $aPIQb$, there exists c such that aPc and $cIQb$; in this case, $b(P \cup Q \cup I \cup \overline{Q})a$ would imply cS_4b and bS_4c, which is impossible, so that $a(P \cup J)b$.

References

1. DOIGNON, J.P., MONJARDET, B., ROUBENS, M. and VINCKE, Ph. Biorder families, valued relations and preference modelling. *J. of Math. Psychology*, 30:435–480, 1986.
2. FISHBURN, P.C. *Interval orders and interval graphs.* J. Wiley and Sons, 1985.
3. FODOR, J. and ROUBENS, M. *Fuzzy preference modelling and multicriteria decision support.* Kluwer, 1994.
4. LUCE, R.D. Semiorders and a theory of utility discrimination. *Econometrica*, 24:178–191, 1956.
5. PIRLOT, M. and VINCKE, Ph. *Semiorders.* Kluwer, 1997.
6. ROUBENS, M. and VINCKE, Ph. A definition of partial interval orders. *Trends in Mathematical Psychology*, pages 309–316, in Degreef, E. and Van Buggenhout, J. (eds), 1984.
7. ROUBENS, M. and VINCKE, Ph. *Preference modelling*, volume 250 of *Lectures Notes in Economics and Mathematical Systems.* Springer, 1985.
8. ROY, B. *Méthodologie multicritère d'aide à la décision.* Economica, 1985.
9. ROY, B. and BOUYSSOU, D. *Aide multicritère à la décision : méthodes et cas.* Economica, 1993.
10. ROY, B. and VINCKE, Ph. Pseudo-orders: definition, properties and numerical representation. *Mathematical Social Sciences*, 62:263–274, 1987.
11. TSOUKIAS, A. and VINCKE, Ph. A new axiomatic foundation of partial comparability. *Theory and Decision*, 39:79–114, 1995.
12. TSOUKIAS, A. and VINCKE, Ph. *Extended preference structure in MCDA.* Climaco,J. (ed), Multicriteria Analysis. Springer Verlag, 1997.
13. TSOUKIAS, A. and VINCKE, Ph. Double threshold orders: a new axiomatization. *Journal of Multicriteria Decision Analysis*, 7:285–301, 1998.
14. VINCKE, Ph. P,Q,I-preference structures. *Lecture Notes in Economics and Mathematical Systems*, (301):72–81, in Kacprzyk, J. and Roubens, M. (eds), Nonconventional preference relations in decision making, 1988.
15. VINCKE, Ph. *Multicriteria Decision-Aid.* Wiley, 1992.

Multi-Objective Fuzzy Linear Programming: The MOFAC Method

Philippe Fortemps and Jacques Teghem

Faculté Polyetchnique de Mons — Mathematics and Operations Research
Rue de Houdain, 9, B-7000 Mons, Belgium
E-mail: {Philippe.Fortemps,Jacques.Teghem}@fpms.ac.be

Summary. Fuzzy set theory is well-suited for modelling imprecision inherent to industrial reality. Whilst a stochastic approach implies the difficult determination of probability informations, fuzzy sets can be understood as imprecise probability distributions. We first recall that the area compensation method for the comparison of two fuzzy numbers is consistent with this framework. We derive then a comparison index in the same interpretative context.

We exemplify the use of the comparison tools for solving multi-objective linear programming problems with imprecision: MOFAC (which stands for Multi-Objective Fuzzy Area Compensation), in a context where the relevant information is assumed as imprecise probabilities. Finally, we perform a comparison with well-known methods, STRANGE and FLIP, in order to exhibit the main features of the proposed approach.

1 Introduction

One of the possible goals for implementing fuzzy sets in mathematical models is to enhance the latter as far as the imprecision is concerned. The literature related to the conjunction of imprecision-minded fuzzy sets and mathematical programming models is particularly wide. For comprehensive surveys, we refer the reader to (Rommelfanger and Słowiński 1998) or, alternatively, to (Lai and Hwang 1992, Sakawa 1993). On the other hand, Roubens and Teghem's (1991) paper on the comparison of fuzzy and stochastic methodologies deserves to be read; the authors draw further prospects in both domains.

Imprecision is the information characteristic arising from partial knowledge. For example, the sentence "we leave Belgium this week–end" gives a piece of incomplete information about the departure day: it is either Saturday or Sunday. Imprecision is always represented by a disjunctive set, i.e. only one value inside this set is allowed. A typical example of imprecision is an error interval, which encodes the set of possible values of one uni-valued variable.

Imprecision is quite inherent to the industrial reality. On the one hand, it makes no sense to consider that industrial data are as precisely measured as it is assumed in academic models. A lot of uncontrollable parameters can influence the value of variables, while precise measurement would require loss of time or intrusive experiments. On the other hand, the current evolution of the market prescribes very fast modification of the production range. There-fore, new products or new production methodologies are to be scheduled with very few information about the data. Before giving any precise value to data, one should remember this maxim: "future is no more what it has been".

Stochastic mathematical programming is a rather well–known field of re-search, but very few has been actually done in the determination of the probability informations required for those models. As a matter of fact, the difficulties of stochastic programming is not only computational. For example, when you want to optimize the assignment of your money amount to portfo-lio, you need precise probability distribution about the value the shares can reach in the future. It is somehow counter-intuitive to ask so precise infor-mation to the DM, especially if new shares have appeared on the market. If he turns himself to stochastic models, it is probably because he lacks of knowledge.

Three main difficulties arise in Multi-Objective Fuzzy Linear Program-ming (MOFLP). The first issue is concerned with a meaningful treatment of the fuzzy objective(s); and the second one is a consistent interpretation of the inequality constraints (for a survey, see Rommelfanger and Słowiński 1998). And last but not least, in case of several objectives, one has to se-lect among the different crisp Multi-Objective Programming approaches (see Vanderpooten and Vincke 1989, Słowiński 1997). There exists also Bellman and Zadeh's (1970) approach to fuzzy linear programming (see also Dubois and Fortemps 1999), but these works are related to flexibilities (i.e. control-lable parameters) rather than to uncertainty.

As far as the interpretation of fuzziness is concerned, it has been shown in Dempster's (1967) framework, that membership functions of fuzzy num-bers can be viewed as *imprecise probability distributions* (Dubois and Prade 1987, Fortemps and Roubens 1996). In other words, we consider in this pa-per the difficult problem of a meaningful and consistent treatment of fuzzy numbers in a mathematical model with imprecision. According to (Fortemps and Roubens 1996), the area compensation method for comparing two fuzzy numbers is recalled, in Section 2, to build a ranking relation between all the fuzzy numbers. Section 3 is devoted to derive a new comparison index in the same interpretative context. This index will be used in the treatment of in-equality satisfaction. Therefore, it makes sense to apply these two methods to mathematical programming models where the relevant information consists of imprecise probabilities.

In Section 4, we exemplify the use of the area compensation methods on fuzzy linear programming. We apply it in Section 5 in the context of interactive multi-objective linear programming. The method is illustrated on a didactic example in Section 5.3. Finally in Section 6, we perform a comparison with a stochastic programming method (STRANGE, Teghem et al. 1986, Teghem 1990) and a fuzzy one (FLIP, Słowiński 1986, Słowiński 1990).

2   The Area Compensation

The literature concerned with the choice among alternatives characterized by fuzzy numbers is particularly productive, since this problem occurs in a cluster of fields like approximate reasoning, multicriteria decision making and mathematical programming. Some of the proposed methods for the comparison of fuzzy numbers have been reviewed by Bortolan and Degani (1985) and, more recently, by Chen and Hwang (1992).

In this paper, we recall the *area compensation* method (Fortemps and Roubens 1996). The authors merged a revised version of the procedure proposed by Roubens (1990) and the ranking by total integral value by Liou and Wang (1992). This leads to a very intuitive ranking method which enjoys a mathematical interpretation in terms of imprecise probabilistic distribution.

2.1   Notations

We consider the set $\mathfrak{R}$ of normalized convex fuzzy numbers. Recall that a fuzzy number A is a fuzzy set on the real line $\mathbb{R}$ defined by the membership function $\mu_A(x), x \in \mathbb{R}$ with

$$\begin{cases} \max_x \mu_A(x) = 1 \\ \mu_A(y) \geq \min\{\mu_A(x), \mu_A(z)\}, \forall x \geq y \geq z \in \mathbb{R} \end{cases}$$

The α-level sets $A_\alpha = \{x \in \mathbb{R} : \mu_A(x) \geq \alpha\}$ are convex subsets of $\mathbb{R}$ whose lower and upper limits are represented by $\underline{a}_\alpha = \inf_{x \in \mathbb{R}}\{x : \mu_A(x) \geq \alpha\}$ and $\overline{a}_\alpha = \sup_{x \in \mathbb{R}}\{x : \mu_A(x) \geq \alpha\}$. For the sake of simplicity, we suppose that both limits are finite. The following results can be adapted to the case of infinite-support fuzzy numbers, but it is not really relevant to the field of mathematical programming.

2.2   The Idea of Area Compensation

Roubens (1990) proposed an intuitive comparison method based on the area compensation determined by the membership functions of two fuzzy numbers. And Fortemps and Roubens (1996) revised it in order to explicitly obtain a ranking as well as a defuzzification procedure. Let us first recall it. We define the area in favour of $A > B$ w.r.t. the left and right parts of the fuzzy numbers:

$$S_L(A > B) = \int_{U(A,B)} [\underline{a}_\alpha - \underline{b}_\alpha]\, d\alpha \qquad S_R(A > B) = \int_{V(A,B)} [\overline{a}_\alpha - \overline{b}_\alpha]\, d\alpha$$

$$\tag{1}$$

where

$$U(A, B) = \{\alpha | 0 \leq \alpha \leq 1,\ \underline{a}_\alpha > \underline{b}_\alpha\} \qquad V(A, B) = \{\alpha | 0 \leq \alpha \leq 1,\ \overline{a}_\alpha > \overline{b}_\alpha\}$$

$$\tag{2}$$

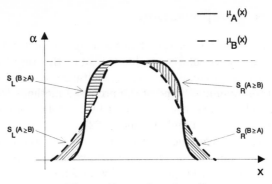

Fig. 1. Comparing A to B

The different areas are drawn on Figure 1.

$C(A \geq B)$, the global degree to which A is larger than B, is naturally computed as the sum of all arguments in favour of $A \geq B$ minus the sum of the antagonistic ones. The magnitude of $C(A \geq B)$ represents how much the coalition in favour of A wins against the one in favour of B.

$$C : \mathfrak{R} \times \mathfrak{R} \to \mathbb{R}$$
$$(A, B) \to C(A \geq B)$$
$$C(A \geq B) = \frac{1}{2} \left\{ \begin{array}{c} S_L(A > B) + S_R(A > B) \\ -S_L(B > A) - S_R(B > A) \end{array} \right\} \tag{3}$$

so that $C(B \geq A) = -C(A \geq B)$. We consider that

$$A \geq B \text{ iff } C(A \geq B) \geq 0 \tag{4}$$

This relation $C(A \geq B)$ induces a complete ranking of all fuzzy numbers, which corresponds to the defuzzification function $\mathfrak{F} : \mathfrak{R} \to \mathbb{R}$ defined in the following theorem.

Theorem 1 *(Fortemps and Roubens 1996)*

$$C(A \geq B) = \mathfrak{F}(A) - \mathfrak{F}(B) \tag{5}$$

where

$$\mathfrak{F}(A) = \frac{1}{2} \int_0^1 (\underline{a}_\alpha + \overline{a}_\alpha) \, d\alpha \tag{6}$$

Therefore, equation (4) can be rewritten as

$$A \geq B \text{ iff } \mathfrak{F}(A) \geq \mathfrak{F}(B) \tag{7}$$

The function $\mathfrak{F} : \mathfrak{R} \to \mathbb{R}$ is a mapping from the set of fuzzy numbers to the set of real numbers $\mathbb{R}$, where the ordering is natural. This defuzzification function is the mean of the two areas defined by the vertical axis and respectively by the left and the right slope of the fuzzy number (see Fig. 2). Both areas describe in fact how much the number A is greater than 0: the first one $(\bar{a}_\alpha)$ in an optimistic way, the second $(\underline{a}_\alpha)$ in a pessimistic one. In the context of imprecise probability distribution and Dempster's (1967) framework, both areas correspond to extreme mean values. Briefly, a fuzzy set can be viewed as describing a set of admissible probability measures. Therefore, the mean value of a fuzzy set can be stated as the interval of mean values w.r.t. all these admissible probability distributions (Dubois and Prade 1987). This interval is denoted by $[E_*(A), E^*(A)]$ for any fuzzy number A, where

$$E_*(A) = \int_0^1 \underline{a}_\alpha \, d\alpha \qquad E^*(A) = \int_0^1 \bar{a}_\alpha \, d\alpha. \qquad (8)$$

and

$$\mathfrak{F}(A) = \frac{E_*(A) + E^*(A)}{2} \qquad (9)$$

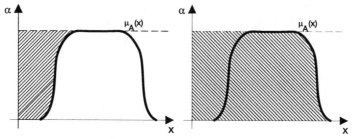

Fig. 2. Mapping a fuzzy number A to the real set $\mathbb{R}$: the first picture represents the area limited by the left slope (or $E_*(A)$), the second one is defined by the right slope (or $E^*(A)$). The mapping $\mathfrak{F}$ consists of computing the arithmetic mean of those two areas.

In (Fortemps and Roubens 1996), further details are presented about the properties of this comparison method for fuzzy numbers; in particular, its linearity: $\forall A, B \in \mathfrak{R}, \forall c \in \mathbb{R}$:

$$\begin{array}{lll} \mathfrak{F}(A) & \in A_0 = \mathrm{cl}\{x : \mu_A(x) > 0\} & (a) \\ \mathfrak{F}(c.A) & = c.\mathfrak{F}(A) & (b) \\ \mathfrak{F}(A + B) = \mathfrak{F}(A) + \mathfrak{F}(B) & (c) \end{array} \qquad (10)$$

where "cl" denotes the set closure.

3 Comparison Index

The comparison method that has been designed in Section 2 on the basis of the area compensation results from a defuzzification procedure. In other words, $C(A \geq B)$ evaluates a slack between A and B, this distance being measured on the same scale as A and B.

In contrast, several other comparison methods give an index with value in the unit interval $[0, 1]$. In such a way, different inequalities can be appreciated on a common scale. In this section, we propose such a comparison index related to the area compensation, as well as to the imprecise probability interpretation of fuzzy numbers.

On the other hand, the comparison of two fuzzy numbers A and B can be considered as a multicriteria problem. Indeed, there may simultaneously exist elements in favour of $A > B$, $A = B$ and $A < B$. When comparing two alternatives A and B in a multicriteria framework, some criteria could be in favour of the preference of A over B, the indifference or the reverted preference.

In fact, our aim is to construct a triple index $(I(A > B), I(A = B), I(A < B))$ such that, $\forall A, B \in \Re$, we have

$$I(A > B) + I(A = B) + I(A < B) = 1 \tag{11}$$

where $I(A > B)$ (resp., $I(A = B)$) represents how much A is strictly greater than (resp., equal to) B. Indices associated with non-strict inequalities will also be defined and used extensively in applications.

3.1 Deriving the Comparison Index

Again, we consider the comparison of two fuzzy numbers A and B, as presented in Section 2. We denote by $S(A > B)$ the total area in favour of $A > B$, i.e., $S(A > B) = S_L(A > B) + S_R(A > B)$ (see Section 2.2). Therefore, we have

$$S(A > B) = \int_0^1 \left[\overline{a}_\alpha - \min\left(\overline{a}_\alpha, \overline{b}_\alpha \right) + \underline{a}_\alpha - \min\left(\underline{a}_\alpha, \underline{b}_\alpha \right) \right] d\alpha \tag{12}$$

In a similar way, it makes sense to consider $S(A = B)$ as the total area claiming that A is equal to B:

$$S(A = B) = \int_0^1 \left[\min\left(\overline{a}_\alpha, \overline{b}_\alpha \right) - \max\left(\underline{a}_\alpha, \underline{b}_\alpha \right) \right] d\alpha \tag{13}$$

We denote by $S(A, B)$ the total area involved in the comparison problem

$$S(A, B) = \int_0^1 \left[\max\left(\overline{a}_\alpha, \overline{b}_\alpha \right) - \min\left(\underline{a}_\alpha, \underline{b}_\alpha \right) \right] d\alpha \tag{14}$$

One could observe that

$$S(A, B) = S(A > B) + S(A = B) + S(A < B) \tag{15}$$

The total area involved in the comparison scheme is partitioned into three separated parts (see Figure 3). It is worth noting that the area marked by a star ($*$) is taken into account two times in $S(A > B)$ and one time negatively in $S(A = B)$. Therefore, the total contribution of this area to $S(A, B)$ is counted one time only.

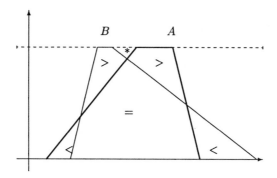

Fig. 3. The partition of the areas

We propose to consider the following indices

$$I(A > B) = \frac{S(A > B)}{S(A, B) + S(A = B)} \tag{16}$$

$$I(A = B) = \frac{2S(A = B)}{S(A, B) + S(A = B)} \tag{17}$$

$$I(A < B) = \frac{S(A < B)}{S(A, B) + S(A = B)} \tag{18}$$

and because of relation (15), we have the desired property that the three indices sum up to one (Eqn. (11)).

It appears that $I(A > B)$ may be greater than 1, or smaller than 0, for example when A and B have disjoint supports. In such a case, there doesn't exist a value x such that $\mu_A(x) > 0$ and $\mu_B(x) > 0$, and $|S(A = B)|$ measures how much A is different from B. Even if this is not a usual behaviour for a comparison index, we decide to keep the current definition of $I(A > B)$ for three main reasons. First, it leads to easy computation (see below). Then, it satisies property (11). Finally, it encompasses the following thresholded index I^*, which can always be used instead of I.

$$I^* = \begin{cases} I \text{ if } 0 \le I \le 1 \\ 0 \text{ if } I < 0 \\ 1 \text{ if } I > 1 \end{cases}$$

See also the Note 3.3 below.

In the definition of our comparison indices, we have decided to concentrate on the shared area as well as on the total area. With such indices, we are able to distinguish between the 3 cases of figure 4. Those three cases are typical. For the middle case, which is the most symmetrical one, the common area is the area of B and neither A nor B may be declared greater than the other. The two other cases can be obtained either by increasing the common area (the left slope of B reaches the one of A) or by reducing it.In both cases, A will be declared greater than B, but with a different degree, since the common area $S(A = B)$ is different.

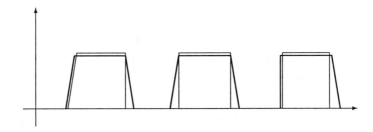

Fig. 4. Three typical cases for the comparison of two fuzzy numbers (A in bold lines and B in thin lines)

For the weak inequality index, we propose to consider

$$I(A \geq B) = I(A > B) + \frac{1}{2}I(A = B) \tag{19}$$

so that $I(A \geq B) + I(A \leq B) = 1$. On the other hand, the difference index is defined as

$$I(A \neq B) = 1 - I(A = B) \tag{20}$$
$$= I(A > B) + I(A < B) \tag{21}$$

In the case where $I(A = B)$ is negative, we have obviously $I(A \neq B) > 1$.

In the next section, we will state some properties of these comparison indices as well as cope with the computational issues. At the same time, we will present a probabilistic interpretation of these indices.

3.2 Properties – Interpretation

As a very first property, one would like to have intuitive results for the comparison of any fuzzy number with itself. Since $S(A > A) = S(A < A) = 0$

and $S(A = A) = S(A, A)$, we have

$$I(A > A) = 0 \quad I(A = A) = 1 \qquad I(A \geq A) = \frac{1}{2} \quad I(A \neq A) = 0 \qquad (22)$$

Indeed, it is desirable that our indices do not declare that A is strictly greater than itself, but that A is equal to A.

There is no doubt that the indices $I(A > B), I(A = B)$ and $I(A \neq B)$ are quite hard to compute, since they involve the integration of minimum function over membership functions. On the other hand, this difficulty disappears for the evaluation of the weak comparison index $I(A \geq B)$, which is quite easy to determine. Hopefully, this index is particularly relevant to Mathematical Programming, since most of the constraints are modelled by weak inequalities.

Proposition 1

$$\forall A, B \in \mathfrak{R}, \; I(A \geq B) = \frac{E^*(A) - E_*(B)}{[E^*(A) - E_*(A)] + [E^*(B) - E_*(B)]} \qquad (23)$$

where $E^*(A)$ (resp., $E_*(A)$) is the upper (resp., lower) mean of A (see Equation (8)).

Recalling that the imprecise probability distribution underlying the fuzzy number A is characterized by an interval mean value $[E_*(A), E^*(A)]$, $I(A \geq B)$ can be understood as the comparison of the relevant intervals. The denominator of the ratio is equal to the sum of the length of both intervals, whilst the numerator is the largest length in favour of $A \geq B$.

The property below establishes a link between the comparison index I and the area compensation method.

Proposition 2

$$\forall A, B \in \mathfrak{R}, \quad I(A \geq B) = \frac{1}{2} + \frac{C(A \geq B)}{[(E^*(A) - E_*(A)] + [E^*(B) - E_*(B)]} \qquad (24)$$

In conclusion, the behaviours of $I(A \geq B)$ and $C(A \geq B)$ are equivalent.

Theorem 2

$$\forall A, B \in \mathfrak{R}, \quad I(A \geq B) \geq \frac{1}{2} \Leftrightarrow C(A \geq B) \geq 0 \Leftrightarrow \mathfrak{F}(A) \geq \mathfrak{F}(B) \qquad (25)$$

3.3 Note

Other comparison indices could be investigated in order to establish the multicriteria aspects of the comparison of two fuzzy numbers.

A priori it could appear relevant to define indices $I'(A > B)$, $I'(A = B)$ and $I'(A < B)$ which still satisfy relation 11:

$$I'(A > B) + I'(A = B) + I'(A < B) = 1$$

but requiring the three indices to be non-negative (whilst in Section 3.1, $I(A = B)$ can be negative).

A possibility — among others — is to consider the positive part of the areas:

$$S'(A > B) = \int_0^1 \left[[\bar{a}_\alpha - \max(\underline{a}_\alpha, \bar{b}_\alpha)]^+ + [\min(\bar{b}_\alpha, \underline{a}_\alpha) - \underline{b}_\alpha]^+ \right.$$
$$\left. + [\underline{a}_\alpha - \bar{b}_\alpha]^+ \right] d\alpha \tag{26}$$

$$S'(A = B) = \int_0^1 \left[[\min(\bar{a}_\alpha, \bar{b}_\alpha) - \max(\underline{a}_\alpha, \underline{b}_\alpha)]^+ \right] d\alpha \tag{27}$$

With respect to the three cases of figure 5, the three indices $S'(A > B)$, $S'(A = B)$ and $S'(A < B)$ correspond[1] to the total areas of regions $(1) + (2) + (3)$, (4) and $(5) + (6) + (2')$, respectively. One of the two regions (2) and $(2')$ has necessarily to be empty.

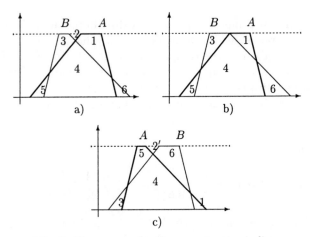

Fig. 5. Three cases for the non negative-indices

The total area $S'(A, B)$ considered in these comparison indices is the same as the total area $S(A, B)$ of Section 3.1:

$$S'(A, B) = S'(A > B) + S'(A = B) + S'(A < B) = S(A, B)$$

---

[1] The values of $S(A > B)$, $S(A = B)$ and $S(A < B)$ from Section 3.1 correspond the total areas of $(1) + 2(2) + (3)$, $(4) - (2) - (2')$ and $(5) + (6) + 2(2')$, respectively.

If we define

$$I'(A > B) = \frac{S'(A > B)}{S'(A, B)} \qquad I'(A = B) = \frac{S'(A = B)}{S'(A, B)}$$

and

$$I'(A \geq B) = \frac{S'(A > B) + S'(A = B)}{S'(A, B)}$$

we have then

$$I'(A \geq B) = \frac{\int_0^1 [\overline{a}_\alpha - \underline{b}_\alpha]^+ \, d\alpha}{\int_0^1 \left(\max(\overline{a}_\alpha, \overline{b}_\alpha) - \min(\underline{a}_\alpha, \underline{b}_\alpha)\right) \, d\alpha} \qquad (28)$$

These indices satisfy the following properties:

$$I'(A = B) = 0 \Leftrightarrow \text{either } I'(A > B) = 1, I'(A < B) = 0$$
$$\text{or } I'(A > B) = 0, I'(A < B) = 1$$
$$I'(A > B) = 1 \Leftrightarrow \overline{b}_\alpha \leq \underline{a}_\alpha, \forall \alpha$$
$$I'(A \geq B) = 1 \Leftrightarrow \underline{b}_\alpha \leq \underline{a}_\alpha, \forall \alpha$$
$$\overline{b}_\alpha \leq \overline{a}_\alpha, \forall \alpha$$

When $\overline{a}_\alpha - \underline{b}_\alpha \geq 0$, $\forall \alpha$, i.e., when $\underline{b}_1 \leq \overline{a}_1$ (see Figure 5a. and b.), the numerator of Equation (28) is the same as the one of relation (23): in this particular case, it is equal to $E^*(A) - E_*(B)$.

However, the indices are definitely more difficult to use than those proposed in Section 3.1 and, in general, they cannot be related to the results of Section 2.

We arrive at the same conclusion with other tentatives to define such non-negative indices.

4 Multi-Objective Fuzzy Linear Programming: The MOFAC Method

There is no need to recall that fuzzy linear programming gives birth to a large literature. Recent surveys of this domain have been made by Lai and Hwang (1992, Chapter 4) and Rommelfanger and Słowiński (1998).

Different models have been investigated, involving imprecise resources, technological coefficients or objective coefficients. Basically, the common procedure consists of a "defuzzification" of the imprecise objective and of the constraints to give rise to an associated deterministic problem. Differences appear in the way the defuzzification is performed.

In case the objective involves fuzzy coefficients, it may be transformed into one crisp criterion through the use of any ranking procedure (see, e.g., Tanaka et al. 1984). Another approach leads to several crisp criteria: Rommelfanger et al. (1989) consider two extreme cases, the "worst" and the "best" ones, and solve the associated multi-objective linear programming (MOLP) problem.

As to fuzziness in the constraints, Ramik and Rimanek (1985) propose to use the set-inclusion concept. Therefore, they transform a fuzzy constraint into several crisp ones, depending on the fuzzy number shape. Tanaka et al. (1984) define an optimism degree α for the DM and compare fuzzy numbers with respect to their α-section. Namely, they transform a fuzzy inequality into two crisp ones corresponding to the boundaries of the α-cut intervals.

By the way, it is nowadays undoubted that the multiobjective paradigm commands attention. In most decision problems, several, generally conflicting, criteria are to be considered. Typically, they arise from various decision makers or from various viewpoints. A single criterion procedure is sometimes possible, when conversion rates between heterogeneous issues can be identified. But, in general, the estimation of a global utility function is not straightforward and the utility approach not always pertinent(Vanderpooten and Vincke 1989).

Uncertainty models and the multiobjective paradigm have been combined. For a recent state-of-the-art, we refer the reader to (Słowiński and Teghem 1990b).

4.1 Problem Statement

We consider the following multiobjective linear program (MOLP):

$$
(\mathcal{P}) \quad
\begin{bmatrix}
\text{``maximize''}
\begin{cases}
Z_1 = \overline{C}_1 \overline{x} \\
\vdots \\
Z_k = \overline{C}_k \overline{x}
\end{cases} \\[2mm]
\text{such that}
\begin{cases}
\overline{A}_1 \overline{x} \leq B_1 \\
\vdots \\
\overline{A}_m \overline{x} \leq B_m
\end{cases} \\[2mm]
\overline{x} \geq \overline{0}
\end{bmatrix}
\qquad (29)
$$

where $\overline{x}$ is a column vector of n crisp positive decision variables, $\overline{C}_1, \ldots, \overline{C}_k$ are row vectors of fuzzy cost coefficients, and $\overline{A}_i$ and B_i $(i = 1, \ldots, m)$ are the row vector of fuzzy coefficients and the fuzzy right-hand side of the i-th constraint, respectively. In this Section, capital letters are used to denote fuzzy numbers, whilst small letters represent crisp variables or values.

As stressed in (Słowiński 1990) and in (Lai and Hwang 1992), the key question in fuzzy MOLP is the comparison of fuzzy numbers, either in the constraints or in the objectives. The comparison principle should meet two basic requirements: it has to be meaningful and computationally efficient.

We have already shown that the area compensation principle induces a comparison that supports the imprecise probability interpretation of a fuzzy set. We still have to prove that it allows a transformation of a fuzzy MOLP into a crisp (also called *deterministic*) multiobjective linear programming problem.

4.2 Problem Defuzzification

First of all, we would like to stress on the distinction between constraints and objectives. The formers help to determine which alternatives are feasible. Their prescription is rather strong and their satisfaction is often in practice the main purpose of a problem solving procedure. Meanwhile, objectives describe preferences among feasible solutions. They provide information on how to choose the final solution. Whilst the satisfaction of the constraints is crucial, the real optimization of the objectives is only a wish !

Therefore, the defuzzification of the constraints commands more attention than the objectives. While a direct treatment of the objectives is performed, it makes sense to allow the DM to interactively set safety levels for the constraints.

The objectives are naturally considered by means of the area compensation method. In fact, the comparison procedure based on the index $C(A \geq B)$ induces a ranking on the set of fuzzy numbers related to the natural ranking on $\mathbb{R}$ by the defuzzification function $\mathfrak{F}$. Therefore, to find the "optimal" solution of a problem with respect to a fuzzy criterion — in the sense of the area compensation principle — amounts to find the optimal solution of the same problem with respect to the defuzzified criterion.

We can thus replace the fuzzy criterion

$$Z_i = \sum_{j=1}^{n} C_{ij} x_j$$

by the defuzzified criterion; and recalling that $\mathfrak{F}$ is linear, we obtain

$$z_i = \mathfrak{F}\left(\sum_{j=1}^{n} C_{ij} x_j\right) = \sum_{j=1}^{n} \mathfrak{F}(C_{ij}) x_j = \sum_{j=1}^{n} c_{ij} x_j \tag{30}$$

where c_{ij} denotes the defuzzified coefficient $\mathfrak{F}(C_{ij})$.

The constraints require a specific, but consistent, treatment. In view of future relaxation or strengthening of the constraints, we need to adopt the same scale to measure all constraint satisfactions. This leads us to prefer the comparison index I. Supporting the same interpretation as $\mathfrak{F}$, the comparison index basically ranges over the unit interval.

Considering the constraint $\overline{A}_i \overline{x} \leq B_i$, we can write

$$C(\overline{A}_i \overline{x} \leq B_i) \geq 0 \Leftrightarrow I(\overline{A}_i \overline{x} \leq B_i) \geq \sigma_i \tag{31}$$

or, equivalently,

$$\frac{E^*(B_i) - E_*(\overline{A}_i\overline{x})}{E^*(B_i) - E_*(B_i) + E^*(\overline{A}_i\overline{x}) - E_*(\overline{A}_i\overline{x})} \geq \sigma_i \tag{32}$$

if we denote by σ_i the satisfaction requirement of this constraint. Since the mean operator E is linear and that every decision variable is to be positive, we may write

$$\frac{E^*(B_i) - \sum_j E_*(A_{ij})x_j}{E^*(B_i) - E_*(B_i) + \sum_j [E^*(A_{ij}) - E_*(A_{ij})]x_j} \geq \sigma_i \tag{33}$$

or

$$\sum_j [\sigma_i E^*(A_{ij}) + (1 - \sigma_i)E_*(A_{ij})]\, x_j \leq (1 - \sigma_i)E^*(B_i) + \sigma_i E_*(B_i) \tag{34}$$

It is worth noting that, with $\sigma_i = 1/2$, this comes down to the initial constraint $\overline{A}_i\overline{x} \leq B_i$ defuzzified via the function $\mathfrak{F}$. But, with other values of σ_i, a stronger (if σ_i increases) constraint or a weaker (if σ_i decreases) one can be obtained. In particular, when $\sigma_i = 1$, we reach the worst case:

$$\sum_j E^*(A_{ij})x_j \leq E_*(B_i)$$

Namely, the upper mean value of $\overline{A}_i\overline{x}$ is constrained to be smaller than the lower mean value of B_i.

In summary , as soon as satisfaction levels σ_i have been specified for the constraints $(i = 1, \ldots, m)$, the MOFAC method transforms the fuzzy MOLP into a crisp one, using either the defuzzification function $\mathfrak{F}$ for the objectives, or the comparison index I for the constraints. This defuzzification is straightforward because the problem is linear. Finally, we obtain

$$(P_{\overline{\sigma}}) \quad \left[\begin{array}{l} \text{``maximize''} \left\{ \begin{array}{l} z_1 = \overline{c}_1 \overline{x} \\ \vdots \\ z_k = \overline{c}_k \overline{x} \end{array} \right. \\[2mm] \text{such that} \left\{ \begin{array}{l} \overline{a}_1^{\sigma_1} \overline{x} \leq b_1^{\sigma_1} \\ \vdots \\ \overline{a}_m^{\sigma_m} \overline{x} \leq b_m^{\sigma_m} \end{array} \right. \\ \overline{x} \geq \overline{0} \end{array} \right. \tag{35}$$

where $a_{ij}^{\sigma_i}$ is obtained as the weighted mean $[\sigma_i E^*(A_{ij}) + (1 - \sigma_i)E_*(A_{ij})]$, $b_i^{\sigma_i} = [(1 - \sigma_i)E^*(B_i) + \sigma_i E_*(B_i)]$ and $c_{ij} = \mathcal{F}(C_{ij})$.

Remark that we allow different satisfaction requirements for the different constraints.

5   Interactive Procedure

In the literature (see, e.g., Steuer 1985, Vanderpooten and Vincke 1989, Słowiński 1997), the authors proposed various iterative methods to determine efficient solutions of a MOLP problem. They consist of successive unicriterion optimization of a weighted aggregated objective. At each step, new efficient solutions are computed and in general the DM is asked to relax objective requirements and/or to modify the weight vector. This kind of procedures ends up with a set of efficient solutions for a given MOLP problem.

Since in our model, the decision maker is allowed to specify lower bounds ($\overline{\sigma}$) for the safety indices, new MOLP problems are iteratively generated. They are solved through the same procedure.

Many procedures for MOLP are available and can be applied to problem ($P_{\overline{\sigma}}$). Moreover, the main interest of this paper is not the use of one method or another. Therefore, for the sake of simplicity in this example, we decide to choose a very basic approach to solve the MOLP problem, relying in some sense on Gonzales et al.'s (1985) work.

5.1   A Multi-Objective Procedure

After the formulation of MOLP problem ($\mathcal{P}$) and the definition of the fuzzy coefficients, the associated deterministic problem ($P_{\overline{\sigma}}$) is built for a uniform vector $\overline{\sigma} = \{\frac{1}{2}, \ldots, \frac{1}{2}\}$. In practice, the DM may stipulate another initial $\overline{\sigma}$-vector.

By individually optimizing each objective of this MOLP problem, one obtains the extremal efficient solutions. In general, k efficient solutions are found. Let S be the set of the currently considered efficient solutions. $S' = \emptyset$ (resp. S'') is the set of new efficient solutions (resp., efficient facets).

From each k-tuple of efficient solutions of S, a new efficient solution is obtained by the optimization of the aggregation of the k objectives with the weights determined as in (Gonzales et al. 1985), i.e., the hyperplane $\mathcal{H}$ going through the k selected points of S is determined and the coefficients of the hyperplane equation are used as weights. Optimizing with these weights, an efficient solution $\overline{y}$ is searched for in the direction orthogonal to the hyperplane $\mathcal{H}$. If $\overline{y}$ belongs to the hyperplane, then the feasible part of $\mathcal{H}$ is an efficient facet F, i.e., a set of efficient solutions, add this facet to S''. Otherwise, add $\overline{y}$ to S'.

Once all the solutions $\overline{y}$'s have been generated — at the first iteration, only one solution $\overline{y}$ is obtained — , the set S' is added to S. The DM is then asked to remove solutions from S until the cardinality of S ($|S|$) is less than, or equal to, $k + 1$.

At this step, the set S contains compromise solutions and S'' is a set of efficient facets. Check for each facet F in S'', if S contains at least one point of F. If not, the facet F has been disqualified by preferred compromise solution in S; thus, remove F from S''. If $|S| < k$, then stop. Otherwise, if the set S has been modified, loop to the computation of new efficient solutions (with $S' = \emptyset$).

The decision maker may perform the final choice among the sets S and S''. If he is fully satisfied by one of these solutions, stop. Otherwise, he may revise the requirements on the constraint satisfaction levels encoded in the vector $\bar{\sigma}$. Graphical tools as well as the value of the slack variables can help the DM in this interactive step.

This leads to a new deterministic MOLP problem $(P_{\bar{\sigma}'})$ which can be treated as previously. To speed up the resolution of this new problem, one can consider the weight vectors used to obtain the solutions of S in the resolution of $(P_{\bar{\sigma}})$. This gives a very efficient starting point for the procedure, since the previous interactive phases can be summarized through this kind of information.

5.2 Some Remarks

It stems from the procedure description that the DM intervenes at two stages. First, he is asked to specify the "safety parameters" $\bar{\sigma}$, determining which constraints require a stronger satisfaction or a weaker one. Moreover, when new efficient solutions are considered for problem $(P_{\bar{\sigma}})$, the DM guides the selection of which solution $\bar{x} \in S$ has to be replaced by $\bar{y}$'s, implicitly revising the weights used in the aggregation of the criteria.

In other words, when trying to improve a criterion value, there are two distinct ways of reacting: either playing with the multiobjective nature of the problem (by changing the weights) or playing with the constraints satisfaction (through the safety levels).

The authors are aware that this method has difficulties to attain some efficient solutions, in particular when the number of objectives if greater than two. Since our purpose is not to design a new interactive procedure but to exemplify the use of our comparison indices, our choice has been guided by simplicity rather than by efficiency.

5.3 On the Example

We consider the following problem (Słowiński and Teghem 1990a):

$$
(\mathcal{P}) \quad
\begin{bmatrix}
\text{``maximize''} \begin{cases} Z_1 = C_{11}x_1 + C_{12}x_2 \\ Z_2 = C_{21}x_1 + C_{22}x_2 \end{cases} \\
\text{such that} \begin{cases} A_{11}x_1 + A_{12}x_2 \le B_1 \\ A_{21}x_1 + A_{22}x_2 \le B_2 \end{cases} \\
x_1 \le 5.5 \\
x_1, x_2 \ge 0
\end{bmatrix}
\tag{36}
$$

The possibility distribution of the uncertain coefficients are depicted on Figure 6.

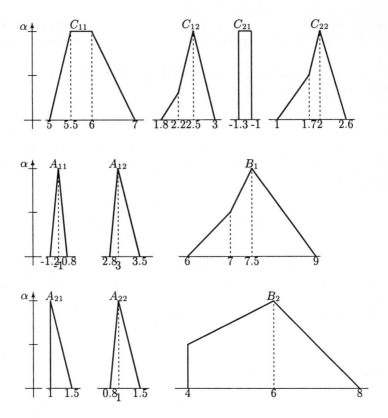

Fig. 6. Possibility distributions of uncertain coefficients (Słowiński and Teghem 1990a)

First Step In the first step of the interactive procedure, vector $\bar{\sigma}$ is fixed to $\left(\frac{1}{2}, \frac{1}{2}\right)$. The associated deterministic problem is

$$
(\mathcal{P}_{\bar{\sigma}}) \quad
\begin{array}{l}
\text{"maximize"} \begin{cases} z_1 = 23.5x_1 + 9.99x_2 \\ z_2 = -4.6x_1 + 7.8x_2 \end{cases} \\[2ex]
\text{such that} \begin{cases} -4x_1 + 12.3x_2 \le 30.25 \\ 4.5x_1 + 4.3x_2 \le 23 \end{cases} \\[1.5ex]
\phantom{\text{such that}} \; x_1 \le 5.5 \\
\phantom{\text{such that}} \; x_1, x_2 \ge 0
\end{array}
\tag{37}
$$

The two extremal efficient solutions obtained by individual optimization of each objective are

	z_1	z_2	x_1	x_2	s_1	s_2
$\bar{u}$	30.03	−5.88	5.11	0.00	50.70	0.00
$\bar{v}$	6.14	4.80	0.00	2.46	0.00	12.42

where s_1 and s_2 are the slack variables associated to the first and second inequality constraint of the problem, respectively. For example, $s_1 = 30.25 + 4x_1 - 12.3x_2$.

The equation of the hyperplane (here a line) containing those two points in the criteria space is

$$z_1 + 2.237z_2 - 16.879 = 0$$

Therefore, to find the next efficient solution, we optimize the aggregated criterion $z = z_1 + 2.237z_2$, subject to the constraints of $(\mathcal{P}_{\overline{\sigma}})$. It provides us with the following efficient solution:

	z_1	z_2	x_1	x_2	s_1	s_2
$\overline{w}$	20.23	3.71	2.11	3.14	0.00	0.00

The decision maker decides to keep the three solutions $\mathcal{S} = \{\overline{u}, \overline{v}, \overline{w}\}$. But, no new efficient solution is obtained, since both facets defined by $\{\overline{u}, \overline{w}\}$ and $\{\overline{v}, \overline{w}\}$ are efficient.

The decision maker is now allowed to modify the requirement levels.

Second Step He decides to consolidate the satisfaction of the first constraint by increasing the value of σ_1. The new level vector is

$$\overline{\sigma}' = (0.93, 0.50)$$

which leads to the MOLP problem

$$(\mathcal{P}_{\overline{\sigma}'}) \quad \left[\text{"maximize"} \begin{cases} z_1 = 23.5x_1 + 9.99x_2 \\ z_2 = -4.6x_1 + 7.8x_2 \end{cases} \right. \\ \text{such that} \begin{cases} -3.656x_1 + 12.902x_2 \le 27.885 \\ 4.5x_1 + 4.3x_2 \le 23 \end{cases} \\ \left. \begin{array}{l} x_1 \le 5.5 \\ x_1, x_2 \ge 0 \end{array} \right. \tag{38}$$

The DM also decides to re-use the same optimization weight sets as in the previous step, namely $(1, 0)$, $(0, 1)$ and $(1, 2.237)$.

	z_1	z_2	x_1	x_2	s_1	s_2
$\overline{u}$	30.03	−5.88	5.11	0.00	46.57	0.00
$\overline{v}$	5.40	4.21	0.00	2.16	0.00	13.71
$\overline{w}$	21.17	2.78	2.40	2.84	0.00	0.00

Here again, two efficient facets are determined and the proposition is made for the DM to revise his satisfaction requirements.

Third Step He is now willing to increase the value of criterion z_1. When considering the unicriterion optimization of z_1 in the previous step, it can be observed that the second constraint was saturated. Therefore, to enhance the value of z_1, we need to relax the σ_2 requirement. For example, we adopt

$$\bar{\sigma}'' = (0.93, 0.30)$$

and solve the MOLP problem

$$(\mathcal{P}_{\bar{\sigma}''}) \quad \left[\begin{array}{l} \text{``maximize''} \begin{cases} z_1 = 23.5x_1 + 9.99x_2 \\ z_2 = -4.6x_1 + 7.8x_2 \end{cases} \\ \text{such that} \begin{cases} -3.656x_1 + 12.902x_2 \le 27.885 \\ \quad 4.3x_1 + \quad 4.02x_2 \le 25 \end{cases} \\ \quad x_1 \le 5.5 \\ \quad x_1, x_2 \ge 0 \end{array} \right. \tag{39}$$

Three efficient solutions are generated, as well as efficient facets,

	z_1	z_2	x_1	x_2	s_1	s_2
$\bar{u}$	33.15	−5.67	5.50	0.34	43.66	0.00
$\bar{v}$	5.40	4.21	0.00	2.16	0.00	13.71
$\bar{w}$	25.14	2.42	2.99	3.01	0.00	0.00

Finally, the decision maker chooses $\bar{w}$ as his best compromise.

This solution is the target point chosen in (Słowiński and Teghem 1990a) for comparison purposes. It allows to "simulate" actions of the DM going in a given direction.

6 Comparison of MOFAC with STRANGE and FLIP

The same example has been treated by both methods STRANGE and FLIP (see Słowiński and Teghem 1990a). Therefore, we may compare our procedure to a typically stochastic approach — namely STRANGE (Teghem et al. 1986) — and to a fuzzy one — FLIP (Słowiński 1986). Both methods are explicitly described in Słowiński and Teghem's (1990b) book and put into competition.

Since we said that any MOLP procedure can be chosen to solve the associate deterministic problem, we will mainly focus on the model differences. Is uncertainty modelled in the same way? What about risk? These are the main viewpoints for the comparison of MOFAC with STRANGE and FLIP.

6.1 Uncertainty Modelling

STRANGE language for input data is based on scenarios; they encodes in a discrete way a set of possible realizations. They are defined globally for each objective as well as for each constraint. In general, the experts estimate extreme cases and a few intermediate ones.

Increasing the number of scenarios leads to a larger number of criteria and, therefore, to a larger number of linear programming problems to be solved in order to compute the pay-off table.

FLIP uses the fuzzy number language. The information about uncertain coefficients is represented separately and in a continuous way. This less schematic representation goes together with a more extensive mathematical treatment.

The number of objectives and constraints are fixed, since the associated deterministic MOLP problem involves one criterion per fuzzy objective and two deterministic constraints per fuzzy one. But, for each objective, a fuzzy goal has to be determined.

MOFAC approach is somewhere in-between those two methods. The imprecise probability distribution on each uncertain coefficient is modelled by a continuous fuzzy number but doesn't require important mathematical effort. The number of criteria and of constraints are equal in the fuzzy problem and in the deterministic one; and no goal is needed.

6.2   Risk and Safety

In the treatment of the risk of violating constraints, two main methodologies can be exhibited (Roubens and Teghem 1991). On the one hand, *Chance Constrained Programming* (CCP) approach considers the risk independently for each uncertain constraint and imposes a bound on this risk; namely, FLIP belongs to this class of procedures. On the other hand, *Stochastic Programming with Recourse* (SPR) consists of a global measure of the constraint violation, through an additional objective aggregating the different slack variables in excess. This class is exemplified by STRANGE. Our approach to safety is more related to FLIP one and to CCP procedures, since each constraint is characterized by one specific satisfaction requirement σ, which can be fixed by the DM. In FLIP, two satisfaction indices (pessimistic and optimistic) are associated to each constraint.

However, a SPR methodology can be easily designed coherently with the probabilistic interpretation of a fuzzy number. For instance, it could be proposed to aggregate in an additionnal objective the slack variables in excess and defuzzified them by means of the proposed function $\mathfrak{F}$.

In MOFAC, the information about the constraint safety may be enhanced by the graphical analysis of the fuzzy numbers ($\overline{A}\overline{x}$ and B) representing the fuzzy constraint ($\overline{A}\overline{x} \leq B$). It will give some clues about constraints that need to be reinforced.

6.3   Interactive Procedure – Computation

In STRANGE, whose interactive spirit is similar to the STEM method, the DM is asked in the interactive phases to indicate an objective on which he is ready to relax as well as the maximum level of this relaxation. In FLIP as well as in our approach, the DM specifies the safety requirements and supervises the generation of successive efficient solutions.

On the other hand, our approach requires much less computational effort as others, since FLIP leads to multiobjective linear fractional programming problems (if the objective memberships are linear!) and STRANGE involves a higher number of constraints and criteria.

It is worth noting that the shape of the membership functions has no influence in MOFAC. Each coefficient is essentially represented by its lower and upper mean values, due to the imprecise probability interpretation. Should this be considered as too restrictive, the defuzzification of each coefficient could take into account weight functions as presented in (Fortemps and Roubens 1996).

In STRANGE, precisely defined probability about scenarios are considered and a global risk objective to be minimized is introduced; FLIP uses fuzzy numbers as a kind of possibility distributions and defines different safety requirements for each constraint. In MOFAC, the imprecision on probability risk is modelled by fuzzy numbers and each constraint satisfaction is managed independently.

References

Bellman, R. and Zadeh, L. (1970). Decision-making in a fuzzy environment, *Management Science* **17**(4): 141–164.

Bortolan, G. and Degani, R. (1985). A review of some methods for ranking fuzzy subsets, *Fuzzy Sets and Systems* **15**(1): 1–19.

Chen, S.-J. and Hwang, C.-L. (1992). *Fuzzy Multiple Attribute Decision Making*, Springer–Verlag.

Dempster, A. P. (1967). Upper and lower probabilities induced by a multiple-valued mapping, *Annals of Mathematical Statistics* **38**: 325–339.

Dubois, D. and Fortemps, P. (1999). Computing improved optimal solutions to max-min flexible constraint satisfaction problems, *European Journal of Operational Research* **118**: 95–126.

Dubois, D. and Prade, H. (1987). The mean value of a fuzzy number, *Fuzzy Sets and Systems* **24**: 279–300.

Fortemps, P. and Roubens, M. (1996). Ranking and defuzzification methods based on area compensation, *Fuzzy Sets and Systems* **82**: 319–330.

Gonzales, J. J., Reeves, G. R. and Franz, L. S. (1985). An interactive procedure for solving multiobjective integer linear programming problems, *in* Y. Y. Haimes and V. Chankong (eds), *Decision Making with Multiple Objectives*, Springer–Verlag, pp. 250–260.

Lai, Y. J. and Hwang, C. L. (1992). *Fuzzy Mathematical Programming: Methods and Applications*, Springer–Verlag.

Liou, T.-S. and Wang, M.-J. (1992). Ranking fuzzy numbers with integral value, *Fuzzy Sets and Systems* **50**: 247–255.

Ramik, J. and Rimanek, J. (1985). Inequality relation between fuzzy numbers and its use in fuzzy optimization, *Fuzzy Sets and Systems* **16**: 123–138.

Rommelfanger, H. and Słowiński, R. (1998). Linear programming with single or multiple objective functions, *in* R. Słowiński (ed.), *Fuzzy sets in decision analysis, operations researck and statistics*, Vol. 4 of *International Handbook of Fuzzy Sets and Possibility Theory*, Kluwer Academic Publishers.

Rommelfanger, H., Hanuscheck, R. and Wolf, J. (1989). Linear programming with fuzzy objectives, *Fuzzy Sets and Systems* **29**: 31–48.

Roubens, M. (1990). Inequality constraints between fuzzy numbers and their use in mathematical programming, *in* R. Słowiński and J. Teghem (eds), *Stochastic Versus Fuzzy Approaches to Multiobjective Mathematical Programming under Uncertainty*, Kluwer Academic Publishers, pp. 321–330.

Roubens, M. and Teghem, J. (1991). Comparison of methodologies for fuzzy and stochastic multi-objective programming, *Fuzzy Sets and Systems* **42**: 119–132.

Sakawa, M. (1993). *Fuzzy Sets and Interactive Multiobjective Optimization*, Plenum Press.

Słowiński, R. (1986). A multicriteria fuzzy linear programming method for water supply system development planning, *Fuzzy Sets and Systems* **19**: 217–237.

Słowiński, R. (1990). FLIP: an interactive method for multiobjective linear programming with fuzzy coefficients, *in* R. Słowiński and J. Teghem (eds), *Stochastic Versus Fuzzy Approaches to Multiobjective Mathematical Programming under Uncertainty*, Kluwer Academic Publishers, pp. 321–330.

Słowiński, R. (1997). Interactive fuzzy multiobjective programming, *in* J. Climaco (ed.), *Multicriteria Analysis – Proceedings of the XIth International Conference on MCDM, 1–6 August 1994, Coimbra (Portugal)*, Springer, pp. 202–212.

Słowiński, R. and Teghem, J. (1990a). A comparison study of STRANGE and FLIP, *in* R. Słowiński and J. Teghem (eds), *Stochastic Versus Fuzzy Approaches to Multiobjective Mathematical Programming under Uncertainty*, Kluwer Academic Publishers, pp. 365–393.

Słowiński, R. and Teghem, J. (eds) (1990b). *Stochastic Versus Fuzzy Approaches to Multiobjective Mathematical Programming under Uncertainty*, Kluwer Academic Publishers.

Steuer, R. (1985). *Multiple Criteria Optimization: Theory, Computation and Applications*, John Wiley and Sons.

Tanaka, H., Ichihashi, H. and Asai, K. (1984). A formulation of linear programming problems based on comparison of fuzzy numbers, *Control and Cybernetics* **13**: 185–194.

Teghem, J. (1990). STRANGE: an interactive method for multiobjective stochastic linear programming, and STRANGE-MOMIX its extension to integer variables, *in* R. Słowiński and J. Teghem (eds), *Stochastic Versus Fuzzy Approaches to Multiobjective Mathematical Programming under Uncertainty*, Kluwer Academic Publishers, pp. 103–115.

Teghem, J., Dufrane, D., Thauvoye, M. and Kunsch, P. L. (1986). "STRANGE":an interactive method for multi-objective linear programming under uncertainty, *European Journal of Operational Research* **26**: 65–82.

Vanderpooten, D. and Vincke, P. (1989). Description and analysis of some representative interactive multicriteria procedures, *Mathematical and Computer Modelling* **12**: 1221–1238.

An Extension of the Axioms of Utility Theory Based on Fuzzy Rationality Measures

Vincenzo Cutello[1] and Javier Montero[2]

[1] Dept. of Math. and C.S.
University of Catania
V.le A. Doria 6
95125 Catania, Italy
E-mail: cutello@dipmat.unict.it

[2] Dept. of Statistics and O.R.
Complutense University
Madrid, Spain
E-mail: Javier_Montero@Mat.UCM.Es

Summary. We present here a (better yet, the problems involved with a) generalization of classical utility theory when basic preferences are stated by means of "rational" fuzzy preference relations. Rationality of fuzzy preference relations will be measured according to general fuzzy rationality measures. A utility function is proposed and introduced by using a "boosting" procedure on the fuzzy preference relations which may assure a linearization of the alternatives, still maintaining or improving rationality.

> *Mathematics is a language in which one cannot express unprecise or nebulous thoughts.*
> H. Poincaré

> *What exactly is Mathematics? Many have tried but nobody has really succeeded in defining mathematics; it is always something else.*
> S.M. Ulam
> (Adventures of a mathematician)

1 Introduction

Fuzzy logic is nowadays a remarkably well formalized mathematical framework for dealing in a precise and formal way with concepts deriving from unprecise knowledge or thoughts. This is particularly true in the general area of decision making. Wherever a finite collection of alternatives must be analyzed, compared so to pick one, it is often the case the human beings tend to loose precision and clarity of mind. Although they are pretty able to pair-wise compare the alternatives. Fuzzy preference relations represent a good formal methodology for producing algorithmic solutions to decision making problems. Utility theory has been traditionally formalized and used in such areas. Its axiomatic foundation, though, relies upon non fuzzy and non contradictory preference relations. Not very human-like in many applications today.

For instance, the amazing growth of the Internet and the WWW, the social and economic issues involved with it have caused an enormous interest in the design, testing and production of software systems which are able to help and interact with human participants in the (virtually handled) economic world. Such software systems are commonly denoted by "Intelligent Systems" and have evolved in body (implementation level), mind (inferential core) and scope from classical expert systems.

In particular, they must *do a good job of acting on their environment* (see [21]). And if we want to define them to be "rational agents" or "ideal rational agents": *for each possible sequence of inputs, an ideal rational agent does whatever action is expected to maximize its performance measure, on the basis of the evidence provided by the inputs and whatever built-in knowledge the agent has.*

Example 1. The first example of intelligent agent is given by one of the aspects of e-commerce. A company who is planning to have a marketing activity using its web server would need a software system which :

- keeps track of the customers requests
- "localizes" the requests to the customer profiles so to offer specific information to specific customers (common advertising activity done already on a simple basis using "cookies")
- "learns" customer preferences from statistical data
- "understands" from customer requests what new products could be of interest and feasible to offer given the company resources and interests;
- "redirects" the customers to other links (friendly company links) when it is necessary
- searches the web for information on competitors activities
- gives general advice and suggestions to the company managers, etc.

    □

Example 2. A second example can be derived by the growing interest on distance education using the web. Many higher education institutions are already working on it and have started offering degrees which are almost entirely done on the web. In such a scenario, one could think of intelligent agents which act as tutors for specific disciplines. For instance, an "interactive mathematics tutor", would check typed formulas and results, would offer suggestions and corrections, would understand the student preferences in terms of material and timing. The agent would have to decide which topics to stress, what exercise to assign, what suggestions to give, etc. □

In both of the examples described above, decisions must be made under probabilistic uncertainty using as well approximate reasoning techniques.

We will now describe a formal framework (see [7,8]) to solve (at least partially) such kind of decision problems. We will start from the classical axioms of utility theory and then we will describe a possible extension by introducing fuzzy preferences and rationality of preferences. To define rationality we will make use of general fuzzy rationality measures (see [4]).

2 The fuzziness of rationality

Rationality of individuals is clearly a fuzzy concept, therefore the closer an intelligent agent is to a human being the fuzzier will be its associated concept of rationality. Rationality can be seen as consistency of (degree of) preferences. Such a consistency of preferences is in fact a combination of explicit and implicit consistency. Explicit consistency is the absence of explicit contradictions, i.e. statements of type $P \wedge \neg P$, and implicit consistency is related to the judgment criteria (and their use) upon which the opinions are ultimately based.

To each individual one can assign a value of rationality between 0 (absolute irrationality) and 1 (absolute rationality). This value (degree) of rationality can be assigned in many different ways, and each of these different assignments corresponds to a different criterion for measuring the rationality of an individual. These criteria are called *fuzzy rationality measures*. Fuzzy rationality measures have been introduced and formalized in [2–5].

2.1 Fuzzy preferences

Fuzzy preference relations were introduced by Zadeh [25] in order to capture degrees of preferences (see also [10,13,14,19,26] for an extensive introduction). Two different alternatives may be considered to be better than a third one, but one preference may not be as intense as the other. In this way, given a finite set of alternatives or states X, a fuzzy binary preference relation is defined as a fuzzy set over all pairs of the cartesian product $X \times X$, so that its membership function, $\mu : X \times X \to [0,1]$, associates to each pair (x,y) the strength or intensity of preference $\mu(x,y)$ between x and y, measured in the unit interval. More intuitively, $\mu(x,y)$ gives the degree to which x is not considered to be worse than y. That is to say, μ is understood as the *weak* fuzzy preference, with a *strict* and an *indifference* part. Reflexivity ($\mu(x,x) = 1$ for all x) is therefore implied. Moreover, we shall be assuming here that such a measure of intensity of preference μ is defined on an absolute scale. This strict cardinal framework is indeed a strong assumption, but it has been justified in the past by some authors, within some particular context (see [23], for example).

Without such an assumption, many operations on preferences may not be meaningful at all. Addition and subtraction on intensities of preference need an interval scale at least, and multiplication requires that intensities are measured at least on a ratio scale (see [18,24] for an extensive discussion on measurement theoretic aspects of fuzzy sets).

2.2 Complete fuzzy preference relations

In some cases, we can also assume that the fuzzy binary preference relations μ are complete, where completeness is defined as

$$\mu(x,y) + \mu(y,x) \geq 1 \quad \forall x, y \in X.$$

Completeness is required in order to assure that the set of states is feasible and comprehensive (see [16], for example, for an axiomatic discussion). Then, the values

$$\mu_I(x,y) = \mu(x,y) + \mu(y,x) - 1$$
$$\mu_B(x,y) = \mu(x,y) - \mu_I(x,y)$$
$$\mu_W(x,y) = \mu(y,x) - \mu_I(x,y)$$

can be understood, respectively, as the degree to which the two alternatives are indifferent (xIy), the degree of strict preference of x over y (xBy, x is *better than* y) and the degree of strict preference of y over x (xWy, x is *worse than* y). In this way, preference between two alternatives x and y will be explained by means of these three intensity values (xBy, xIy, xWy), each one associated to one possible crisp relation between both alternatives in such a way that

$$\mu_B(x,y) + \mu_I(x,y) + \mu_W(x,y) = 1 \quad \forall x, y \in X.$$

2.3 Incomplete fuzzy preference relations

If $\mu(x,y) + \mu(y,x) < 1$, the value $1 - \mu(x,y) - \mu(y,x)$ can be understood either as the degree to which the comparison has not been accepted or the two alternatives are both rejected (see [1]).

Therefore, given an arbitrary fuzzy preference relation μ for any fixed pair of alternatives, x, y we define

$$\mu_{PI}(x,y) = \max(\mu(x,y) + \mu(y,x) - 1, 0)$$
$$\mu_{NI}(x,y) = \max(1 - \mu(x,y) - \mu(y,x), 0)$$

in order to capture the degrees of possitive indifference and negative indifference (incomparability). Notice, in particular that $\mu_{PI}(x,y)$ is the *Lukasiewicz* T-norm representing in this case $x \geq y$ and $y \geq x$ (see [16,13]). It is then obvious that the meaning of the expressions

$$\mu_B(x,y) = \mu(x,y) - \mu_{PI}(x,y)$$
$$\mu_W(x,y) = \mu(y,x) - \mu_{PI}(x,y)$$

is kept. Obviously, this model is based on the assumption that both positive and negative indifference are basically indifferences, so that standardized (complete) preferences can be defined

$$\mu^*(x,y) = \mu(x,y) + \mu_{NI}(x,y) = 1 - \mu_W(y,x)$$

The μ^* will be called the *completion* of μ.

Moreover, each value

$$\sigma(x,y) = 1 - \mu_{NI}(x,y) = \min\{\mu(x,y) + \mu(y,x), 1\} \tag{1}$$

can be associated to the degree to which the comparison between the pair of alternatives x, y is being supported.

2.4 Fuzzy rationality measures

Given now a complete (or the completion of a non complete one) fuzzy preference relation μ, we must assign to μ a degree or rationality. In the context of fuzzy binary preference relations, a standard assumption to characterize consistency or rationality is max-min transitivity (see [25] and [10,26]). Under this hypothesis if x is better than y with intensity $\mu(x,y)$ and y is better than z with intensity $\mu(y,z)$ then the degree to which x is better than z, i.e. $\mu(x,z)$, can never be lower than both values $\mu(x,y)$ and $\mu(y,z)$. The intuitive meaning of this property which extends transitivity is clear. As pointed out in [10], the strength of the link between two elements must be greater than or equal to the strength of any chain involving other elements. However, the property of being max-min transitive is crisp, that is, each relation either is or is not max-min transitive. Therefore, assuming max-min transitivity as key property for consistency and therefore rationality, does not allow a fuzzy classification.

General fuzzy rationality measures, that is to say functions ρ which map fuzzy preference relations into the interval $[0,1]$ and which allow a fuzzy classification have been introduced in [4]. Let us recall the axiomatic definition of any fuzzy rationality measure ρ.

(R1) **Foundation:** *If X is a finite set of alternatives, then $\rho(\mu) = 1$ for any crisp binary preference μ being a strict chain on X.*

(R2) Name Invariance: *Given* $\mu : X \times X \to [0,1]$ *and a permutation* $\pi : X \to X$ *then*

$$\rho(\mu^{\pi}) = \rho(\mu)$$

where $\mu^{\pi}(x,y) = \mu(\pi(x), \pi(y))$ *for all* $x, y \in X$.

(R3) Symmetry:

$$\rho(\neg\mu) = \rho(\mu)$$

where

$$\neg\mu(x,y) = \mu(y,x).$$

for all $x, y \in X$.

(R4) Principle of persistent degree of rationality *Let Y be a non-empty finite set of alternatives and let x be an extra alternative not belonging to Y. Let us consider a fuzzy preference $\mu : Y \times Y \to [0,1]$ such that $\mu(y,z) = 1, \mu(z,y) = 0, \forall y \in Y_1, \forall z \in Y_2$ for some Y_1, Y_2 partition of Y, and an extension μ' such that*

$$\mu'(y,z) = \mu(y,z), \forall y, z \in Y$$

$$\mu'(y,x) = 1, \mu'(x,y) = 0, \forall y \in Y_1$$

$$\mu'(x,z) = 1, \mu'(z,x) = 0, \forall z \in Y_2$$

$$\mu'(x,x) = 1$$

Then it must be

$$\rho(\mu') \geq \rho(\mu).$$

The last axiom of fuzzy rationality measures partitions the set of rationality measures into three sets: normal, pessimistic and optimistic.

(R5) Regularity: Given $\mu : X \times X \to [0,1]$ defined over X, $(\bar{x}, \bar{y})$ arbitrary pair of alternatives, let $P_{\mu}(\bar{x}, \bar{y})$ be the collection of pair of real numbers (a, b) such that
(i) $0 \leq \mu(\bar{x}, \bar{y}) + a \leq 1$
(ii) $0 \leq \mu(\bar{y}, \bar{x}) + b \leq 1$
(iii) $\mu(\bar{x}, \bar{y}) + \mu(\bar{y}, \bar{x}) + a + b \geq 1$
For every pair $(a, b) \in P_{\mu}(\bar{x}, \bar{y})$ we will denote by

$$\Delta_{\mu}((\bar{x}, \bar{y}), (a, b))$$

the fuzzy preference relation defined as follows

$$\Delta_{\mu}((\bar{x}, \bar{y}), (a, b))(x, y) = \begin{cases} \mu(\bar{x}, \bar{y}) + a \text{ if } (x, y) = (\bar{x}, \bar{y}) \\ \mu(\bar{y}, \bar{x}) + b \text{ if } (x, y) = (\bar{y}, \bar{x}) . \\ \mu(x, y) \qquad \text{otherwise} \end{cases}$$

Let ρ be a fuzzy rationality measure, then

(1) ρ is normal if

$$\rho(\Delta_\mu((\bar{x},\bar{y}),(a,0))), \quad \rho(\Delta_\mu((\bar{x},\bar{y}),(a,-a))), \quad \rho(\Delta_\mu((\bar{x},\bar{y}),(a,a)))$$

are monotone functions of a.

(2) ρ is pessimistic if there exists a value $a \in [0,1]$ such that

(2.1) $\rho(\Delta_\mu((\bar{x},\bar{y}),(b,0))) \geq \rho(\Delta_\mu((\bar{x},\bar{y}),(c,0)))$

(2.2) $\rho(\Delta_\mu((\bar{x},\bar{y}),(b,-b))) \geq \rho(\Delta_\mu((\bar{x},\bar{y}),(c,-c)))$

(2.3) $\rho(\Delta_\mu((\bar{x},\bar{y}),(b,b))) \geq \rho(\Delta_\mu((\bar{x},\bar{y}),(c,c)))$

for all b, c such that either $a > b > c$ or $a < b < c$.

(3) ρ is optimistic if there exists a value $a \in [0,1]$ such that

(3.1) $\rho(\Delta_\mu((\bar{x},\bar{y}),(b,0))) \leq \rho(\Delta_\mu((\bar{x},\bar{y}),(c,0)))$

(3.2) $\rho(\Delta_\mu((\bar{x},\bar{y}),(b,-b))) \leq \rho(\Delta_\mu((\bar{x},\bar{y}),(c,-c)))$

(3.3) $\rho(\Delta_\mu((\bar{x},\bar{y}),(b,b))) \leq \rho(\Delta_\mu((\bar{x},\bar{y}),(c,c)))$

for all b, c such that either $a > b > c$ or $a < b < c$.

2.5   Some examples

We will now give some examples of fuzzy rationality measures. The proofs that they satisfy the appropriate axioms can be found in [4].

- A fuzzy preference relation μ is *max-min transitive* whenever

$$\mu(x,y) \geq \min\{\mu(x,z),\mu(z,y)\}$$

for all z and for any fixed pair of alternatives x, y.
Let us define

$$\rho_{maxmin}(\mu) = \begin{cases} 1 \text{ if } \mu \text{ is max-min transitive} \\ 0 \text{ otherwise} \end{cases}.$$

The above is a pessimistic fuzzy rationality measure.

- Next example is based upon Orlovsky's choice set of unfuzzy nondominated alternatives. Let us define for any arbitrary non-empty subset Y of alternatives

$$Y^\mu_{UND} = \{x \in Y | \mu(x,y) \geq \mu(y,x), \forall y \in Y\}$$

for any given fuzzy preference $\mu : X \times X \to [0,1]$. Then the following map is an optimistic fuzzy rationality measure:

$$\rho_N(\mu) = \begin{cases} \min\{\frac{1}{|Y^\mu_{UND}|} | Y^\mu_{UND} \neq \emptyset\} \text{ if } Y^\mu_{UND} \neq \emptyset, \forall Y \subseteq X, Y \neq \emptyset, \\ 0 \hspace{5.5cm} \text{otherwise} \end{cases}.$$

Note that ρ_N will take value 1 if and only if there is just one unfuzzy non-dominated alternative for each non-empty set of alternatives. Moreover, value 0 is reached if and only if there exists some subset with no unfuzzy nondominated alternatives. In between these two cases, the larger the choice sets are, the lower is the degree of rationality. Therefore, this rationality measure captures the fact that usually a unique final decision must be chosen, and the bigger is the choice the more complex will be the procedure required to select an alternative.

- If we just assign value 1 whenever all choice sets Y_{UND}^{μ} are not empty and value 0 otherwise, we will get the following *normal* fuzzy rationality measure (see [15] for a necessary and sufficient condition for the existence of Orlovsky's choice set):

$$\rho_{UND}(\mu) = \begin{cases} 1 \text{ if } Y_{UND}^{\mu} \neq \emptyset, \forall Y \subseteq X, Y \neq \emptyset \\ 0 \text{ otherwise} \end{cases}.$$

If we consider the dual set of the set of unfuzzy nondominated alternatives, i.e., the set of unfuzzy dominated alternatives, defined as follows:

$$Y_{UD}^{\mu} = \{x \in Y | \mu(x, y) \leq \mu(y, x), \forall y \in Y\}$$

for any non empty set of alternatives $Y \subseteq X$. Then the following mapping defines another normal fuzzy rationality:

$$\rho_D(\mu) = \begin{cases} 1 \text{ if } X_{UND}^{\mu} \cup X_{UD}^{\mu} \neq \emptyset \\ 0 \text{ otherwise} \end{cases}.$$

This last fuzzy rationality measure captures the fact that from a decision point of view, a fuzzy binary preference relation will become a decision aid procedure whenever either a set of alternatives which is equivalent from a decision point of view has been given, or we are able to choose a smaller subset (best or worst alternatives), in such a way that the number of alternatives to be considered in the next step is reduced.

2.6 Some more comments on fuzzy rationality measures

There is a significant computational problem related with fuzzy rationality measures and the feasibility of their use in real life applications. Indeed, some of the rationality measures proposed, though intuitively (and axiomatically) sound, appear to be quite complex from a computational point of view (see [6]).

Finally, we must point out the importance of the completeness assumption. Rationality measures, as considered in this paper, do not apply to non complete fuzzy preference relation, although incomparable alternatives indeed appear in practice (see [11–13,16] for a general approach to valued preference binary relations, where weak and strict intensity preferences, together with indifference and incomparability, are simultaneously modeled). Rationality under incomparability (as modeled in [12]) appears then to be a very interesting subject for future research.

3 The axioms of utility theory

First of all, we will introduce a reminder about the axioms of utility theory, following [21].

Let us assume a "rational" agent and a set of basic alternatives or states, $A_1, \ldots, A_n$. Such states can be combined to obtain new ones which are basically lotteries. In details, if we have the states $A_1, A_2, \ldots, A_l$ then for any probability value $p_1, p_2, \ldots, p_l$ such that $\sum_{i=1}^{l} p_i = 1$ we obtain the lottery $\begin{pmatrix} p_1 & \cdots & p_l \\ A_1 & \cdots & A_l \end{pmatrix}$, that is to say, the state where with probability p_i we have A_i. The axioms of utility theory which would follow, will not be concerned with utility but with preferences. Preferences can be modeled as a binary relation $\mu(A_i, A_j) \in \{0, 1\}$ defined over the set of states. In particular,

- if $\mu(A_i, A_j) > \mu(A_j, A_i)$ we say that the agent strictly prefers A_i to A_j, i.e. $A_i \succ A_j$;
- if $\mu(A_i, A_j) = \mu(A_j, A_i)$ we say that the agent is indifferent to the two states, i.e. $A_i \sim A_j$; (and such an indifference could be either "positive" or "negative");
- if $\mu(A_i, A_j) \geq \mu(A_j, A_i)$ we say that the agent does not prefer A_j over A_i, i.e. $A_i \succeq A_j$. Such a preference is denoted as "weak" preference.

The agent rationality can be characterized, for example, with the absence of (either strict or weak) preference cycles (see [20]). If the binary relation is complete (i.e. $\mu(A_i, A_j) = 1$ or $\mu(A_j, A_i) = 1$ holds for every pair $A_i, A_j \in X$) weak *acyclity* condition is equivalent to classical crisp transitivity of weak binary relations. Classical crisp binary order preference relations, that is, those relations verifying reflexivity and transitivity, represent ideal examples of consistent crisp preference relations. An alternative weaker proposal of consistency for crisp binary relations based on the idea of quasi-transitivity has been given in [22], by assuming transitivity just for the associated strict preferences. This alternative assumption can be justified from a theoretical point of view because it is well known that transitivity does not in practice hold for indifferences (see also [20]).

The above considerations are formally translated into the first two axioms below. The remaining four axioms are, instead, related to the way the preference relation evolves when we move onto lotteries built from the given states.

(A1) Orderability: given any two states A_i, A_j it must be true

$$(A_i \succ A_j) \vee (A_i \sim A_j) \vee (A_i \prec A_j)$$

(A2) Transitivity: given any three states A_i, A_j, A_h it must be true

$$(A_i \succ A_j) \wedge (A_j \succ A_h) \rightarrow (A_i \succ A_h)$$

(A3) Continuity: this axiom expresses the fact that if $(A_i \succ A_j \succ A_h)$ then there exists a probability value p such that the agent is indifferent between A_j and the lottery where that yields A_i with probability p and A_h with probability $1 - p$, that is to say

$$A_i \succ A_j \succ A_h \rightarrow \exists p \mid \begin{pmatrix} p & 1-p \\ A_i & A_h \end{pmatrix} \sim A_j$$

(A4) Substitutability:

$$A_i \sim A_j \rightarrow \begin{pmatrix} p & 1-p \\ A_i & A_h \end{pmatrix} \sim \begin{pmatrix} p & 1-p \\ A_j & A_h \end{pmatrix}$$

(A5) Monotonicity:

$$A_i \succ A_j \rightarrow \{p \geq q \leftrightarrow \begin{pmatrix} p & 1-p \\ A_i & A_j \end{pmatrix} \succeq \begin{pmatrix} q & 1-q \\ A_i & A_j \end{pmatrix}\}$$

(A6) Decomposability:

$$\begin{pmatrix} p & 1-p \\ A_i & \begin{pmatrix} q & 1-q \\ A_j & A_h \end{pmatrix} \end{pmatrix} \sim \begin{pmatrix} p & (1-p)q & (1-p)(1-q) \\ A_i & A_j & A_h \end{pmatrix}$$

3.1 The utility principle

Given the above axioms, there exists a real valued function U which verifies

$$U(A_i) > U(A_j) \leftrightarrow A_i \succ A_j$$
$$U(A_i) = U(A_j) \leftrightarrow A_i \sim A_j$$

Such a function, defined over the set of states and lotteries, can be supposed to be normalized, that is to say, to have values between 0 (minimal utility) and 1 (maximal utility). A possible way to define a utility function is the following:

- let A be a state of maximal utility and A' be a state of minimal utility;
- define $U(A) = 1$ and $U(A') = 0$;
- for any other state A_i, in view of axiom (A3), there exists a probability value p such that

$$A_i \sim \begin{pmatrix} p & 1-p \\ A & A' \end{pmatrix}$$

Put then $U(A_i) = p$.

4 The axioms of fuzzy utility theory

Let $A_1, \ldots, A_n$ be a set of basic alternatives or states. Since our intelligent agent is supposed to be rational, we suppose that its preference relation μ defined over the set of basic alternatives must verify $\rho(\mu) > 0$, for some fuzzy rationality measure ρ. Such a property is obviously the extension to the fuzzy case of the axioms (A1) and (A2) of utility theory, above described.

(FA1) Rationality:

$$\rho(\mu) > 0$$

4.1 Extending the set of alternatives

Next question we need to address is the following: how do we extend μ when a lottery $\begin{pmatrix} p & 1-p \\ A_i & A_j \end{pmatrix}$ is added to the set of alternatives, in such a way that the rationality value does not decrease ? Let A_h be a basic state, then

$$\mu(A_h, \begin{pmatrix} p & 1-p \\ A_i & A_j \end{pmatrix})$$

must clearly be equal to

- $\mu(A_h, A_i)$ if $p = 1$
- $\mu(A_h, A_j)$ if $p = 0$

In general, we will assume

(FA2) Extension: for any probability value p, and basic alternatives A_i, A_j, and A_h

$$\min(\mu(A_h, A_i), \mu(A_h, A_j)) \leq \mu(A_h, \begin{pmatrix} p & 1-p \\ A_i & A_j \end{pmatrix})$$

and

$$\mu(A_h, \begin{pmatrix} p & 1-p \\ A_i & A_j \end{pmatrix}) \leq \max(\mu(A_h, A_i), \mu(A_h, A_j))$$

Analogously,

$$\min(\mu(A_i, A_h), \mu(A_j, A_h)) \leq \mu(\begin{pmatrix} p & 1-p \\ A_i & A_j \end{pmatrix}, A_h)$$

and

$$\mu(\begin{pmatrix} p & 1-p \\ A_i & A_j \end{pmatrix}, A_h) \leq \max(\mu(A_i, A_h), \mu(A_j, A_h))$$

In particular, we have

- for $\mu(A_h, A_i) = 1$ and for any p,

$$\mu(A_h, A_j) \le \mu(A_h, \begin{pmatrix} p & 1-p \\ A_i & A_j \end{pmatrix})) \le 1$$

- for $\mu(A_i, A_h) = 1$ and for any p,

$$\mu(A_j, A_h) \le \mu(\begin{pmatrix} p & 1-p \\ A_i & A_j \end{pmatrix}, A_h) \le 1$$

As a consequence, if $\mu(A_h, A_i) = \mu(A_i, A_h) = 1$

$$\mu_I(A_h, A_j) \le \mu_I(A_h, \begin{pmatrix} p & 1-p \\ A_i & A_j \end{pmatrix})).$$

Axiom (FA2) is justified by the axiom of persistent rationality. Indeed, if we can partition the set of basic alternatives into Y_1 and Y_2 such that

$$\mu(A, A') = 1, \mu(A', A) = 0, \forall A \in Y_1, \forall A' \in Y_2$$

the above assumption will guarantee us that the rationality of the extended preference relation will not decrease.

In view of axiom (FA2) we can propose an analytical definition of the fuzzy preference relation, to be axiomatically justified.

Definition 1 (F-def). For any probability value p, and alternatives $A_i, A_j,$ and A_h

$$\mu(A_h, \begin{pmatrix} p & 1-p \\ A_i & A_j \end{pmatrix})) = p\mu(A_h, A_i) + (1-p)\mu(A_h, A_j)$$

and

$$\mu(\begin{pmatrix} p & 1-p \\ A_i & A_j \end{pmatrix}, A_h) = p\mu(A_i, A_h) + (1-p)\mu(A_j, A_h).$$

Moreover, given any $k \ge 2$, $X_1, \ldots, X_k$ alternatives and $p_1, \ldots, p_k$ such that $\sum_{i=1}^k p_i = 1$ we extend μ as follows

- let $B = \begin{pmatrix} p_1 & \cdots & p_k \\ X_1 & \cdots & X_k \end{pmatrix}$,
- given any alternative A and probability value q let

$$C = \begin{pmatrix} q & (1-q)p_1 & \cdots & (1-q)p_k \\ A & X_1 & \cdots & X_k \end{pmatrix}$$

then

$$\mu(\begin{pmatrix} q & 1-q \\ A & B \end{pmatrix}, C) = \mu(C, \begin{pmatrix} q & 1-q \\ A & B \end{pmatrix})) = 1.$$

From (F-def) it follows that

$$\mu_I(A_h, \begin{pmatrix} p & 1-p \\ A_i & A_j \end{pmatrix}) = p\mu_I(A_i, A_h) + (1-p)\mu_I(A_j, A_h).$$

It also follows that the decomposability axiom is properly extended.

Notice that in case μ is crisp, and $A_i \succ A_h \succ A_j$, then we may suppose that $\mu(A_h, \begin{pmatrix} p & 1-p \\ A_i & A_j \end{pmatrix}) = 1$ if $p \leq 1/2$ and 0 otherwise. Analogously, we may suppose that $\mu(\begin{pmatrix} p & 1-p \\ A_i & A_j \end{pmatrix}, A_h) = 1$ if $p \geq 1/2$ and 0 otherwise. That is to say, we put $1/2$ as a threshold and we increase μ to 1 if it is at least $1/2$, whereas we decrease to 0 if it less than $1/2$. In this case, for $p = 1/2$, we obtain $A_h \sim \begin{pmatrix} p & 1-p \\ A_i & A_j \end{pmatrix}$, which, without differences in intensity of preferences, seems to be the only appropriate understanding of axiom (A3) of continuity. We can conclude then that axiom (FA2) as extended by (F-def) is also a fuzzy extension of axiom (A3).

4.2   The problem of indifference

Let now $X = \begin{pmatrix} p & 1-p \\ A_i & A_h \end{pmatrix}$ and $Y = \begin{pmatrix} p & 1-p \\ A_j & A_h \end{pmatrix}$. If $\mu_I(A_i, A_j) = 1$ can we automatically claim that $\mu_I(X, Y) = 1$? The answer is no! Indeed, we must take into account the preference values which relate A_i and A_j to A_h. Following (F-def) we have

- for $p = 1$, $\mu_I(X, Y) = \mu_I(A_i, A_j)$
- for $p = 0$, $\mu_I(X, Y) = 1$

In general, we have

$$\mu_I(X, Y) = p^2 \mu_I(A_i, A_j) + p(1-p)(\mu_I(A_i, A_h) + \mu_I(A_j, A_h)) + (1-p)^2$$

4.3   Monotonicity

The monotonicity condition is implied by (F-def). Specifically, suppose that $\mu(A_i, A_j) > \mu(A_j, A_i)$ and let $X = \begin{pmatrix} p & 1-p \\ A_i & A_j \end{pmatrix}$ and $Y = \begin{pmatrix} q & 1-q \\ A_i & A_j \end{pmatrix}$ then for all probability values p, q we have

$$\mu(X, Y) = pq + (1-p)q\mu(A_j, A_i) + p(1-q)\mu(A_i, A_j) + (1-p)(1-q)$$

and

$$\mu(Y, X) = pq + (1-q)p\mu(A_j, A_i) + q(1-p)\mu(A_i, A_j) + (1-p)(1-q)$$

Thus

$$\mu(X, Y) - \mu(Y, X) = \alpha(\mu(A_j, A_j) - \mu(A_j, A_i))$$

where $\alpha = p(1-q) - (1-p)q$ and it is clear that $\alpha \geq 0$ if and only if $p \geq q$.

4.4   How do we define a utility function?

We use the 5-th and last axiom of fuzzy rationality measures
    We have the following

Theorem 1 (Boosting Theorem). *If ρ is either a normal or an optimistic fuzzy rationality measure, by using the regularity axiom we can obtain from μ a fuzzy preference relation μ^* such that*

- $\rho(\mu^*) \geq \rho(\mu)$
- *for every pair of alternatives (x, y) such that $\mu(x, y) \leq \mu(y, x)$ we have*

$$\mu^*(x, y) \leq \mu^*(y, x)$$

- *for every pair of alternatives (x, y) either*
    - $\mu^*(x, y) = \mu^*(y, x)$, *or*
    - $\max\{\mu^*(x, y), \mu^*(y, x)\} = 1$, *or*
    - $\min\{\mu^*(x, y), \mu^*(y, x)\} = 0$.

Proof. Let $(\bar{x}, \bar{y})$ be an arbitrary pair of alternatives. Suppose, w.l.o.g. that $\mu(\bar{x}, \bar{y}) \geq \mu(\bar{y}, \bar{x})$.
    Suppose first that ρ is normal. Since from the regularity condition we have that $\rho(\Delta_\mu((\bar{x}, \bar{y}), (a, -a)))$ is a monotone function of a then

- if for $a > 0$ we have that $\rho(\Delta_\mu((\bar{x}, \bar{y}), (a, -a)))$ does not decrease we can reach either the value $\Delta_\mu((\bar{x}, \bar{y}), (a, -a))(\bar{x}, \bar{y}) = 1$ or the value $\Delta_\mu((\bar{x}, \bar{y}), (a, -a))(\bar{y}, \bar{x}) = 0$.
- if instead for $a > 0$ we have that $\rho(\Delta_\mu((\bar{x}, \bar{y}), (a, -a)))$ decreases then by choosing $a = -(\mu(\bar{x}, \bar{y}) - \mu(\bar{y}, \bar{x}))/2 < 0$ we have that
    - $\Delta_\mu((\bar{x}, \bar{y}), (a, -a))(\bar{x}, \bar{y}) = \Delta_\mu((\bar{x}, \bar{y}), (a, -a))(\bar{y}, \bar{x})$.
    - $\rho(\Delta_\mu((\bar{x}, \bar{y}), (a, -a)))$ increased.

In both cases the theorem is proven when ρ is normal.
    Suppose now that ρ is optimistic. We know that there exists a value $a \in [0, 1]$ such that

$$\rho(\Delta_\mu((\bar{x}, \bar{y}), (b, 0))) \leq \rho(\Delta_\mu((\bar{x}, \bar{y}), (c, 0)))$$

for all b, c such that either $a > b > c$ or $a < b < c$.

- If $\mu(\bar{x}, \bar{y}) + a < 1$ and $\mu(\bar{y}, \bar{x}) - a > 0$ then $\rho(\Delta_\mu((\bar{x}, \bar{y}), (b, -b)))$ is a non decreasing function of b for $b > a$ and so we can reach either the value $\Delta_\mu((\bar{x}, \bar{y}), (b, -b))(\bar{x}, \bar{y}) = 1$ or the value $\Delta_\mu((\bar{x}, \bar{y}), (b, -b))(\bar{y}, \bar{x}) = 0$.
- if $a = 1 - \mu(\bar{x}, \bar{y})$ then $\rho(\Delta_\mu((\bar{x}, \bar{y}), (b, -b)))$ increases when b decreases from $1 - \mu(\bar{x}, \bar{y})$ to $\mu(\bar{y}, \bar{x}) - \mu(\bar{x}, \bar{y})$. So we reach a situation where $\Delta_\mu((\bar{x}, \bar{y}), (b, 0))(\bar{x}, \bar{y}) = \mu(\bar{y}, \bar{x})$.
- Analogously if $\mu(\bar{y}, \bar{x}) - a = 0$
    $\square$

Remark 1. The proof of the theorem is quite easy although technically tedious. It can be done locally by taking two alternatives at a time x, y and either decreasing (alt. increasing) $\mu(x, y)$ and/or increasing (alt. decreasing) $\mu(y, x)$. For pessimistic f.r.m. our intuition suggests that it is possible to take two alternatives, increase on one hand and then readjust things all over so to have a higher degree of rationality. It can be easily seen by considering some examples with max-min transitivity which is a pessimistic fuzzy rationality measure. Therefore, it can be also somehow generalized to the pessimistic case, although we have no formal and definite proof yet.

We can now pick the best and worst alternatives by respectively maximizing and minimizing the function

$$u(x) = \sum_{y \neq x} \mu_B(x, y) - \sum_{y \neq x} \mu_W(x, y)$$

Whenever, the boosting theorem allows us to partition X in several subsets $X_1, \ldots, X_k$ such that for every $x \in X_i$ and $y \in X_j$ if $i < j$ then either $\mu(x, y) = 1$ and $\mu(y, x) < 1$, or $\mu(x, y) > 0$ and $\mu(y, x) = 0$, the above choices are in some sense the result of a *linearization* of the alternatives. Note also that the above definition is consistent with the famous Debreu's theorem ([9]) that for mutual preferential independent preference values (i.e. for each pair (x, y) the value $\mu(x, y)$ does not depend on the other alternatives) the utility function can be seen as a linear combination of utility values dependent only on the single alternative.

Finally, once we find the alternatives of maximal and minimal utility we can act as in the crisp case.

5 A simple example

Consider the following fuzzy preference values over a set of four alternatives.

1	0.2	0.8	0.6
0.9	1	0.5	0.4
0.5	0.6	1	0.3
0.6	0.7	0.8	1

Suppose the entry (i, j) of the array gives us the value $\mu(x_i, x_j)$. It can be easily seen that $\rho_N(\mu) = 0$ since $Y^{\mu}_{UND} = \emptyset$ for $Y = \{x_1, x_2, x_3\}$.

We now try to boost the preference values hoping to linearize and improving the rationality.

For instance, if we put $\mu(x_2, x_3) = 0.6$ then $\{x_1, x_2, x_3\}^{\mu}_{UND} = \{x_2\}$ and $\rho_N(\mu) = 1/2$

Now, we remember that

$$\mu_I(x, y) = \mu(x, y) + \mu(y, x) - 1$$
$$\mu_B(x, y) = \mu(x, y) - \mu_I(x, y)$$
$$\mu_W(x, y) = \mu(y, x) - \mu_I(x, y)$$

and we have the following table for the values (μ_I, μ_B, μ_W)

	0.1, 0.1, 0.8	0.3, 0.5, 0.2	0.2, 0.4, 0.4
0.1, 0.8, 0.1		0.2, 0.4, 0.4	0.1, 0.3, 0.6
0.3, 0.2, 0.5	0.2, 0.4, 0.4		0.1, 0.2, 0.7
0.2, 0.4, 0.4	0.1, 0.6, 0.3	0.1, 0.7, 0.2	

It follows that

$$u(x_1) = 1 - 1.4 = -0.4$$
$$u(x_2) = 1.5 - 1.1 = 0.4$$
$$u(x_3) = 0.8 - 1.6 = -0.8$$
$$u(x_4) = 1.7 - 0.9 = 0.8$$

Therefore, x_4 is the alternative of maximal utility whereas x_3 is the alternative of minimal utility.

6   Final comments

We described a possible fuzzy extension of the classical axioms of utility theory. Our goal is to provide a framework for decision making under uncertainty and approximate knowledge to be a part of any "intelligent system" inferential core. We would like to stress the fact that our formalization is certainly not the only possible one (for another formalization see for instance [17]). The novelty of this approach rests in the use of fuzzy rationality measures to formalize "reasonable orderings" of alternatives or lotteries and in the mathematical possibility to partially readjust the fuzzy preferences so to make the decisional problem easier. Many questions about the proposed formalization remain unanswered and seem to us to be good topics for future investigations. Let us mention two which are both related to the boosting theorem.

1. Clarify what happens when we are dealing with pessimistic fuzzy rationality measures.
2. Even when dealing with normal or optimistic fuzzy rationality measures, the proposed theorem is not an algorithm. How do we algorithmically proceed and when do we stop ?

References

1. V. Cutello and J. Montero, A model for amalgamation in group decision making, in: J. Villareal, Ed., *NAFIPS '92*, vol. 1 (N.A.S.A. Conference Publications, Houston, 1992) 215–223.
2. V. Cutello and J. Montero. An axiomatic approach to fuzzy rationality. In: K.C. Min, Ed., *IFSA '93* (Korea Fuzzy Mathematics and Systems Society, Seoul, 1993), 634–636.

3. V. Cutello and J. Montero. Equivalence of Fuzzy Rationality Measures. In: H.J. Zimmermann, Ed., *EUFIT'93* (Elite Foundation, Aachen, 1993), vol. 1, 344–350.

4. V. Cutello and J. Montero. Fuzzy rationality measures. *Fuzzy sets and Systems* 62:39–54, 1994.

5. V. Cutello and J. Montero. Equivalence and Composition of Fuzzy rationality measures. *Fuzzy sets and Systems*, 85(1):31–43, 1997.

6. V. Cutello, J. Montero and G. Sorace On the computational complexity of computing fuzzy rationality degrees In *Proceedings of IPMU'96, Information Processing and Management of Uncertainty in Knowledge-Based Systems*, B. Bouchon-Meunier, M. Delgado, J.L. Verdegay, M.A. Vila and R.R. Yager, Eds.; pp. 471-475, Granada, July 1-5, 1996, Spain.

7. V. Cutello and J. Montero. Intelligent agents, fuzzy preferences and utilities. In *Proceedings of IPMU'98, Information Processing and Management of Uncertainty in Knowledge-Based Systems*, July 1998, Paris, France.

8. V. Cutello and J. Montero. Fuzzy Rationality and Utility theory axioms. In *Proceedings of NAFIPS'99*, North American Fuzzy Information Processing Society Conference, New York, NY, 1999, pp. 332-336.

9. G. Debreu Topological methods in cardinal utility theory In K.J. Arrow, S. Karlin, P. Suppes, Eds. *Mathematical Methods in the Social Sciences*, Stanford University Press, 1959.

10. D. Dubois and H. Prade, *Fuzzy Sets and Systems: Theory and Applications* (Academic Press, New York, 1980).

11. J.C. Fodor and M. Roubens. Preference modelling and aggregation procedures with valued binary relations. In: R. Lowen and M. Roubens, Eds., *Fuzzy Logic* (Kluwer Academic Press, Amsterdam, 1993), 29–38.

12. J.C. Fodor and M. Roubens. Valued preference structures. *European Journal of Operational Research* 79:277–286 (1994).

13. J. Fodor and M. Roubens *Fuzzy modelling and multicriteria decision support.* Kluwer, Dordrecht, 1994.

14. L. Kitainik. *Fuzzy Decision Procedures with Binary Relations.* Kluwer Academic Pub., Boston, 1993.

15. J. Montero and J. Tejada, A necessary and sufficient condition for the existence of Orlovsky's choice set, *Fuzzy Sets and Systems* 26 (1988) 121–125.

16. J. Montero, J. Tejada and V.Cutello. A general model for deriving preference structures from data. *European Journal of Operational Research*, 98:98–100, 1997.

17. K. Nakamura. Preference relations on a set of fuzzy utilities as a basis for decision making. *Fuzzy Sets and Systems*, 20:147–162, 1986.

18. A.M. Norwich and I.B. Turksen. A model for the measurement of membership and the consequences of its empirical implementation. *Fuzzy Sets and Systems*, 12:1–25 (1984).

19. S.E. Orlovski. *Calculus of Decomposable Properties, Fuzzy Sets and Decisions.* Allerton Press, New York, 1994.

20. P.K. Pattanaik, *Voting and collective choice* (Cambridge University Press, Cambridge, 1971).

21. S. Russell and P. Norvig. Artificial Intelligence: A modern approach. Prentice Hall, 1995.

22. A.K. Sen, *Collective choice and social welfare* (Holden-Day, San Francisco, 1970).

23. U. Thole, H.J. Zimmermann and P. Zysno. On the suitability of minimum and product operators for the intersection of fuzzy sets. *Fuzzy sets and Systems*, 2:167–180 (1979).

24. I.B. Turksen. Measurement of membership functions and their acquisition. *Fuzzy sets and Systems*, 40:5–38 (1991).

25. L.A. Zadeh, Similarity relations and fuzzy orderings, *Information Science* 3 (1971) 177–200.

26. H.J. Zimmerman, *Fuzzy Sets Theory and its Applications* (Kluwer-Nijhoff, Boston, 1985).

Hybrid Probabilistic-Possibilistic Mixtures and Utility Functions *

Didier Dubois[1], Endre Pap[2], and Henri Prade[1]

[1] I.R.I.T., Université Paul Sabatier, 118 route Narbonne, 31062 Toulouse Cedex 4, France, e-mail: dubois@irit.fr, e-mail:prade@irit.fr
[2] Institute of Mathematics, University of Novi Sad, 21000 Novi Sad, Yugoslavia, e-mail: pap@unsim.ns.ac.yu , pape@eunet.yu

Abstract. A basic building block in the standard mathematics of decision under uncertainty is the notion of probabilistic mixture. In order to generalize decision theory to non probabilistic uncertainty, one approach is to generalize mixture sets. In the recent past it has been proved that generalized mixtures can be non trivially defined, and they have been instrumental in the development of possibilistic utility theory. This paper characterizes the families of operations involved in generalized mixtures, due to a previous result on the characterization of the pairs of continuous t-norm and t-conorm such that the former is conditionally distributive over the latter. What is obtained is a family of mixtures that combine probabilistic and possibilistic mixtures via a threshold. It is based on a restricted family of t-conorm/ t-norm pairs which are very special ordinal sums. Any practically useful theory of pseudo-additive measures must use such special pairs of operations in order to extend the additivity property, and the notion of probabilistic independence.

1   Introduction

Utility theory is based on the notion of mathematical expectation. Its axiomatic foundations, following von Neumann and Morgenstern [19] rely on the notion of probabilistic mixtures, see [15]. It has been recently shown by Dubois et al. in [6] that the notion of mixtures can be extended to pseudo-additive measures (sometimes called decomposable measures, see [9,16,20]), including the case of possibility theory (see [12]). Possibilistic mixtures strikingly differ from probabilistic measures, because they account for a non-convex structure. However, changing sum into maximum, and the product into a triangular norm, possibilistic mixtures have properties that parallel those of probabilistic mixtures. In particular, possibilistic mixtures form the underpinnings of possibilistic utility theory, as proposed by Dubois and Prade in [11] and more recently systematized by Dubois, Godo et al. in [7].

The aim of this paper is to address the following question: what else remains possible beyond possibilistic and probabilistic mixtures? This question is addressed, from a mathematical point of view, by taking advantage of a

---

* The paper was written during the stay of the second author as visiting professor at University Paul Sabatier, in Toulouse, in June, 1999.

result of Klement et al. obtained in [16] on the relaxed distributivity of triangular norm over a triangular conorm (called conditional distributivity). This result has a drastic consequence on the notion of mixtures. Beyond possibilistic and probabilistic mixtures, only a form of hybridization is possible such that the mixture is possibilistic under a certain threshold, and probabilistic above.

A related question is the one of a counterpart to probabilistic independence for pseudo-additive measures. Namely what type of operation is mathematically consistent for obtaining the uncertainty of a conjunction of prescribed events as a function of the individual uncertainty of such events? Such events are called separable. The same distributivity property must be satisfied between the t-conorm characterizing the pseudo-additive measure, and the triangular norm expressing separability.

Mixtures and separability are closely linked within utility theory, see [5]. The role of separability is to let the probability of a sequence of independent events in composite lotteries to be evaluated. And mixtures enable the reduction of such composite lotteries to be carried out. This paper thus addresses a key question in the theory of pseudo-additive measures, since the possibility of specifying separable events is a basic practical issue in any uncertainty theory.

The paper is organized as follows. Section 2 is a refresher on triangular norms. Section 3 states the mathematical result concerning the conditional distributivity on t-norm theory. Section 4 is a refresher on pseudo-additive measures. Section 5 motivates the rest of the paper on the problem of separable events and lays down the families of pseudo-additive measures where this notion makes sense. Section 6 recalls the notion of generalized mixtures and presents the hybrid mixture. Section 7 is devoted to decomposition of S-measure in binary trees. Section 8 displays the hybrid utility functions they induce in details.

2 Triangular conorms and norms

Triangular conorms and norms are applied in many fields as fuzzy sets, fuzzy logics and their applications, in the theory of generalized measures and in nonlinear differential and difference equations (see [16,20,22]).

Definition 1. A triangular conorm (t-conorm for short) is a binary operation on the unit interval $[0, 1]$, i.e., a function $S : [0, 1]^2 \to [0, 1]$ such that for all $x, y, z \in [0, 1]$ the following four axioms are satisfied:

(S1) *Commutativity* $S(x, y) = S(y, x)$,
(S2) *Associativity* $S(x, S(y, z)) = S(S(x, y), z)$,
(S3) *Monotonicity*
       $S(x, y) \leq S(x, z)$ whenever $y \leq z$,
(S4) *Boundary Condition* $S(x, 0) = x$.

If S is a t-conorm, then its dual t-norm $T : [0,1]^2 \rightarrow [0,1]$ is given by

$$T(x,y) = 1 - S(1-x, 1-y).$$

Example 1. The following are the four basic t-norms together with their dual t-conorms:

(i) Minimum T_M and maximum S_M given by

$$T_M(x,y) = \min(x,y), \quad S_M(x,y) = \max(x,y),$$

(ii) Product T_P and probabilistic sum S_P given by

$$T_P(x,y) = x \cdot y, \quad S_P(x,y) = x + y - x \cdot y,$$

(iii) Lukasiewicz t-norm T_L and Lukasiewicz t-conorm S_L given by

$$T_L(x,y) = \max(x+y-1, 0), \quad S_L(x,y) = \min(x+y, 1),$$

(iv) The weakest t-norm, the drastic product T_D, and the strongest t-conorm S_D given by

$$T_D(x,y) = \begin{cases} \min(x,y) & \text{if } \max(x,y) = 1, \\ 0 & \text{otherwise,} \end{cases}$$

$$S_D(x,y) = \begin{cases} \max(x,y) & \text{if } \min(x,y) = 0, \\ 1 & \text{otherwise.} \end{cases}$$

A general way of constructing new t-norms (t-conorms) from given t-norms (t-conorms) is given in the following theorem, see [16]:

Theorem 1. *Let $(T_k)_{k \in K}$ be a family of t-norms and let $\{]\alpha_k, \beta_k[\}_{k \in K}$ be a family of pairwise disjoint open subintervals of the unit interval $[0,1]$ (i.e., K is an at most countable index set). Consider the linear transformations $(\varphi_k : [\alpha_k, \beta_k] \rightarrow [0,1])_{k \in K}$ given by*

$$\varphi_k(u) = \frac{u - \alpha_k}{\beta_k - \alpha_k}.$$

Then the function $T : [0,1]^2 \rightarrow [0,1]$ defined by

$$T(x,y) = \begin{cases} \varphi_k^{-1}(T_k(\varphi_k(x), \varphi_k(y))) & \text{if } (x,y) \in]\alpha_k, \beta_k[^2, \\ \min(x,y) & \text{otherwise,} \end{cases} \tag{1}$$

is a triangular norm, which is called ordinal sum of summands $T_k, k \in K$. We shall write $T = (<\alpha_k, \beta_k, T_k>)_{k \in K}$.

In a quite analogous way, a triangular conorm S can be defined as an ordinal sum of a family $(S_k)_{k \in K}$ of t-conorms, putting max instead of min in (1) and we shall write $S = (<\alpha_k, \beta_k, S_k>)_{k \in K}$.

The following representations hold, see [16,22]:

Theorem 2. *A function* $S : [0,1]^2 \to [0,1]$ *is a continuous Archimedean triangular conorm,i.e., for all* $x \in]0,1[$ *we have* $S(x,x) > x$, *if and only if there exists a continuous, strictly increasing function* $s : [0,1] \to [0,+\infty]$ *with* $s(0) = 0$ *such that for all* $x,y \in [0,1]$

$$S(x,y) = s^{-1}(\min(s(x) + s(y), s(1))).$$

The analogous theorem holds for continuous Archimedean triangular norms:

Theorem 3. *A function* $T : [0,1]^2 \to [0,1]$ *is a continuous Archimedean triangular norm,i.e., for all* $x \in]0,1[$ *we have* $T(x,x) < x$, *if and only if there exists a continuous, strictly decreasing function* $t : [0,1] \to [0,+\infty]$ *with* $t(1) = 0$ *such that for all* $x,y \in [0,1]$

$$T(x,y) = t^{-1}(\min(t(x) + t(y), t(0))).$$

The functions s and t from Theorems 2 and 3 are then called additive generators of S and T, respectively. They are uniquely determined by S and T, respectively, up to a positive multiplicative constant.

We have the following representation for arbitrary continuous t-conorm and t-norm, see [16].

Theorem 4. *A function* $S : [0,1]^2 \to [0,1]$ *(a function* $T : [0,1]^2 \to [0,1]$*) is a continuous t-conorm (t-norm) if and only if* S *(* T *) is an ordinal sum whose summands are continuous Archimedean t-conorms (t-norms).*

The t-conorm S (t-norm T) is called strict if it is continuous and strictly monotone on the open square $]0,1[^2$. The continuous t-conorm S (t-norm T) is called nilpotent if each $a \in]0,1[$ is a nilpotent element of S (of T), i.e., for every $a \in]0,1[$ there exists $n \in \mathbb{N}$ such that $a_S^{(n)} = 1$ (respectively $a_T^{(n)} = 0$), where $a_S^{(n)}$ is the n-th power of a given by $S(a, \ldots, a)$ (respectively $T(a, \ldots, a)$) repeating a n-times. The class of continuous Archimedean t-conorms (t-norms) consists of two disjoint classes: strict and nilpotent.

The following important characterization of a strict t-norm and a nilpotent t-conorm will enable us to simplify the approach in this paper, see [16].

Theorem 5. *A function* $T : [0,1]^2 \to [0,1]$ *is isomorphic to* T_P, *i.e., there is a strictly increasing bijection* $\varphi : [0,1] \to [0,1]$ *such that for all* $x,y \in [0,1]$ *we have*
$$T(x,y) = \varphi^{-1}(T_P(\varphi(x), \varphi(y))$$

if and only if it is a strict t-norm.

Theorem 6. *A function* $S : [0,1]^2 \to [0,1]$ *is isomorphic to* S_L, *i.e., there is a strictly increasing bijection* $\varphi : [0,1] \to [0,1]$ *such that for all* $x,y \in [0,1]$ *we have*
$$S(x,y) = \varphi^{-1}(S_L(\varphi(x), \varphi(y))$$

if and only if it is a nilpotent t-conorm.

3   Conditional distributivity

It is well-known (see [16]) that a t-norm T is distributive over a t-conorm on the whole square $[0,1]^2$ if and only if $S = S_M$. We shall relax this condition to require distributivity only on a smaller region, see [3,2,16].

Definition 2. A t-norm T is conditionally distributive over a t-conorm S if for all $x, y, z \in [0,1]$ we have

$$(CD) \quad T(x, S(y,z)) = S(T(x,y), T(x,z)) \quad \text{whenever} \quad S(y,z) < 1.$$

The continuity of T and S implies that distributivity can be extended for a wider domain.

Proposition 1. *Let a continuous t-norm T be conditionally distributive over a continuous t-conorm S. Let $x, y, z \in [0,1]$ and y and z are such that $S(y,z) = 1$ and for every $b < y$ we have $S(b,z) < 1$ or for every $c < z$ we have $S(y,c) < 1$, then the distributivity $T(x, S(y,z)) = S(T(x,y), T(x,z))$ holds.*

We shall need the following theorem from [16] which gives the complete characterization of the family of continuous pairs (S, T) which satisfy the condition (CD).

Theorem 7. *A continuous t-norm T is conditionally distributive over a continuous t-conorm S if and only if there exist $a \in [0,1]$, a strict t-norm T' and a nilpotent t-conorm S^* such that the additive generator s^* of S^* satisfying $s^*(1) = 1$ is also a multiplicative generator of T' such that*

$$T = (< 0, a, T_1 >, < a, 1, T' >)$$

where T_1 is an arbitrary continuous t-norm and

$$S = (< a, 1, S^* >).$$

We denote by $(< S_M, S^* >, < T_1, T' >)_a$ the pair of continuous t-conorm S and t-norm T from Theorem 7.

Example 2. (i) The extreme case $a = 0$ for the pair $(< S_M, S_L >, < T_1, T_P >)_0$, T_1 arbitrary, gives us the pair S_L and T_P represented in Figure 1

(ii) The other extreme case $a = 1$ for the pair $(< S_M, S_L >, < T_1, T_P >)_1$, where T_1 is an arbitrary continuous t-norm, gives us the pair S_M and T_1 represented in Figure 2

(iii) Let $a = 0.2$. Then the pair $(< S_M, S_L >, < T_1, T_P >)_{0.2}$ is given on the Figure 3

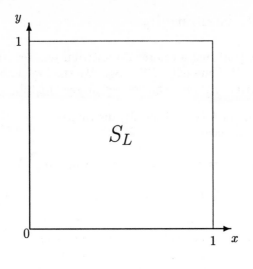

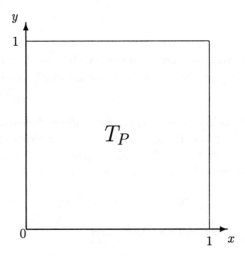

Fig. 1. Case $a = 0$

4 Pseudo-additive measures

Let X be a fixed non-empty finite set.

Definition 3. Let S be a t-conorm and let $\mathcal{A}$ be a σ-algebra of subsets of X. A mapping $m : \mathcal{A} \to [0, 1]$ is called a pseudo-additive measure, shortly S-measure, if $m(\emptyset) = 0, m(X) = 1$ and if for all $A, B \in \mathcal{A}$ with $A \cap B = \emptyset$ we have

$$m(A \cup B) = S(m(A), m(B)).$$

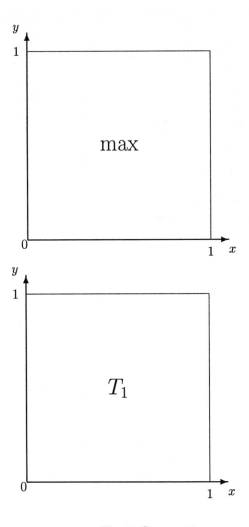

Fig. 2. Case $a = 1$

Each S-measure $m : \mathcal{P}(X) \to [0,1]$ is uniquely determined by the values $m(\{x\})$ with $x \in X$.

Remark 1. In the general case when X is an arbitrary non-empty set (also infinite) there is an additional condition on m in Definition 3 namely that it is continuous from below. In this case, if S is a left continuous t-conorm, then a set function $m : \mathcal{A} \to [0,1]$ satisfying $m(\emptyset) = 0$ is an S-measure if and

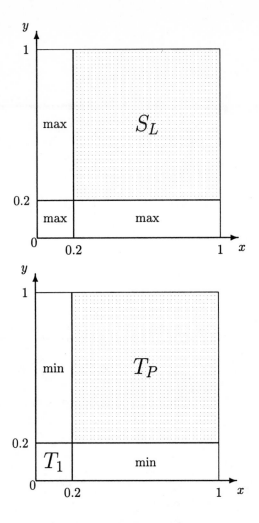

Fig. 3. Case of $0 < a < 1$

only if for each sequence (A_n) of pairwise disjoint elements of $\mathcal{A}$ we have

$$m\Big(\bigcup_{n=1}^{\infty} A_n\Big) = S_{n=1}^{\infty} m(A_n).$$

Example 3. Each measure $m : \mathcal{A} \to [0, \infty]$ with $\mathrm{Range}(m) \subseteq [0, 1]$ is an S_L-measure. Let $P : \mathcal{A} \to [0, 1]$ be a probability measure. Then for each $\alpha \in \,]-1, \infty[\, \setminus \{0\}$ the set function $m_\alpha : \mathcal{A} \to [0, 1]$ defined by

$$m_\alpha(A) = \frac{1}{\alpha}\Big((1 + \alpha)^{P(A)} - 1\Big)$$

is an S_α^{SW}-measure for the Sugeno-Weber t-conorm $S_\alpha^{SW}(x,y) = \min(x + y + \alpha xy, 1)$, see [16]. We have $m_\lambda = (s_\alpha^{SW})^{-1} \circ P$, where s_α^{SW} is the unique additive generator of S_α^{SW} which satisfies $s_\alpha^{SW}(1) = 1$.

Example 4. A set function $m : \mathcal{P}(X) \to [0,1]$ is S_M-measure if and only if for all $A, B \in \mathcal{A}$ we have

$$m(A \cup B) = S_M(m(A), m(B)).$$

Usually it is called possibility measure, denoted by Π and the corresponding distribution by π, see [12,20,26]. Namely for an arbitrary function $\pi : X \to [0,1]$, the set function $\Pi : \mathcal{P}(X) \to [0,1]$ defined by $\Pi(A) = \sup\{\pi(x) \mid x \in A\}$ is an S_M-measure. We remark that only for X finite the notions of S_M-measure and possibility measures coincide.

Remark 2. If $m : \mathcal{A} \to [0,1]$ is an S-measure and $\psi : [0,1] \to [0,1]$ an increasing bijection, then $\psi^{-1} \circ m : \mathcal{A} \to [0,1]$ is an S_ψ-measure, where S_ψ is defined by

$$S_\psi(x,y) = \psi^{-1}\left(S(\psi(x), \psi(y))\right).$$

The S-measures presented in Examples 3 and 4 are special cases of $(\sigma\text{-})$ S-decomposable measures [9,20,25].

5 Separable events

A basic notion in probability theory is independence. Beyond its philosophical appeal, probabilistic independence is instrumental for simplifying computations in stochastic modeling (as in Markov processes and Bayesian networks). If a theory of pseudo-additive measures has to be useful in practical applications for uncertainty modeling, some counterpart of independence must be exhibited for them.

The main issue in probabilistic independence is the existence of special events $A_1, \ldots, A_n$ such that

$$P(A_1 \cap \ldots \cap A_n) = \prod_{i=1}^{n} P(A_i).$$

Such events are called independent events. In order to preserve the computational advantages of independence, any operation $*$ for which it could be established that

$$P(A_1 \cap \ldots \cap A_n) = *_{i=1}^{n} P(A_i),$$

would do. However the Boolean structure of sets of events and the additivity of the probability measure, impose considerable constraint on the choice of operation $*$. Especially for any pair of events A and B such that the following properties are requested for a single operation $*$

Condition $(*)$:

$$P(A \cap B) = P(A) * P(B)$$
$$P(\overline{A} \cap B) = P(\overline{A}) * P(B)$$
$$P(A \cap \overline{B}) = P(A) * P(\overline{B})$$
$$P(\overline{A} \cap \overline{B}) = P(\overline{A}) * P(\overline{B}),$$

the only possible choice for $*$ covering all possible ranges of P is the product. See [5] for the case when $*$ may depend on A and B (that is $*_{AB} \neq *_{\overline{A}B}$). Here we shall study the possible operations $*$ in the condition $(*)$ when changing P for a pseudo-additive measure based on a t-conorm S. A first remark is that it is natural to require that $*$ be a continuous triangular norm. If $A = X$ is a sure event, then A and X are independent, and it follows that

$$m(A \cap X) = m(A) * m(X) = m(A) * 1 = m(A).$$

Commutativity and associativity of $*$ reflect the corresponding properties for conjunctions. It is also very natural that $*$ be non-decreasing in each place and continuous.

Remark 3. We set aside the exotic cases of non-continuous operations, or the problems resulting from finite setting, namely when operation $*$ would not be regular (e.g., associative, non monotonic) on the finite set $\{m(A) \mid A \subset X\}$, see Halpern [14].

We try to find which triangular norms can be used for extending the notion of independence for pseudo-additive measures in the sense of a prescribed triangular conorm. Since the term independence has a precise meaning in probability theory, we shall speak of separability instead. In particular

Definition 4. Two events A and B are said to be $*$-separable if

$$m(A \cap B) = m(A) * m(B)$$

for a triangular norm $*$.

Let A, B, C be three events such that $B \cap C = \emptyset$ and that the pairs (A, B) and (A, C) are made of separable events. Suppose m is an S- measure. Then only the equality

$$A \cap (B \cup C) = (A \cap B) \cup (A \cap C)$$

induces strong constraints on the choice of $*$ when S is fixed. Namely, we have

$$m(A \cap (B \cup C)) = S(m(A \cap B), m(A \cap C))$$
$$= S(m(A) * m(B), m(A) * m(C)).$$

Now, in probability theory, if disjoint sets B and C are independent from A, then $B \cup C$ is independent of A as well. Here again, in order to make the separability a computationally attractive property, the same property is taken for granted, i.e.,

$$m(A \cap (B \cup C)) = m(A) * m(B \cup C).$$

Hence the following identity must hold

$$m(A) * S(m(B), m(C)) = S(m(A) * m(B), m(A) * m(C)) \qquad (2)$$

for all (A, B, C) such that $B \cap C = \emptyset$, (A, B) separable, (A, C) separable. Note that if $m(A) = 1$ or 0, this property is always satisfied.

Assume $m(B \cup C) < 1$ in (2). Then the above equation coincides with the conditional distributivity property. It must hold for all S- measures. Then Theorem 7 (using Theorems 5, 6 which reduce all situations to the case in Example 2 for some $a \in [0, 1]$) provides the only possible choices for the pair $(S, *)$. Namely for some $a \in [0, 1]$

- for S the ordinal sum of max on $[0, a]$ and S_L on $[a, 1]$ for some $a \in [0, 1]$;
- for $*$ the ordinal sum of any continuous t-norm T_1 on $[0, a]$ and the product T_P on $[a, 1]$.

Hence the pseudo-additive measure is an hybrid set function $m : \mathcal{P}(X) \to [0, 1]$ such that for $A \cap B = \emptyset$ we have (see Theorem 1)

$$m(A \cup B) = \begin{cases} a + (1 - a) \min \left(\frac{m(A) - a}{1 - a} + \frac{m(B) - a}{1 - a}, 1 \right) & \text{if } m(A) > a, m(B) > a \\ \max(m(A), m(B)) & \text{otherwise.} \end{cases}$$

There is no way of satisfying (2) if m is such that $m(B) + m(C) > 1$ for some B, C that are independent. So the only reasonable pseudo-additive measures that prevent this situation from happening while ensuring the normalization, and admitting of an independence concept, are

- probability measures (and $* = $ product);
- possibility measures (and $*$ is any t-norm);
- pure hybrid measures m such that there is $a \in]0, 1[$ which gives for A and B disjoint

$$m(A \cup B) = \begin{cases} m(A) + m(B) - a & \text{if } m(A) > a, m(B) > a \\ \max(m(A), m(B)) & \text{otherwise,} \end{cases}$$

and for independence:

$$m(A \cap B) = \begin{cases} a + \frac{(m(A) - a)(m(B) - a)}{1 - a} & \text{if } m(A) > a, m(B) > a \\ a \cdot T_1(\frac{m(A)}{a}, \frac{m(B)}{a}) & \text{if } m(A) \leq a, m(B) \leq a \\ \min(m(A), m(B)) & \text{otherwise,} \end{cases}$$

and the normalization condition reads

$$\sum_{\{x\},m(\{x\})>a} m(\{x\}) = 1 + (\text{card}(\{x, m(\{x\}) > a\}) - 1) \cdot a.$$

The following example of S-measure will be used for the construction of hybrid probabilistic-possibilistic mixture.

Example 5. We take $(<S_M, S_L>, <T_1, T_P>)_{0.2}$ and define an S-measure $m : \mathcal{P}(\{1, 2, 3, 4, 5\}) \to [0, 1]$ for the one point sets as:

$$m_1 = 0.75, m_2 = 0.4, m_3 = 0.25, m_4 = 0.15, m_5 = 0.05.$$

We see that $m_1 + m_2 + m_3 = 1 + 2a = 1.4$. Then the other values of S-measure m are given , for two points sets by:

$$m_{12} = 0.95, m_{13} = 0.8, m_{14} = m_{15} = 0.75,$$

$$m_{23} = 0.45, m_{24} = m_{25} = 0.4,$$

$$m_{34} = m_{35} = 0.25, m_{45} = 0.15,$$

for three points sets by:

$$m_{123} = 1, m_{124} = 0.95, m_{125} = 0.95, m_{134} = 0.8; m_{135} = 0.8; m_{145} = 0.75,$$

$$m_{234} = 0.45, m_{235} = 0.45, m_{245} = 0.4, m_{345} = 0.25,$$

for four points sets by:

$$m_{1234} = 1, m_{1235} = 1, m_{1245} = 0.95, m_{1345} = 0.8, m_{2345} = 0.45,$$

and $m_{12345} = 1, m(\emptyset) = 0$.

We see that the behavior of this S-measure is probabilistic-like if the values of all elements which are in the considered set are greater than 0.2. The behavior of this S-measure is purely possibilistic if the values of all elements which are in the considered set are less than or equal to 0.2.

6 Hybrid mixtures

We shall use here the results of [6], Section 5, in a somewhat modified version. Namely, we shall start with a pair of t-conorm and t-norm instead of taking a pair of more general operations $(\oplus, \odot)$ on $[0, 1]$ called in [6] semisum and semiproduct, respectively. This gives no restrictions by [6], Corollary 2.

Let (S, T) be a pair of continuous t-conorm and t-norm, respectively, which satisfy the condition (CD). Then by Theorem 7 they are of the form

$$(<S_M, S^*>, <T_1, T'>)_a,$$

for $a \in [0, 1]$, where S^* is a nilpotent t-conorm, T_1 an arbitrary t-norm and T' a strict t-norm. We define the set Φ_S of ordered pairs (α, β) in the following way

$$\Phi_S = \{(\alpha, \beta) \mid (\alpha, \beta) \in [0, 1], S(\alpha, \beta) = 1\}.$$

Definition 5. An extended mixture set is a quadruple $(\mathcal{G}, M, T, S)$ where $\mathcal{G}$ is a set and $M : \mathcal{G}^2 \times \Phi_S \to \mathcal{G}$ is a function (extended mixture operation) such that the following conditions are satisfied:

M1. $M(x, y; 1, 0) = x$;

M2. $M(x, y; \alpha, \beta) = M(y, x; \beta, \alpha)$;

M3. $M(M(x, y; \alpha, \beta), y; \gamma, \delta) = M(x, y; T(\alpha, \gamma), S(T(\beta, \gamma), T(\delta, 1)))$.

The conditions **M1-M3** imply by [6],Lemma 1, the following condition

M4. $M(x, x; \alpha, \beta) = x$.

In the classical framework (see [15]) **M1-M3** imply one further important property of mixture operation. This property holds for extended mixture under some additional supposition, [6], Lemma 1 (second part). We formulate it in a slightly more general form (actually in [6], Section 6., it is used just in this form).

Lemma 1. *Suppose M is an extended mixture, i.e.,***M1-M3** *holds for M. Then*

M5 $M(M(x, y; \alpha, \beta), M(x, y; \gamma, \delta); \lambda, \mu)$

$= M(x, y; S(T(\alpha, \lambda), T(\gamma, \mu)), S(T(\beta, \lambda), T(\delta, \mu)))$ *holds for all $x, y \in \mathcal{G}$ and all $(\alpha, \beta), (\gamma, \delta), (\lambda, \mu) \in \Phi'$, where Φ' is a non-empty subset of Φ_S, if and only if*

$$T(\gamma, S(\alpha, \beta)) = S(T(\gamma, \alpha), T(\gamma, \beta)),$$

i.e., T is distributive over S on Φ'.

Let (S, T) be a pair of continuous t-conorm and t-norm, respectively, such that they satisfy the condition (CD) with $a \in [0, 1]$. We restrict ourselves to the situation $(< S_M, S_L >, < T_1, T_P >)_a$, since this is the most important case and all other cases can be obtained by isomorphisms (see Theorems 5, 6).

We define the set $\Phi' = \Phi_{S,a}$ of ordered pairs (α, β) in the following way

$$\Phi_{S,a} = \{(\alpha, \beta) \mid (\alpha, \beta) \in]a, 1[, \alpha + \beta = 1 + a \text{ or } \min(\alpha, \beta) \le a, \max(\alpha, \beta) = 1\}.$$

We have $\Phi_{S,a} \subset \Phi_S$. By Proposition 1 we have that for every $\alpha, \beta, \gamma \in \Phi_{S,a}$ the distributivity holds.

We define now the hybrid mixture set, which is an extension of the mixture sets investigated in [15] and [6].

Definition 6. A hybrid mixture set is a quadruple $(\mathcal{G}, M, T, S)$ where $\mathcal{G}$ is a set, (S, T) is a pair of continuous t-conorm and t-norm, respectively, which satisfy the condition (CD) and $M : \mathcal{G}^2 \times \Phi_{S,a} \to \mathcal{G}$ is a function (hybrid mixture operation) given by

$$M(x, y; \alpha, \beta) = S(T(\alpha, x), T(\beta, y)).$$

As shown above, it is enough to restrict to the case

$$(< S_M, S_L >, < T_1, T_P >)_a.$$

Then it is easy to verify that M satisfies the axioms **M1-M5** on $\Phi_{S,a}$. This kind of mixtures exhausts the possible solutions to **M1-M5**, but were not considered in [6] in their full generality.

7 Decomposition of S-measure in binary trees

Let us show the main appeal of **M1-M5**. Any probability distribution on a finite set X can be represented as a sequence of binary lotteries. A binary lottery is 4-uple (A, α, x, y) where $A \subset X$ and $\alpha \in [0, 1]$ such that $P(A) = \alpha$, and it represents the random event that yields x if A occurs and y otherwise. Let p be a probability on X such that $p_i = p(x_i), x_i \in X$. Assume $X = \{x_1, x_2, x_3\}$ then p can be described by the following trees on Figure 4

The binary tree is obtained as follows: First partition X into $\{x_1\}$ and $\{x_2, x_3\}$ with probabilities p_1 and $p_2 + p_3$, respectively, then partition $X \setminus \{x_1\}$ into $\{x_2\}$ and $\{x_3\}$ with probabilities $p_2/(p_2 + p_3)$ and $p_3/(p_2 + p_3)$, respectively. The two trees of Figure 4 are equivalent, provided that the probability of x_i is calculated by performing the product of weights on the path from the root of the tree until the leaf x.

More generally, suppose m is a S-measure on $X = \{x_1, x_2, x_3\}$ and $m_i = m(\{x_i\})$. Suppose we want to decompose the ternary tree on the Figure 5 into the binary tree so that they are equivalent.

Then the reduction of lottery property enforces the following equations

$$S(v_1, v_2) = 1, \quad T(\mu, v_1) = m_2, \quad T(\mu, v_2) = m_3,$$

where T is the triangular norm that expresses separability for S-measures. The first condition expresses that (v_1, v_2) is in the mixture set (with no truncation for t-conorm S allowed). If these equations have unique solutions, then by iterating this construction, any distribution of a S-measure can be decomposed into a sequence of binary lotteries. This property is basic in probability theory since it explains why probability trees can be used as a primitive notion for developing the notion of probability after Shafer [23].

The problem of normalization takes us to the following system of equations

$$\alpha_1 = T(\mu, v_1), \quad \alpha_2 = T(\mu, v_2), \quad S(v_1, v_2) = 1 \tag{3}$$

for given α_1 and α_2. Applying Corollary 2 from [6] we know that there generally exists an unique solution (μ, v_1, v_2). We are interested in the analytical forms of (μ, v_1, v_2). We suppose without loss of generality that $\alpha_1 \geq \alpha_2$. In the following we assume that $T_1 = \min$.

Then we have the following cases:

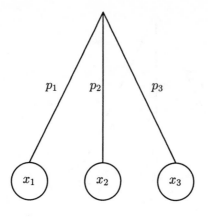

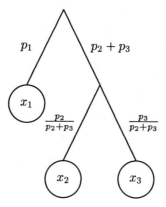

Fig. 4. Probability tree and the corresponding binary trees

Case I. Let $\alpha_1 > a, \alpha_2 > a$. Then (3) reduces to

$$\alpha_1 = a + \frac{(\mu - a)(v_1 - a)}{1 - a},$$

$$\alpha_2 = a + \frac{(\mu - a)(v_2 - a)}{1 - a},$$

$$1 = v_1 + v_2 - a.$$

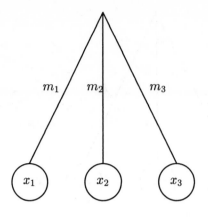

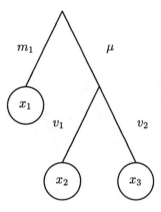

Fig. 5. S-measure tree and the corresponding binary trees

We obtain the unique solution

$$(\mu, v_1, v_2) = (\alpha_1 + \alpha_2 - a, a + \frac{(1-a)(\alpha_1 - a)}{\alpha_1 + \alpha_2 - 2a}, a + \frac{(1-a)(\alpha_2 - a)}{\alpha_1 + \alpha_2 - 2a}).$$

Case II. Assume $\alpha_1 > a \geq \alpha_2$. From (3), it follows that $\mu > a$. Hence $T = \min$ in the second equation of (3) since the result is less that a. Hence $v_2 = \alpha_2$. Hence $S = \max$ and it enforces $v_1 = 1$, and $\mu = \alpha_1$. So the triple

$$(\mu, v_1, v_2) = (\alpha_1, 1, \alpha_2)$$

is the unique solution to :

$$\max(v_1, v_2) = 1,$$

$$\alpha_1 = a + \frac{(\mu - a)(v_1 - a)}{1 - a},$$

$$\alpha_2 = \min(\mu, v_2).$$

Case III. Assume $\alpha_2 < \alpha_1 \leq a$. Then $S = \max$. Namely, to prove that $S = \max$ we have to prove that the solutions $v_1 > a$ and $v_2 > a$ are impossible. Indeed if this is assumed, then $T = \min$ and it follows that $\mu = \alpha_1 = \alpha_2$, a contradiction. Hence $S = \max$. Assume $v_1 = 1$. Then the first equation in (3) yields $\mu = \alpha_1$. Assuming $T = T_1 = \min$ the second equation of (3) leads to $v_2 = \alpha_2$. Hence the same solution $(\alpha_1, 1, \alpha_2)$ as in case II. Note that assuming $v_2 = 1$ leads to a contradiction since then $\mu = \alpha_2$ and equation $\alpha_1 = T(\alpha_2, v_1)$ has no solution.

The remaining case is when $\alpha_1 = \alpha_2 = \alpha \leq a$. If $S = \max$, one of v_1 and v_2 is 1 and $\mu = \alpha$. It is easy to check that if T is not $T_M = \min$, the solution to (3) is $v_1 = v_2 = 1$. However this solution is not unique if $T = \min$. We can choose any triple $(\mu, v_1, v_2) = (\alpha, 1, v_2)$ with $v_2 \in [\alpha, 1]$. However it is natural, by symmetry, to request that $v_1 = v_2$. In that case we always find the unique solution $v_1 = v_2 = 1$ if $S = \max$. Unfortunately $S = \max$ is not compulsory either. Indeed we may look for values v_1 and v_2 in $]a, 1[$ such that $v_1 + v_2 = 1 + a$, and $T(\mu, v_1) = \alpha$, and $T(\mu, v_2) = \alpha$. Clearly in this case $T = \min$ (since $v_1 > a, v_2 > a$ and $\alpha \leq a$), and $\mu = \alpha$. Again we are entitled to request , by symmetry, that $v_1 = v_2$. It yields $v_1 = v_2 = (1 + a)/2$ as another symmetric solution. From a practical point of view a natural objection against this probabilistic-like solution is that the limit of case III solution when α_1 comes close to α_2 is $(\mu, v_1, v_2) = (\alpha, 1, 1)$, and not $(\mu, v_1, v_2) = (\alpha, (1+a)/2, (1+a)/2)$. To conclude, although the binary decomposition equation (3) has many solutions in this symmetric pathological case, the only plausible one is $(\alpha, 1, 1)$.

Example 6. Considering Example 5 we have the following tree of binary lotteries given at Figure 6

It can be checked for instance that the weight of x_2 is $m_2 = T(0.45, 0.84)$.

8   Hybrid utility

Let (S, T) be a pair of continuous t-conorm and t-norm, respectively, of the form $(< S_M, S_L >, < T_1, T_P >)_a$. Let u_1, u_2 be two utilities taking values in the unit interval $[0, 1]$ and let μ_1, μ_2 be two degrees of plausibility from $\Phi_{S,a}$. Then we define *the optimistic hybrid utility function* by means of the hybrid mixture as

$$U(u_1, u_2; \mu_1, \mu_2) = S(T(u_1, \mu_1), T(u_2, \mu_2)).$$

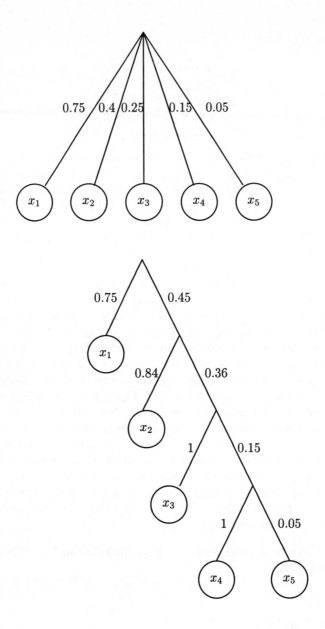

Fig. 6. *S*-measure tree and the corresponding binary trees

We shall examine in details this utility function.

Case I. Let $\mu_1 > a, \mu_2 > a$, i.e., $\mu_1 + \mu_2 = 1 + a$. Then we have the following subcases:

(a) Let $u_1 > a, u_2 > a$. Then we have

$$U(u_1, u_2; \mu_1, \mu_2) = S(a + \frac{(u_1 - a)(\mu_1 - a)}{1 - a}, a + \frac{(u_2 - a)(\mu_2 - a)}{1 - a}). \quad (4)$$

Then $a + \frac{(u_i - a)(\mu_i - a)}{1 - a} > a$ for all $i = 1, 2$. Hence by (4)

$$U(u_1, u_2; \mu_1, \mu_2) = \frac{u_1(\mu_1 - a) + u_2(1 - \mu_1)}{1 - a}$$

(b) Let $u_1 \leq a, u_2 > a$. Then we have

$$U(u_1, u_2; \mu_1, \mu_2) = S(u_1, a + \frac{(u_2 - a)(\mu_2 - a)}{1 - a}) = a + \frac{(u_2 - a)(\mu_2 - a)}{1 - a}.$$

(c) In a quite analogous way it follows for $u_1 > a, u_2 \leq a$ that

$$U(u_1, u_2; \mu_1, \mu_2) = a + \frac{(u_1 - a)(\mu_1 - a)}{1 - a}.$$

(d) Let $u_1 \leq a, u_2 \leq a$. Then

$$U(u_1, u_2; \mu_1, \mu_2) = \max(u_1, u_2).$$

Case II. Let $\mu_1 \leq a, \mu_2 = 1$ (in a quite analogous way we can consider the case $\mu_2 \leq a, \mu_1 = 1$). Then we have the following subcases, where $S = \max$:

(a) Let $u_1 > a, u_2 > a$. Then we have

$$U(u_1, u_2; \mu_1, \mu_2) = S(\mu_1, u_2) = u_2.$$

(b) Let $u_1 \leq a, u_2 > a$. Then we have

$$U(u_1, u_2; \mu_1, \mu_2) = S(a \cdot T_1(\frac{u_1}{a}, \frac{\mu_1}{a}), u_2) = u_2.$$

(c) Let $u_1 > a, u_2 \leq a$. Then we have

$$U(u_1, u_2; \mu_1, \mu_2) = S(\mu_1, u_2) = \max(\mu_1, u_2).$$

(d) Let $u_1 \leq a, u_2 \leq a$. Then we have

$$U(u_1, u_2; \mu_1, \mu_2) = \max(a \cdot T_1(\frac{u_1}{a}, \frac{\mu_1}{a}), u_2).$$

For $T_1 = $ min the case II and case Id are exactly possibilistic utility.

Although the above description of optimistic hybrid utility is rather complex, it can be easily explained, including the name optimistic.

Case I is when the decision-maker is very uncertain about the state of nature: both μ_1 and μ_2 are high and the two involved states have high plausibility. Case Ia is when the reward is high in both states- then the behavior of utility is probabilistic. Case Ib (analogously for the case Ic) is when the reward is low in state x_1 ($u_1 \leq a$) but high on the other state. Then the decision-maker looks forward to the best outcome and the utility is a function of u_2 and μ_2 only. In case Id when both rewards are low, the decision-maker is possibilistic and again focuses on the best outcome. Case II is when state x_1 is unlikely. In cases IIa,b when the plausible reward is good, then the decision-maker looks forward to this reward. In case IIc where the most plausible reward is low then the decision maker still keeps some hope that state x_1, will prevail if u_2 is really bad, but weakens the utility of state x_1, because of its lack of plausibility. This phenomena subsides when the least plausible outcome is also bad, but the (bad) utility of x_1, participates in the calculation of the resulting utility, by discounting μ_1, even further. From the analysis, the optimistic attitude of an agent ranking decisions using the hybrid utility is patent.

We introduce *the pessimistic hybrid utility function* $\overline{U}$ using the utility function U in the following way

$$\overline{U}(u_1, u_2; \mu_1, \mu_2) = 1 - U(1 - u_1, 1 - u_2; \mu_1, \mu_2).$$

Then we can give the corresponding interpretations of $\overline{U}$ as dual interpretations to the preceding cases of U. Just go again through the above behavior analysis, interpreting u_1 and u_2 and $\overline{U}$ as disutilities instead of utilities. For instance, in case IIa,b, the decision-maker is afraid that the worst outcome occurs ($u_2 > a$ is interpreted as penalty).

Example 7. We take $(< S_M, S_L >, < T_1, T_P >)_{0.2}$. and S-measure

$$m : \mathcal{P}(\{1, 2, 3, 4, 5\}) \to [0, 1]$$

as in Example 5. For five utilities

$$u_1 = 0.3, u_2 = 0.1, u_3 = 0.9, u_4 = 0.2, u_5 = 0.1$$

we can calculate the corresponding utility using the binary tree at Figure 6. and we represent the procedure in Figure 7

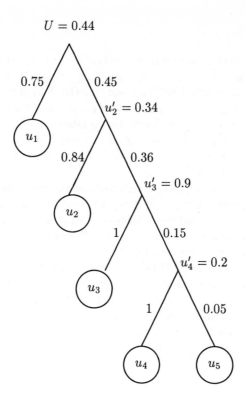

Fig. 7. Utility binary trees

For u_3', we are in case IIb, and for u_4' we are in case IId. Then $u_4' = \max(0.2, \min(0.05, 0.1)) = 0.2$. For u_3', again $u_3' = \max(0.9, \min(0.2, 0.15)) = 0.9$. Then

$$u_2' = 0.2 + \frac{(0.36 - 0.2)(0.9 - 0.2)}{0.8} = 0.34 \text{ (case Ic)},$$

and finally

$$U = \frac{0.3 \cdot 0.55 + 0.34 \cdot 0.55}{0.8} = 0.44 \text{ (case Ia)}.$$

9 Conclusions

More details and proofs of theorems stated in this paper can be found in [8]. It remains a pending problem to find a corresponding axiomatization for hybrid utility as was done for classical utility theory in [19] and possibility utility theory in [7,11]. Of interest too is the study of properties of independence in the setting of hybrid possibility-probabilistic measures.

We remark that the pair of t-conorm S and t-norm T which satisfies (CD) and the corresponding S-measure give a basis for an integration theory, so called (S, T)-integral, see [16,17].

Cox's well-known theorem [4,21], which justifies the use of probability for treating uncertainty, was discussed in many papers. This approach justifies both the additivity property and the conditioning rule. Recently, some critical comments have been made on the universal validity of Cox's statement, and some relaxed axioms have been proposed, enabling non-additive functions to be admissible solutions, see [10,14]. Especially, possibility measures are examples of such solutions when the set function is no longer requested to be self-dual. It is clear that the family of pseudo-additive measures exhibited in this paper is worth studying in Cox relaxed framework, since a natural form of conditioning can be defined on the basis of the triangular norm in the pair (S, T) satisfying (CD), leading to an almost regular independence notion exhibited here.

References

1. Aczél, J. (1969) Lectures on Functional Equations and their Applications. Academic Press, New York
2. Benvenuti, P., Mesiar, R. (submitted) Pseudo-arithmetical operations as a basis for the general measure and integration theory. Inf. Sciences
3. Bertoluzza, C. (1993) On the distributivity between t-norms and t-conorms. In Proc. Second Internat. Conference on Fuzzy Systems,FUZZ-IEEE '93, San Francisco, volume I, 140-147
4. Cox, R. (1946) Probability, frequency, and reasonable expectation. American Journal of Physics 14 (1) , 1-13
5. Dubois D. (1986) Generalized probabilistic independence and its implications for utility. Operations Res. Letters 5, 255-260
6. Dubois D., Fodor,J.C., Prade, H., Roubens,M. (1996) Aggregation of decomposable measures with applications to utility theory. Theory and Decision 41, 59-95
7. Dubois D., Godo,L., Prade, H., Zapico, A. (1998) Making decision in a qualitative setting: from decision under uncertainty to case-based decision.(Eds. A.G. Cohn, L. Schubert, S.C. Shapiro) Proceedings of the Sixth International Conference "Principles of Knowledge Representation and Reasoning" (KR ' 98), Morgan Kaufman Publishers, Inc, San Francisco, 594-605
8. Dubois D., Pap, E., Prade, H. (in preparation) Non-additive measures, generalized mixtures and utility function .

9. Dubois D., Prade, H. (1982) A class of fuzzy measures based on triangular norms, Internat. J. Gen. System **8** , 43–61

10. Dubois D., Prade,H. (1990) The logical view of conditioning and its application to possibility and evidence theories. Internat. J. of Approximate Reasoning **4** (1), 23-46

11. Dubois, D.,Prade, H.(1995) Possibility theory as a basis for qualitative decision theory. In Proc. of the 14th Int. Joint Conf. on Artificial Intelligence (IJCAI '95), Montreal, 1924-1930

12. Dubois, D., Prade, H. (1998) Possibility theory: qualitative and quantitative aspects. The Handbook of Defeasible Reasoning and Uncertainty Management Systems Vol I (Ed. Ph. Smets), Kluwer, Dordrecht, 169-226

13. Golan, J.S. (1992) The theory of semirings with applications in mathematics and theoretical computer science. Longman

14. Halpern, J.Y. (1999) A counterexample to theorems of Cox and Fine. Journal of Artif. Int. Research **10**, 67-85

15. Herstein, I.N., Milnor, J. (1953) An axiomatic approach to measurable utility. Econometrica **21** , 291-297

16. Klement,E.P., Mesiar,R., Pap, E. (to appear) Triangular Norms. Kluwer Academic Publishers, Dordrecht

17. Klement,E.P., Mesiar, R., Pap, E. (1999) (S, U)-integral. Proc. EUSFLAT - 99, Palma de Mallorca, 371-374.

18. Klement,E.P., Weber,S. (1991) Generalized measures. Fuzzy Sets and Systems **40**, 375–394

19. von Neumann, J., Morgenstern, O. (1944) Theory of Games and Economic Behavior. Princeton Univ. Press, Princeton, NJ

20. Pap, E. (1995) Null-Additive Set Functions, Kluwer Academic Publishers, Dordrecht and Ister Science, Bratislava

21. Paris, J.B. (1994) The Uncertain Reasoner's Companion, A Mathematical Perspective. Cambridge, U.K.: Cambridge University Press

22. Schweizer, B.,Sklar, A. (1983) Probabilistic Metric Spaces. North-Holland, Amsterdam

23. Shafer, G. (1996) The Art of Causal Conjecture. The MIT Press, Cambridge, Massachusetts

24. Sugeno, M., Murofushi, T. (1987) Pseudo-additive measures and integrals. J. Math. Anal. Appl. **122**, 197-222

25. Weber, S. (1984) $\perp$ −decomposable measure and integrals for Archimedean t−conorms. J. Math. Anal. Appl. **101**, 114-138

26. Zadeh, L. (1978) Fuzzy sets as a basis for a theory of possibility. Fuzzy Sets and Systems **1**, 3-28.

Additive Recursive Rules

D 80

Javier Montero[1], Ana del Amo[1], and Elisenda Molina[2]

[1] Faculty of Mathematics
Complutense University
Madrid, Spain
E-mail: Javier_Montero@Mat.UCM.Es
[2] Faculty of Applied Sciences
Miguel Hernández University
Elche, Spain

Summary. Recursiveness is a generalization of associativity, initially introduced in order to explain what an *Ordered Weighted Averaging (OWA)* rule is. In this paper, additive recursive rules are presented, showing the relevance of some particular OWA recursive rules.
Key words: Fuzzy Connective Rules, Recursiveness, Associativeness

1 Introduction

Fuzzy connectives use to be assumed commutative and associative binary operators in the unit real interval. But key operators, like Yager's OWA operators (see, e.g., [17]), and in particular the standard mean, are not binary operators, despite they are very often applied in order to aggregate information. As pointed out in [2–5], associativity is just an easy assumption in order to define a rule, which must allow us to aggregate information no matter the number of items to be amalgamated. Of course such a rule must proceed always in a consistent way, in order to be consider a proper rule.

A *rule* here is a *consistent* family of connectives

$$\{\phi_n : [0,1]^n \to [0,1]\}_{n>1}$$

being each operator ϕ_n the one to be applied when the number of items is n. By definition we also assume that all these connectives are continuous and non-decreasing in each coordinate.

The key problem is then how such *consistency* should be defined.

Obviously, *consistency* is not just a matter of finding a *compact* mathematical formula, but a true constructive idea leading the process of defining such a family of operations, so we can really understand we are being *coherent* all through out the different problems we are faced to.

Recursiveness was introduced in order to guarantee such a consistency, so there is a unique *rule* working on different situations (different numbers of items). *Operationality* is assured imposing that the aggregation process is always based upon binary operations. In this way, the existence of an easy calculus is assured.

Classical approach assumes the existence of a unique commutative binary operator (see, e.g., [8,9], or the more general approach given in [18,12]). But as pointed out in [4], key aggregation operators can not be explained by means of a sequential application of a unique binary operator. Then it happens that we may find serious difficulties in understanding the rule to which a given operator belongs to, i.e., we get confused about how to proceed when we get more items to be aggregated (see also [5]).

Recursiveness shows that *consistency* can be also assured allowing the binary operators evolve, depending on the number of items to be aggregated.

2   Recursiveness

First of all, we realize that many aggregation procedures require a previous re-arrangement of data. For example, most facts need to be analyzed according time.

Such a re-arrangement of data must of course define an *ordering rule*, so additional data can be allocated keeping all previous re-arrangements. Otherwise most people will consider that our ordering process is not being *consistent*.

Definition 1. Let us denote

$$\pi_n(a_1, a_2, \ldots, a_n) = \left(a_{\pi_n(1)}, a_{\pi_n(2)}, \ldots, a_{\pi_n(n)}\right)$$

An *ordering rule* π is a *consistent* family of permutations $\{\pi_n\}_{n>1}$ such that for any possible finite collections of numbers, each extra item a_{n+1} is allocated keeping relative positions of items, i.e.,

$$\pi_{n+1}(a_1, a_2, \ldots, a_n, a_{n+1}) =$$
$$= \left(a_{\pi_n(1)}, \ldots, a_{\pi_n(j-1)}, a_{\pi_{n+1}(j)}, a_{\pi_n(j+1)} \cdots, a_{\pi_n(n)}\right),$$

for some $j \in \{1, \ldots, n+1\}$.

For example, OWA operators arrange numbers in a decreasing (or increasing) sequence. In this case, we are re-arranging data according to a pre-existent linear order on the real line. A linear order defined on the item space defines an *ordering rule*. But notice that an *ordering rule* does not assume a pre-existent order. For example, we may decide to keep data in its *natural* sequence, just in the order each one is reaching to us, real time. Such an *identity ordering rule* indeed keeps the relative position of previously ordered elements.

The following definition was then proposed in [5].

Definition 2. A left-recursive connective rule is a family of connective operators

$$\{\phi_n : [0,1]^n \to [0,1]\}_{n>1}$$

such that there exists a sequence of binary operators

$$\{L_n : [0,1]^2 \to [0,1]\}_{n>1}$$

verifying

$$\phi_2(a_1, a_2) = L_2(a_{\pi(1)}, a_{\pi(2)})$$
$$\phi_n(a_1, \dots, a_n) = L_n(\phi_{n-1}(a_{\pi(1)}, \dots, a_{\pi(n-1)}), a_{\pi(n)}) \quad \forall n > 2$$

for some ordering rule π.

Right recursiveness can be analogously defined, and then we talk about a *recursive rule* when both left and right representations hold for the same ordering rule. *Commutative* recursive rules will be those recursive rules leading always to the same result for any possible ordering rule. We talk about *standard* recursive rules when they are based upon the identity ordering rule.

In this way recursiveness generalizes the property of associativity, still assuring an operational constructive consistency, but allowing to explain key rules in practice, like the *mean rule*. Alternative approaches can be found in [10,11,15] and [16].

3 Main result

The main result of this paper follows from the fact that a connective rule $\{\phi_n\}_{n>1}$ is recursive if and only if a set of general associativity equations (in the sense of Mak [14]) hold for each n, once the ordering rule π has been already applied:

$$\phi_n(a_1, \dots, a_n) = R_n(a_{\pi(1)}, \phi_{n-1}(a_{\pi(2)}, \dots, a_{\pi(n)}))$$
$$= L_n(\phi_{n-1}(a_{\pi(1)}, \dots, a_{\pi(n-1)}), a_{\pi(n)})$$

must hold for all n.

If each one of these binary connectives L_n, R_n can be assumed to be defined in the Cartesian product of two non-trivial compact intervals on the real line, being all of them continuous strictly increasing in each coordinate, then it can be shown (see Koopmans [13]) that they are commutative and basically additive, in such a way that it takes the expression

$$\phi_n(a_1, \dots, a_n) = \psi^{-1}(\psi(a_1) + \dots + \psi(a_n))$$

More in general, we consider Mak's representation result [14]. In order to apply such a result, we shall restrict ourselves to a certain family of recursive connective rules: the family of connective rules such that Mak's assumptions do apply (see [14], or [1] for an overview).

Definition 3. A *regular recursive connective rule* is a family of connective operators

$$\{\phi_n : [0,1]^n \to [0,1]\}_{n>1}$$

such that there exists a sequence of binary operators

$$\{L_n : [0,1]^2 \to [0,1]\}_{n>1}$$

and

$$\{R_n : [0,1]^2 \to [0,1]\}_{n>1}$$

which are surjective continuous mappings verifying the following conditions:

1. If $x' \leq x''$ and $y' \leq y''$, then $L_n(x',y') \leq L_n(x'',y'')$ and $R_n(x',y') \leq R_n(x'',y'')$
2. If $x' < x''$, then $L_n(x',y) < L_n(x'',y)$ for some y and $R_n(x',y') < R_n(x'',y')$ for some y'
   If $y' < y''$, then $L_n(x,y') < L_n(x,y'')$ for some x and $R_n(x',y') < R_n(x',y'')$ for some x'
3. There is no $x_i \in (0,1)$ such that $L_n(x_i,\bar{x}) = 0$, $\forall \bar{x}$
   There is no $x'_i \in (0,1)$ such that $R_n(x'_i,\bar{x}) = 0$, $\forall \bar{x}$
   There is no $x_i \in (0,1)$ such that $L_n(\bar{x},x_i) = 0$, $\forall \bar{x}$
   There is no $x'_i \in (0,1)$ such that $R_n(\bar{x},x'_i) = 0$, $\forall \bar{x}$
4. $L_n(0,y') = 0$, $\forall y'$ if and only if $fL_n(y',0) = 0$ $\forall y'$
   $R_n(0,y'') = 0$ $\forall y''$ if and only if $R_n(y'',0) = 0$ $\forall y''$
   $L_n(1,y') = 1$ $\forall y'$ if and only if $L_n(y',1) = 1$ $\forall y'$
   $R_n(1,y'') = 1$ $\forall y''$ if and only if $R_n(y'',1) = 1$ $\forall y''$

If we restrict to such a family of operators then we shall be able to characterize *basically additive* recursive rules, as obtained from Mak's theorem [14]. We shall consider first *standard rules*, where ordering rules do not play any role. Generalization will be direct.

Theorem 1. *Let*

$$\{\phi_n : [0,1]^n \to [0,1]\}_{n>1}$$

be a regular standard recursive rule. If ϕ_n is strictly increasing in each coordinate for all $n > 1$, then there exists:

(a) $p : [0,1] \to \mathbb{R}_+$, continuous and strictly increasing function
(b) $\{\delta_n : [0,1] \to \mathbb{R}_+\}_{n>1}$, family of continuous and strictly increasing functions, and
(c) $\{c_n\}_{n\geq1}$, sequence of positive real numbers

in such a way that for all $(a_1, \ldots, a_n) \in [0,1]^n$ and for all $n \geq 2$ we have

$$\phi_n(a_1, \ldots, a_n) = \delta_n^{-1}\left(\prod_{j=2}^{n-2} c_j \sum_{k=1}^{n} c_1^{k-1} p(a_k)\right), \tag{1}$$

where $\prod_{j=2}^{\ell} c_j$ is taken as 1 whenever $\ell \leq 2$.

Proof: Obviously, from the definition $\{\phi_n\}_{n>1}$ is a standard recursive rule if, and only if, for all $n \geq 3$, the following generalized associativity equation (in the sense of Mak) holds:

$$L_n\big(R_{n-1}(u,v),w\big) = R_n\big(u, L_{n-1}(v,w)\big) \tag{2}$$

Thus, having $(a_1, \ldots, a_n) \in [0,1]^n$, taking $u = a_1$, $v = \phi_{n-2}(a_2, \ldots, a_{n-2})$ and $w = a_n$ assures the above equation.

Keeping in mind the above relation, we know from [14] that under Mak assumptions (i.e., $\{L_n\}_{n>1}$ and $\{R_n\}_{n>1}$ binary operators, continuous and strictly increasing in proper compact non empty intervals) the solution for equation (2) is basically additive (see also [13]). That is, there exist σ_n, θ_n, δ_n, p_n, q_n and r_n, continuous and strictly increasing functions over the compact interval $[0,1]$, which verify:

$$R_{n-1}(u,v) = \sigma_n^{-1}\big(p_n(u) + q_n(v)\big) \tag{3}$$
$$L_{n-1}(v,w) = \theta_n^{-1}\big(q_n(v) + r_n(w)\big) \tag{4}$$
$$R_n(u,b) = \delta_n^{-1}\big(p_n(u) + \theta_n(b)\big) \tag{5}$$
$$L_n(a,w) = \delta_n^{-1}\big(\sigma_n(a) + r_n(w)\big) \tag{6}$$

Next, we will prove by induction on n that there exist $\{c_n\}_{n\geq1}$, $\{\delta_n\}_{n\geq2}$ and p in the theorem conditions such that for all $n \geq 4$,

$$\theta_n(x) = c_1 c_{n-2}\delta_{n-1}(x)$$
$$\sigma_n(x) = c_{n-2}\delta_{n-1}(x)$$
$$p_n(x) = \prod_{j=2}^{n-2} c_j p(x)$$
$$q_n(x) = c_1 c_{n-2}\sigma_{n-1}(x)$$
$$r_n(x) = c_1^{n-1} \prod_{j=2}^{n-2} c_j p(x)$$

Being for $n = 3$:

$$\theta_3(x) = c_1 \delta_2(x)$$
$$\sigma_3(x) = \delta_2(x)$$
$$p_3(x) = p(x)$$
$$q_3(x) = c_1 p(x)$$
$$r_3(x) = c_1^2 p(x)$$

Previous to the induction on n, we will try out first that it is verified for $n = 3$.

Let's consider

$$L_3\big(R_2(u,v),w\big) = R_3\big(u, L_2(v,w)\big)$$

where $R_2(a_1,a_2) = \phi_2(a_1,a_2) = L_2(a_1,a_2)$, for all (a_1,a_2). That way, from R_2 and L_2 being (3) and (4) respectively, it is concluded that $\{\sigma_3, p_3, q_3\}$ and $\{\theta_3, q_3, r_3\}$ are solutions for the functional equation

$$\phi_2(x,y) = f^{-1}(g(x) + h(y))$$

Therefore, there exist a, b, c, real numbers, such that the following relation is verified:

$$\theta_3(x) = c\sigma_3(x) + a + b$$
$$q_3(x) = cp_3(x) + a$$
$$r_3(x) = cq_3(x) + b$$

Without a loss of generality, $\sigma_3(0) = p_3(0) = q_3(0) = 0$ and $\theta_3(0) = q_3(0) = r_3(0) = 0$ can be assumed. Otherwise, if the three first ones are not equal 0, then it is possible to define

$$\widetilde{\sigma}_3(x) = \sigma_3(x) - \sigma_3(0), \quad \widetilde{p}_3(x) = p_3(x) - p_3(0) \quad \text{and} \quad \widetilde{q}_3(x) = q_3(x) - q_3(0)$$

Let us check that

$$\phi_2(u,v) = R_2(u,v) = \widetilde{\sigma}_3^{-1}(\widetilde{p}_3(u) + \widetilde{q}_3(v))$$

still holds. Notice that

$$\widetilde{\sigma}_3\big(R_2(u,v)\big) = \sigma_3\big(R_2(u,v)\big) - \sigma_3(0)$$

On the other hand,

$$\widetilde{p}_3(u) + \widetilde{q}_3(v) = p_3(u) + q_3(v) - p_3(0) - q_3(0)$$

Since $\phi_2(0,0) = 0$, then

$$\sigma_3(0) = \sigma_3\big(R_2(0,0)\big) = p_3(0) + q_3(0)$$

Therefore,

$$\widetilde{\sigma}_3^{-1}(\widetilde{p}_3(u) + \widetilde{q}_3(v)) = R_2(u,v).$$

In parallel, it would be assumed $\theta_3(0) = q_3(0) = r_3(0) = 0$. Consequently, $a = b = 0$. Therefore, $\theta_3(x) = c\sigma_3(x)$, $q_3(x) = cp_3(x)$ and $r_3(x) = cq_3(x)$. Assuming $p \equiv p_3$, $\delta_2 \equiv \sigma_3$ and $c_1 = c$, then it is true for $n = 3$. Particularly,

$$L_3(a,w) = \delta_3^{-1}\big(\delta_2(a) + c_1^2 p(w)\big) \tag{7}$$
$$R_3(u,b) = \delta_3^{-1}\big(p(u) + c_1\delta_2(b)\big) \tag{8}$$

Let's consider if the same relation holds for $n = 4$.

Absolutely, from the above expression of R_3 and taking into account the general solution of the Mak equation for $n = 4$, it is concluded that $\{\sigma_4, p_4, q_4\}$ and $\{\delta_3, p, c_1\delta_2\}$ are solutions for the functional equation

$$R_3(x, y) = f^{-1}(g(x) + h(y))$$

Therefore, following the same reasoning above and taking into account that

$$L_3(0, 0) = L_3(\phi_2(0, 0), 0) = \phi_3(0, 0, 0) = 0$$

it follows that there exists $k_1 \in \mathbb{R}$ such that:

$$\sigma_4(x) = k_1\delta_3(x) \tag{9}$$
$$p_4(x) = k_1 p(x) \tag{10}$$
$$q_4(x) = k_1 c_1 \delta_2(x) \tag{11}$$

Analogously, $\{\theta_4, q_4, r_4\}$ and $\{\delta_3, \delta_2, c_1^2 p\}$ are solutions for the functional equation

$$L_3(x, y) = f^{-1}(g(x) + h(y))$$

Where tracking the same scheme, it is inferred that there exists $k_2 \in \mathbb{R}$ verifying:

$$\theta_4(x) = k_2\delta_3(x) \tag{12}$$
$$q_4(x) = k_2\delta_2(x) \tag{13}$$
$$r_4(x) = k_2 c_1^2 p(x) \tag{14}$$

From the expressions (11) and (13) it can be deduced that $k_2 = ck_1$. Therefore, assuming $c_2 = k_1$, the recurrent expression for $n = 4$ is concluded.

To finish, let's check if the recurrent expression hold for $n-1$, and likewise for n. From general solution of Mak's equation for $n - 1$, it follows

$$R_{n-1}(u, b) = \delta_{n-1}^{-1}\left(p_{n-1}(u) + \theta_{n-1}(b)\right) \tag{15}$$
$$L_{n-1}(a, w) = \delta_{n-1}^{-1}\left(\sigma_{n-1}(a) + r_{n-1}(w)\right) \tag{16}$$

And for n, the expressions result to be:

$$R_{n-1}(u, v) = \sigma_n^{-1}\left(p_n(u) + q_n(v)\right)$$
$$L_{n-1}(v, w) = \theta_n^{-1}\left(q_n(v) + r_n(w)\right)$$

where, following the scheme used above, and considering that

$$L_{n-1}(0, 0) = L_{n-1}(\phi_{n-2}(0, \cdots, 0), 0) = 0$$

and

$$R_{n-1}(0, 0) = R_{n-1}(0, \phi_{n-2}(0, \cdots, 0)) = 0$$

there exist k_1, $k_2 \in I\!R$, such that:

$$\sigma_n(x) = k_1 \delta_{n-1}(x)$$
$$p_n(x) = k_1 p_{n-1}(x)$$
$$q_n(x) = k_1 \theta_{n-1}(x)$$

whereas

$$\theta_n(x) = k_2 \delta_{n-1}(x)$$
$$q_n(x) = k_2 \sigma_{n-1}(x)$$
$$r_4(x) = k_2 r_{n-1}(x)$$

By induction hypothesis, it follows

$$\theta_{n-1}(x) = c_1 c_{n-3} \delta_{n-2}(x) = c_1 \sigma_{n-1}(x)$$

Therefore, from the expressions of q_n, it follows that $k_2 = c_1 k_1$. Hence, assuming $c_{n-2} = k_1$ and using induction hypothesis to deduce p_{n-1} and r_{n-1} from p and $\{c_1, \ldots, c_{n-3}\}$, the partial result that was to be proved is satisfied.

The condition imposed about the positiveness of the constants c_n, $n \geq 1$, is justified by the fact that

$$\theta_n(0) = \sigma_n(0) = p_n(0) = q_n(0) = r_n(0) = 0, \quad \forall\ n \geq 3$$

being those strictly increasing functions, which assure the non negativeness of all the functions we have been dealing with.

Once we have obtained the expression for the binary operators $\{R_n\}_{n>1}$ and $\{L_n\}_{n>1}$ depending on

$$\{c_n\}_{n \geq 1}, \quad \{\delta_n\}_{n \geq 2}, \quad p$$

the expression (1) of ϕ_n is trivially inferred using induction on n by applying the recursive definition of ϕ_n, thus proving the theorem. $\square$

As a consequence, it can be shown that given $\{\phi_n : [0,1]^n \to [0,1]\}_{n>1}$ a recursive connective rule in the above theorem conditions, then $\{L_n\}_{n>1}$ and $\{R_n\}_{n>1}$, are unique in their range (see [1]).

The result established in the above theorem 1 can be extended to the case in which the recursive rule is not necessarily standard: if the rule is not standard, let π be the ordering rule such that

$$\phi_n(a_1, \ldots, a_n) = R_n\big(a_{\pi(1)}, L_{n-1}(\phi_{n-2}(a_{\pi(2)}, \ldots, a_{\pi(n-1)}), a_{\pi(n)})\big) \quad (17)$$
$$= L_n\big(R_{n-1}(a_{\pi(1)}, \phi_{n-2}(a_{\pi(2)}, \ldots, a_{\pi(n-1)}), a_{\pi(n)})\big) \quad (18)$$

hold $\forall n \geq 3$.

We can consider

$$F_n : S_n \longrightarrow [0,1]$$

with

$$S_n = \{(\pi(x_1), \ldots, \pi(x_n))/(x_1, \ldots, x_n) \in [0,1]^n\}$$

in such a way that

$$F_n(\pi(x_1), \ldots, \pi(x_n)) = \phi_n(x_1, \ldots, x_n), \quad \forall(\pi(x_1), \ldots, \pi(x_n)) \in S_n \; \forall n > 1$$

Let F_n be extended over $[0,1]^n$. For example, if ϕ_n is an OWA operator

$$\phi_n(x_1, \ldots, x_n) = w_{1,n}x_{[1]} + \ldots + w_{n,n}x_{[n]} \quad \forall(x_1, \ldots, x_n) \in [0,1]^n$$

then it would be

$$F_n(x_1, \ldots, x_n) = w_{1,n}x_1 + \ldots + w_{n,n}x_n \quad \forall(x_1, \ldots, x_n) \in [0,1]^n$$

Assuming that $\{F_n\}_{n\geq 2}$, $\{L_n\}_{n\geq 2}$, $\{R_n\}_{n\geq 2}$ (L_n, R_n extended in the same way) verify the recursivity equation (17) we have for all $(x_1, \ldots, x_n) \in [0,1]^n$

$$\begin{aligned}
F_n(x_1, \ldots, x_n) &= R_n\big(x_1, L_{n-1}(F_{n-2}(x_2, \ldots, x_{n-1}), x_n)\big) \\
&= L_n\big(R_{n-1}(x_1, F_{n-2}(x_2, \ldots, x_{n-1}), x_n)\big)
\end{aligned}$$

4 Idempotent additive rules

The above result shows a quite restrictive solution. It is then easy to understand that extra degrees of freedom will vanish by fixing some of the parameters $\{\delta_n\}_{n>1}$, $\{c_n\}_{n\geq 1}$ and p. Each particular rule is fully characterized as soon all this family of parameters is fixed.

For example, a quite frequent assumption is *idempotency*.

Theorem 2. *Let*

$$\{\phi_n : [0,1]^n \to [0,1]\}_{n>1}$$

be a regular standard recursive rule such that ϕ_n is strictly increasing and idempotent, for all $n > 1$. Then there exists $p : [0,1] \to \mathbb{R}_+$, continuous and strictly increasing function, and a real number $c > 0$, such that for all $(a_1, \ldots, a_n) \in [0,1]^n$, $n \geq 2$ we have

$$\phi_n(a_1, \ldots, a_n) = \begin{cases} p^{-1}\left(\frac{1-c}{1-c^n}\sum_{k=1}^n c^{k-1}p(a_k)\right), & \text{if } c \neq 1 \\ p^{-1}\left(\frac{1}{n}\sum_{k=1}^n p(a_k)\right), & \text{if } c = 1 \end{cases}$$

Proof: From Theorem 1 we know that for all $(a_1, \ldots, a_n) \in [0,1]^n$ and $n \geq 2$

$$\phi_n(a_1, \ldots, a_n) = \delta_n^{-1}\left(\prod_{j=2}^{n-2} c_j \sum_{k=1}^n c_1^{k-1}p(a_k)\right).$$

Then, since ϕ_n is an idempotent aggregator, for all $a \in [0, 1]$

$$a = \phi_n(a, \ldots, a) = \delta_n^{-1}(e_n p(a)),$$

being

$$e_n = \prod_{j=2}^{n-2} c_j \sum_{k=1}^{n} c_1^{k-1} = \begin{cases} \dfrac{1 - c_1^n}{1 - c_1} \displaystyle\prod_{j=2}^{n-2} c_j, & \text{if } c_1 \neq 1 \\[2ex] n \displaystyle\prod_{j=2}^{n-2} c_j, & \text{if } c_1 = 1 \end{cases}$$

That means, $\delta_n \equiv e_n p$. Then, the family of functions $\{\delta_n\}_{n>1}$ would be determined from the sequence of real numbers $\{c_n\}_{n\geq 1}$ and the unique function p. Furthermore, ϕ_n would be

$$\phi_n(a_1, \ldots, a_n) = p^{-1}\left(\frac{1}{e_n} \prod_{j=2}^{n-2} c_j \sum_{k=1}^{n} c_1^{k-1} p(a_k)\right)$$

$$= p^{-1}\left(\frac{1 - c_1}{1 - c_1^n} \sum_{k=1}^{n} c_1^{k-1} p(a_k)\right), \qquad c_1 \neq 1$$

$$\phi_n(a_1, \ldots, a_n) = p^{-1}\left(\frac{1}{n} \sum_{k=1}^{n} p(a_k)\right), \qquad c_1 = 1$$

for all $(a_1, \ldots, a_n) \in [0, 1]^n$, for all $n \geq 2$. Then, taking $c = c_1$, ϕ_n exclusively depend on c and p.

Taking into account the recurrent expression of the following functions θ_n, σ_n, p_n, q_n and r_n, for $n \geq 2$, that was obtained in the theorem 1 proof, if follows that the binary operators $\{L_n\}_{n>1}$ and $\{R_n\}_{n>1}$ in function of c and p can be expressed:

$$L_n(a, b) = \delta_n^{-1}(\sigma_n(a) + r_n(b))$$

$$= p^{-1}\left(\frac{\sigma_n(a)}{e_n} + \frac{r_n(b)}{e_n}\right)$$

$$= p^{-1}\left(\frac{c_{n-2} e_{n-1}}{e_n} p(a) + \frac{c_1^{n-1} \prod_{j=2}^{n-2} c_j}{e_n} p(b)\right)$$

$$= p^{-1}\left(\frac{1 - c^{n-1}}{1 - c^n} p(a) + \frac{c^{n-1}(1 - c)}{1 - c^n} p(b)\right),$$

and

$$R_n(a,b) = \delta_n^{-1}\big(p_n(a) + \theta_n(b)\big)$$

$$= p^{-1}\left(\frac{p_n(a)}{e_n} + \frac{\theta_n(b)}{e_n}\right)$$

$$= p^{-1}\left(\frac{\prod_{j=2}^{n-2} c_j}{e_n}\,p(a) + \frac{c_1 c_{n-2} e_{n-1}}{e_n}\,p(b)\right)$$

$$= p^{-1}\left(\frac{1-c}{1-c^n}\,p(a) + \frac{c(1-c^{n-1})}{1-c^n}\,p(b)\right)$$

if $c_1 \neq 1$, whereas

$$L_n(a,b) = p^{-1}\left(\Big(1 - \frac{1}{n}\Big)p(a) + \frac{1}{n}p(b)\right)$$

$$R_n(a,b) = p^{-1}\left(\frac{1}{n}p(a) + \Big(1 - \frac{1}{n}\Big)p(b)\right)$$

if $c_1 = 1$. □

Hence, being $\{\phi_n : [0,1]^n \to [0,1]\}_{n>1}$ a rule verifying the above theorem conditions, for each $n > 2$, there exists a weights system $w_{i,n}$, $i = 1, \ldots, n$, and a function p, such that:

$$\phi_n(a_1,\ldots,a_n) = p^{-1}\big(w_{1,n}p(a_1) + \cdots + w_{n,n}p(a_n)\big), \quad \forall(a_1,\ldots,a_n) \in [0,1]^n$$

where

(i) For all $i = 1,\ldots,n$, and for all $n \geq 2$

$$w_{i,n} = \begin{cases} \frac{1-c}{1-c^n}c^{i-1} = \frac{1-c^{n+1}}{1-c^n}w_{i,n+1} \in (0,1), & \text{if } c \neq 1 \\[2mm] \frac{1}{n} = \frac{n+1}{n}w_{i,n+1} \in (0,1), & \text{if } c = 1 \end{cases}$$

(ii) $\displaystyle\sum_{i=1}^{n} w_{i,n} = 1.$

Furthermore, $\forall n > 1$, there exist:

$$\ell_n = \begin{cases} \frac{1-c^{n-1}}{1-c^n} \in (0,1), & \text{if } c \neq 1 \\[2mm] 1 - \frac{1}{n} \in (0,1), & \text{if } c = 1 \end{cases}$$

and

$$r_n = \begin{cases} \frac{1-c}{1-c^n} \in (0,1), & \text{si } c \neq 1 \\[2mm] \frac{1}{n} \in (0,1), & \text{if } c = 1 \end{cases}$$

such that

$$L_n(a,b) = p^{-1}\big(\ell_n p(a) + (1 - \ell_n)p(b)\big)$$
$$R_n(a,b) = p^{-1}\big(r_n p(a) + (1 - r_n)p(b)\big)$$

Therefore, every regular standard recursive rule that is strictly increasing and idempotent, is made up of aggregation operators that are *quasilinear means* with *generator function p* and weights ℓ_n, $1 - \ell_n$ and r_n, $1 - r_n$ for L_n and R_n, respectively (see [6,7] and [15]).

When dealing with non-standard rules, the above theorem can be extended as follows:

Theorem 3. *Let*

$$\{\phi_n : [0,1]^n \to [0,1]\}_{n>1}$$

be a regular recursive rule and π the underlying ordering rule. If ϕ_n is strictly increasing and idempotent, for all $n > 1$, then there exist $p : [0,1] \to \mathbb{R}_+$, continuous and strictly increasing function, and a real number $c > 0$, such that for all $(a_1, \ldots, a_n) \in [0,1]^n$ and $n \geq 2$ we have

$$\phi_n(a_1, \ldots, a_n) = p^{-1}\left(\frac{1-c}{1-c^n} \sum_{k=1}^{n} c^{k-1} p(a_{\pi(k)})\right). \tag{19}$$

Notice that when $c = 1$ then $\{\phi_n : [0,1]^n \to [0,1]\}_{n>1}$ is a commutative rule:

$$\phi_n(a_1, \ldots, a_n) = p^{-1}\left(\frac{1}{n} \sum_{k=1}^{n} p(a_k)\right), \quad \forall \ (a_1, \ldots, a_n) \in [0,1]^n \tag{20}$$

Being π the natural decreasing order, a recursive rule family of special interest shows up. Concretely, being $\{\phi_n : [0,1]^n \to [0,1]\}_{n>1}$ the regular recursive rule and π the underlying ordering rule, all the connective operators are *quasi–OWA* operators (see Fodor-Marichal-Roubens [10]).

It is very important to notice that adding idempotency is almost fixing the whole rule from the first aggregation operator. For example, if ϕ_2 is an OWA operator then the whole rule is settled of OWA operators, and the list of weights is univocally determined.

5   Final comments

This paper shows how usual additive aggregation rules can be explained in terms of a recursive approach, and which ones of those additive rules are in fact recursive.

Moreover, it is shown how easily we fall into a quite intuitive practical observation: we have very few *consistent* choices for the rule as soon as the aggregation operator of the first two items has been defined.

Acknowledgements: This research has been supported by grant PB95-0407 from the Government of Spain.

References

1. A. del Amo, J. Montero and E. Molina: Representarion of consistent recursive rules (submitted)
2. V. Cutello, E. Molina and J. Montero: Associativeness versus recursiveness. In: *Proceedings of 26-th IEEE International Symposium on Multiple-valued Logic*, Santiago de Compostela (Spain), May 29-31, 1996; pp. 154–159.
3. V. Cutello, E. Molina and J. Montero: Binary operators and connective rules. In: M.H. Smith, M.A. Lee, J. Keller and J. Yen, Eds., *Proceedings of NAFIPS'96 (North American Fuzzy Information Processing Society)*. IEEE Press, Piscataway, NJ (1996); pp. 46–49.
4. V. Cutello and J. Montero: Recursive families of OWA operators. In: P.P. Bonissone, Ed., *Proceedings of the Third IEEE Conference on Fuzzy Systems*. IEEE Press, Piscataway, NJ (1994); pp. 1137–1141.
5. V. Cutello and J. Montero: Recursive connective rules, *Int. J. Intelligent Systems* (to appear)
6. H. Dyckoff: Basic concepts for a theory of evaluation: hierarchical aggregation via autodistributive connectives in fuzzy set theory, *European Journal of Operational Research* 20:221–233 (1985)
7. H. Dyckoff and W. Pedrycz: Generalized means as model of compensative connectives, *Fuzzy sets and Systems* 14:143–154 (1984).
8. J. Dombi: Basic concepts for a theory of evaluation: the aggregative operator, *European Journal of Operational Research* 10:282–293 (1982).
9. J. Dombi: A general class of fuzzy operators, the De Morgan class of fuzzy operators and fuzziness measures induced by fuzzy operators, *Fuzzy Sets and Systems* 8:149–163 (1982).
10. J.C. Fodor, J.L. Marichal and M. Roubens: Characterization of the ordered weighted averaging operators. *Institut de Mathématique, Université de Liège*, Prépublication 93.011.
11. J.C. Fodor and M. Roubens: Fuzzy Preference Modelling and Multicriteria Decision Support (Kluwer, Dordrecht, 1994)
12. J.C. Fodor, R.R. Yager and A. Rybalov: Structure of uninorms, *Int. J. Uncertainty, Fuzziness and Knowledge-Based Systems* 5:411–427 (1997)
13. T.C. Koopmans: Representation of preference ordering with independent components of consumption. In: C.B. McGuire and R. Radner, Eds., *Decision and Organization*. North-Holland, Amsterdam (1972), 57–78 (2nd edition by the University of Minnesota Press, 1986).
14. K.T. Mak: Coherent continuous systems and the generalized functional equation of associativity. *Mathematics of Operations Research* 12:597–625 (1987).

15. J.L. Marichal, P. Mathonet and E. Tousset: Characterization of some aggregation functions stable for positive trasnformations. *Fuzzy Sets and Systems* 102:293–314 (1999).
16. M. Mas, G. Mayor, J. Suñer and J. Torrens: Generation of multi-dimensional aggregation functions, *Mathware and Soft Computing* 5:233–242 (1998).
17. R.R. Yager: On ordered weighted averaging aggregation operators in multicriteria decision making, *IEEE Transactions on Systems, Man and Cybernetics* 18:183–190 (1988).
18. R.R. Yager and A. Rybalov: Uninorm aggregation operators, *Fuzzy Sets and Systems* 80:111–120 (1996)

Maximizing the Information Obtained from Data Fusion

Ronald R. Yager

DF3

Machine Intelligence Institute
Iona College
New Rochelle, NY 10801
yager@panix.com

ABSTRACT. We consider the question of conjuncting data and in particular the issue of the amount of information that results. It is shown that if the data being fused is non-conflicting then the maximal information is obtained by simply taking the intersection of the data. When the data is conflicting the use of the intersection can result in the fused value having less information then any of its components. In order to maximize the resulting information in this conflicting environment some meta knowledge must be introduced to adjudicate between conflicting data. Two approaches to address this problem are introduced. The first considers using only a subset of the observations to construct the fused value, a softening of the requirement that all observations be used. The basic rational of this approach is to calculate the fused value from a subset of observations that are not to conflicting and consisting of enough of the observations to be considered a credible fusion. Central to this approach is the introduction of meta-knowledge in the form of a measure of credibility associated with the use of different subsets of the observations. The second approach is based upon the introduction of a prioritization of the observations. In this approach an observation is essentially discounted if conflicts with higher priority observations.

1. Introduction

An integral part of any decision making process is the determination of the value of relevant variables. This generally involves a gathering of information about these variables. When multiple sources of information exist we often must fuse the knowledge provided by these different sources. A fundamental problem that can arise when we fuse multiple pieces of knowledge from different sources is that they are conflicting. The resolution of conflict requires the introduction of some meta-knowledge in order to help adjudicate the conflict. In this work we consider two approaches to the adjudication of conflict. One approach is based upon the idea of only using some subset of the provided knowledge to form the fused value. Central to this approach is the introduction of meta-knowledge in the form of a measure of credibility indicating the appropriateness of using a given subset of observations to calculate the fused value. The basic rational of this approach is to calculate the fused value from a subset of observations that are not to conflicting and consist of enough of the observations to be considered a credible fusion. In helping to decide which of the possible subsets of observations to use in calculating the fused value we are guided by the principle of trying maximize the amount of information contained in the fused value. The second approach to conflict adjudication is based upon the introduction of a prioritization of the observations. In this approach an observation is essentially discounted if it conflicts with higher priority knowledge. Again, as we shall see, the process of information optimization plays a central role in implementing this process.

2. Information Measurement in Approximate Reasoning

In this work we shall use the framework of the theory of approximate reasoning (AR) [1-3] as it provides a very powerful formalism for the representation, measurement and subsequent fusion of information. Assume V is some variable which can take its value in the set X within AR a piece of knowledge about V by a statement of the form V *is $\mathcal{A}$* where $\mathcal{A}$ is some specific value, set of values or linguistic concept. Using the capabilities of fuzzy set theory we can represent $\mathcal{A}$ as a fuzzy subset over the domain X, we shall denote this fuzzy subset as A. As suggested by Zadeh [4] this type of statement induces a possibility distribution on X such that for any element $x \in X$ its membership grade in A, $A(x)$, is the possibility that x is the value of V.

A possibility distribution (fuzzy subset) A associated with a variable V is called normal if there exists at least one element x^* in X such that $A(x^*) = 1$ otherwise it is called sub–normal. A sub-normal possibility distribution is some indication of inconsistency or conflict between our knowledge and the fact that V must be an element in X. We shall indicate this degree of conflict as $Con(A) = 1 - Max_X[A(x)]$.

Yager [5-8] describes the specificity of a possibility distribution (fuzzy subset) as a measures of the degree to which the distribution has one element as its manifestation., it measures the truth of the proposition *A has one element and not many others*. Formally a specificity measure is a mapping, $Sp: I^X \to [0, 1]$ where $Sp(A)$ indicates the specificity of the fuzzy subset A and which satisfies the following conditions:

1. $Sp(A) = 1$ iff A has exactly one element with membership grade one and all other elements have membership grade zero (a singleton set).
2. $Sp(A) = 0$ if all the elements have the same membership grade.
3. If A is normal, has at least one element with membership grade one, and if $A \subset B$ then $Sp(A) \geq Sp(B)$.
4. If A and B are non-empty crisp sets and $Card(B) \geq Card(A)$ then $Sp(A) \geq Sp(B)$.

Specificity can be used to measure amount of information contained in a possibility distribution [7,8], the larger the specificity the more information. In spirit it plays the same role in possibility theory as entropy does in probability theory. Let us look at this connection between specificity and the information in a possibility distribution. Uncertainty arises in a situation in which we are not sure what is the value of a variable, information is a commodity that helps clarify uncertainty. A proposition V *is* A, inducing a possibility distribution on V, can be seen as providing information about the value of V. The more specific a possibility distribution, the more it points to one element as the actual value of V, the less the uncertainty and hence the more information.

There are many possible measures of specificity in order to compare these the following definition is useful. If Sp and Sp' are two specificity measures over X we shall say that Sp is a stricter measure of specificity than Sp' if $Sp'(A) \geq Sp(A)$ for all A. In [8] Yager introduced a class of specificity measures called linear specificity measures.

Definition: Assume X is a set of cardinality n. Let A be a fuzzy subset of X. The **linear measure** of specificity of A is defined as $Sp(A) = b_1 - \sum_{i=2}^{n} b_i w_i$ where b_i is the ith largest of the membership grades in A. The w_i's are a collection of weights having the following properties: 1. $\sum_{i=2}^{n} w_i = 1$, 2. $w_i \in [0, 1]$ and 3. $w_i \geq w_j$ if $i < j$.

One property associated with this measure is the fact that $Sp(A) \leq Max_x[A(x)]$. We see that as the maximum membership grade of a fuzzy subset decreases, all other membership grades remaining the same, the information in the fuzzy subset decreases. The specificity is always greater then the difference between the largest and second largest membership grade, $Sp(A) \geq b_1 - b_2$. We see that any measure of specificity in this class is bounded as follows $b_1 \geq Sp(A) \geq b_1 - b_2$.

The weights, the w_i's, distinguish the specificity measures in this class. Two special members of this class are worth noting. The first measure is when $w_2 = 1$ and $w_i = 0$ for $i > 2$, we shall denote this as S_p^*. In this case $S_p^*(A) = b_1 - b_2$. If Sp is any specificity measure then for any fuzzy subset A $Sp(A) \geq S_p^*(A)$, $S_p^*(A)$ is the most strict measure of specificity.

Another special specificity measure is the one where $w_i = \dfrac{1}{n-1}$, for $i = 2, ..., n$, we shall denote as $\widehat{S}p$, for this measure $\widehat{S}p(A) = b_1 - \dfrac{1}{n-1}\sum_{i=2}^{n} b_2$. This measures the difference between the maximum membership grade and the average of all the others.. We can show that this is the most lax measure in our class.

Given a piece of knowledge, a fundamental concern is the determination the truth of some other statement. In general it is impossible to precisely determine the truth if the specificity of our knowledge is not one. In an attempt to circumvent this problem Zadeh [9] introduced two surrogate measures, the measures of *possibility* and *certainty*. Dubois and Prade [10] have investigated these concepts in considerable detail.

Assume *V is A* is a piece of knowledge and let *V is B* be a proposition whose validity we are interested in determining. The possibility of *V is B* given *V is A*, denoted Poss[*V is B/V is A*], is defined as Poss[*V is B/V is A*] = $Max_x[A(x) \wedge B(x)]$. Essentially this measure captures the degree of intersection of the two proposition. It is the upper bound on the truth of *V is B* given *V is A*, as such it provides an optimistic measure of the truth of *V is B* given *V is A*.

The second measure called the measure of certainty is denoted as Cert[*V is B/V is A*] and is defined as Cert[*V is B/V is A*] = 1 - Poss[*V is not B/V is A*]. We note that Dubois and Prade [10] refer to this as the measure of necessity. This concept measures the degree to which A is contained in B. It is the lower bound on the truth of *V is B* given *V is A*, as such it provides a pessimistic measure of the truth of *V is B* given *V is A*.

The value

$$\text{Range}[V \text{ is } B/V \text{ is } A] = \text{Poss}[V \text{ is } B/V \text{ is } A] - \text{Cert}[V \text{ is } B/V \text{ is } A]$$

is a measure of our uncertainty with regard to our knowledge of the truth of *V is B* given *V is A*. Let us see how this uncertainty is effected by the quality of the information we have with respect to V is A. In the following we shall assume that B is normal. Let us first consider the situation in which our knowledge, *V is A*, is non-conflicting, A is normal, there exists some element x^* such that $A(x^*) = 1$. In this situation we have $\text{Poss}[V \text{ is } B/V \text{ is } A] \geq B(x^*)$ and $\text{Cert}[V \text{ is } B/V \text{ is } A] \leq B(x^*)$. In the the most specific case when A is a singleton, $A = \{x^*\}$, we get $\text{Poss}[V \text{ is } B/V \text{ is } A] = \text{Cert}[V \text{ is } B/V \text{ is } A] = B(x^*)$, here we know exactly the truth of *V is B*, it is $B(x^*)$. Now consider the situation where A and A' are two normal sets and $A \subset A'$, A is more specific then A'. In this situation $\text{Poss}[V \text{ is } B/V \text{ is } A] \geq \text{Poss}[B/A']$ and $\text{Cert}[V \text{ is } B/V \text{ is } A] \leq \text{Cert}[B/A']$ and therefore $\text{Range}[B/A] \leq \text{Range}[B/A']$.

3. Certainty Qualified Propositions

Given a piece of information often we associate with it a measure indicating the belief we attribute to this information. Zadeh [11, 12], Yager [13], and Dubois and Prade [14] have investigated this issue. Assume *V is A* is a statement let $\alpha \in [0, 1]$ be the certainty we assign to this proposition, the larger α the more certain, we shall denote this as

V is A is α - certainty

and call it a certainty qualified proposition. In [13] it was suggested that a certainty qualified proposition can be transformed into an unqualified proposition *V is B* where $B(x) = A(x) \vee (1 - \alpha)$. We note that if $\alpha = 1$, then A = B and if $\alpha = 0$ then B = X.

It appears natural that the more certain a proposition the more information it should contain. As a matter of fact if $\alpha = 0$ since B = X and $\text{Sp}(X) = 0$ this conjecture is somewhat reinforced. Assume A is a proposition, let $\alpha_1 > \alpha_2$ and let B_1 and B_2 be the transformed propositions under these values respectively. From the above definition of certainty transformation we can see that $B_1 \subset B_2$. Furthermore, if A is normal then both B_1 and B_2 are normal and hence our properties of specificity tells us that $\text{Sp}(B_1) \geq \text{Sp}(B_2)$. It can be shown [15] that this is indeed the case whether A is normal or not that is for all A if $\alpha_1 > \alpha_2$ then $\text{Sp}(A \text{ is } \alpha_1 - certain) \geq \text{Sp}(A \text{ is } \alpha_2 - certain)$. From this it follows that for all A and any α, $\text{Sp}(A) \geq \text{Sp}(A \text{ is } \alpha - certain)$.

While the standard definition for certainty qualification is $B(x) = (1 - \alpha) \vee A(x)$, one can consider the use of other t-conorms instead of the Max, $B(x) = S(\overline{\alpha}, A(x))$. In order for a t-conorm to provide a good definition of certainty qualification it should satisfy monotonicity, if $\alpha_1 \geq \alpha_2$ then $Sp(A \text{ is } \alpha_1 \text{ - certain}) \geq Sp(A \text{ is } \alpha_2 \text{ - certain})$.

Consider the algebraic sum t-conorm, $S(u, v) = u + v - uv$. If $\alpha_1 > \alpha_2$ then the elements of the respective certainty qualified propositions are

$$b_j = a_j + (1 - \alpha_1) - a_j(1 - \alpha_1) = \overline{\alpha}_1 + \alpha_1 a_j$$
$$c_j = \overline{\alpha}_2 + \alpha_2 a_j$$

Furthermore if $j < k$ then $b_j \geq b_k$ and $c_j \geq c_k$. Since $\alpha_1 > \alpha_2$ and $a_j \leq 1$ we also have $c_j \geq b_j$ for all j.

With $Sp(A) = a_1 - \sum_{j=2}^{n} w_j a_j$ we see that

$$Sp(B) = b_1 - \sum_{j=2}^{n} w_j b_j = \overline{\alpha}_1 + \alpha a_1 - \sum_{j=2}^{n} w_j (\overline{\alpha}_1 + \alpha_1 a_j)$$

$$Sp(B) = \overline{\alpha}_1 + \alpha a_1 - (\overline{\alpha}_1 + \alpha \sum_{j=2}^{n} w_j a_j) = \alpha_1 a_1 - \alpha_1 \sum_{j=2}^{n} w_j a_j$$

$$= \alpha_1 Sp(A).$$

Similarly $Sp(C) = \alpha_2 Sp(A)$. Since $\alpha_1 > \alpha_2$ we have $Sp(B) \geq Sp(C)$, and the desired property holds.

However as the following example illustrates all t-conorms don't satisfy this condition.

Example. Assume $X = \{x_1, x_2\}$ and let $A = \{\frac{0.2}{x_1}, \frac{0}{x_2}\}$. Here the specificity is $Sp(A) = 0.2 - 0 = 0.2$. Consider the Sugeno class of t–conorms

$$S(u, v) = Min(1, u + v + K\, uv)$$

where $K = 2$. If B is the α - certainty transformed proposition where $\alpha = 0.5$ we get $B = \{\frac{1}{x_1}, \frac{0.5}{x_2}\}$ and the specificity of this is $Sp(B) = 1 - 0.5 = 0.5$ and thus we have increased our information.

Let us see if we can make some generalization regarding the relationship between t-conorm operation used in certainty qualification and the monotonicity of information. Again assume A is a fuzzy subset with membership grades $a_1 > a_2 > a_3 ...> a_n$. Let $\alpha_1 > \alpha_2$ (both in the unit interval). Let

$$B = A \text{ is } \alpha_1 \text{ - certain}$$
$$C = A \text{ is } \alpha_2 \text{ - certain}$$

If S is a t-conorm $b_j = S(a_j, \overline{\alpha}_1)$ and $c_j = S(a_j, \overline{\alpha}_2)$. We note from the ordering of the a_i's we have $b_i \geq b_j$ and $c_i \geq c_j$ if $i < j$. In this situation $Sp(B) = b_1 - \sum_{j=2}^{n} w_j b_j$ and $Sp(C) = c_1 - \sum_{j=2}^{n} w_j c_j$. Since $\sum_{j=2}^{n} w_j = 1$ then we can obtain $b_1 = \sum_{j=2}^{n} w_j b_1$ and $c_1 = \sum_{j=2}^{n} w_j c_1$. From this we get

$$Sp(B) = \sum_{j=2}^{n} w_j (b_1 - b_j)$$

$$Sp(C) = \sum_{j=2}^{n} w_j(c_1 - c_j).$$

A sufficient condition for having $Sp(B) \geq Sp(C)$ is for $b_1 - b_j \geq c_1 - c_j$ for all $j = 2, ..., n$, that is if $S(a_1, \overline{\alpha}_1) - S(a_j, \overline{\alpha}_1) \geq S(a_1, \overline{\alpha}_2) - S(a_j, \overline{\alpha}_2)$. Since $\alpha_1 > \alpha_2$ $\overline{\alpha}_2 > \overline{\alpha}_1$) and $a_1 \geq a_j$ we can more generally express this requirement as

$$S(a, u) - S(b, u) \geq S(a, v) - S(b, v)$$

with $a \geq b$ and $v > u$. We note in the special case when $u = 0$ ($\alpha_1 = 1$) we have

$$a - b \geq S(a, v) - S(b, v).$$

This requires the t-conorm to be of such a nature that the addition of a constant disjunct causes a decrease in the difference.

More generally denoting $v = u + \Delta$ we have

$$S(a, u) - S(b, u) \geq S(a, u + \Delta) - S(b, u + \Delta).$$

Rearranging terms we get

$$S(b, u + \Delta) - S(b, u) \geq S(a, u + \Delta) - S(a, u).$$

Dividing by Δ and taking the limit as $\Delta \to 0$ w get as sufficient functions for the t-conorm that

$$\frac{\partial S(b, u)}{\partial u} \geq \frac{\partial S(a, u)}{\partial u}$$

for $a > b$. We shall call a t-conorm satisfying this condition *differentially non–increasing*. In the following we shall assume all t-conorms used have this property.

We shall here consider one form of certainty qualification which is not a t–conorm, the exponential type qualification. Let A be a proposition we define *A is α - certain* as B where $b_j = a_j^{\alpha}$. Let α_1 and α_2 be two values where α_1 and α_2, then the transformations of A using these values are B and C respectively where $b_j = a_j^{\alpha_1}$ and $c_j = a_j^{\alpha_2}$. In this case

$$Sp(B) = a_1^{\alpha_1} - \sum_{j=2}^{n} w_j a_j^{\alpha_1}$$

Since $\sum_{j=2}^{n} w_j = 1$ we express this as

$$Sp(B) = \sum_{j=2}^{n} w_j (a_1^{\alpha_1} - a_j^{\alpha_2})$$

We see that

$$Sp(B) - Sp(C) = \sum_{j=2}^{n} w_j [(a_1^{\alpha_1} - a_j^{\alpha_1}) - (a_1^{\alpha_2} - a_j^{\alpha_2})]$$

If $a_1^{\alpha_1} - a_j^{\alpha_1} \geq a_1^{\alpha_2} - a_j^{\alpha_2}$ for all $a_1 \geq a_j$, $\alpha_1 > \alpha_2$ then $Sp(B) \geq Sp(C)$. Consider the term $a^{\alpha} - b^{\alpha}$ where $0 \leq b \leq a \leq 1$. If we take the derivative of this we get

$$a^\alpha \ln(a) - b^\alpha \ln(b).$$

Since both a and b are less then or equal to 1 then $\ln(b) \le \ln(b) \le 0$ and therefore

$$a^\alpha \ln(a) - b^\alpha \ln(b) \ge 0.$$

Thus $a^\alpha - b^\alpha$ doesn't decrease as α increases and hence $a_1^{\alpha_1} - a_j^{\alpha_1} \ge a_1^{\alpha_2} - a_j^{\alpha_2}$ and our desired result follows.

4. Fusing Fuzzy Information

We now turn to the issue of fusing pieces of fuzzy information. Assume V is A and V is B are two pieces of information the fusion of these two pieces of information is V is D where D = A ∩ B, that is $D(x) = T(A(x), B(x))$ where T is a t–norm operator. Since $T(a, b) \le a$.it is always the case that A ∩ B ⊂ A and A ∩ B ⊂ B. It is also noted that $T(a, b) \le Min(a, b)$.

Let A and B be two fuzzy subsets on the space X, A and B are non-conflicting if D is normal, $Max_x[D(x)] = 1$. For any t-norm two pieces of information are non-conflicting if and only if there exists some value x^* for which $A(x^*) = B(x^*) = 1$. We shall say A and B are conflicting to degree $w = 1 - Max_x[D(x)]$. If D is normal, A and B are non conflicting, then $w = 0$. Non conflicting data will have $w = 0$ for any choice of t-norm, for conflicting data w will depend upon the t-norm used, although it will always be greater then zero.

We now consider the issue of information transmission under the conjunction. Generally we would anticipate that fusing information should result in statements containing at least as much information that any of the constituents of the fusion, it should be an **information increasing operation (IIO)**. Indeed if the data being combined are non-conflicting then their fusion indeed always results in a non-decrease, in information (specificity) over that contained in either of the individual constituent pieces. Formally if D = A ∩ B is normal, then for any specificity measure $Sp(D) \ge Sp(A)$ and $Sp(D) \ge Sp(B)$. Thus the fusion of non-conflicting knowledge can be seen as generally an information increasing operation.

In the case of conflicting information, $Max_x[D(x)] < 1$, as the following example illustrates, it is possible to obtain less information as a result of conjunction then is contained in either of the constituents.

Example: In this example we shall use Min for conjunction and assume the weights in the specificity measure are all equal, $w_j = \dfrac{1}{n-1}$. Assume A = $\{\dfrac{1}{x_1}, \dfrac{0.7}{x_2}, \dfrac{0.5}{x_3}\}$ and B = $\{\dfrac{0.8}{x_1}, \dfrac{1}{x_2}, \dfrac{0.6}{x_3}\}$ then $Sp(A) = 1 - \dfrac{1}{2}(0.7 + 0.5) = 0.4$ and $Sp(B) = 1 - \dfrac{1}{2}(0.8 + 0.6) = 0.3$. Since D = $\{\dfrac{0.8}{x_1}, \dfrac{0.7}{x_2}, \dfrac{0.5}{x_3}\}$ then $Sp(D) = 0.2$

However it is not always the case that the fusion of conflicting data results in a decrease in specificity, examples to illustrate this can easily be constructed. In general the effect on the specificity in the case of conjuncting conflicting datum is rather complex, however we can make some observation. we see that the specificity decreases as $Max_x[D(x)]$ decreases, since $Con(D) = 1 - Max_x[D(x)]$, it decreases as the conflict increases. Secondly we see that it decreases as other membership grades increase. More generally we see a decrease in specificity, information, occurs as the difference between the biggest and the remaining membership grades decrease.

As we have just illustrated the standard method for fusing multiple sources of information, the intersection operation, allows for the possibility of losing information. In the spirit of building intelligent information systems it would be desirable to try to obtain information fusion techniques which are able to avoid any loss of information during fusion. In the following we shall consider some methods for data fusion which try to maximize the resulting information, we shall call these **information enhancing intersections (IEI)**. As we have noted the loss of information during fusion is closely related to the occurrence of conflict between the data being fused, hence operations which can serve as conflict adjudication methods appear to be a promising direction. In the following we shall look at some approaches to constructing IEI"s.

5. Softening of Fusion Requirements

Here we suggest an approach to information maximization based upon a softening of the requirement that all datum need be considered in the fusion. Assume P_i: V *is* A_i, i = 1 to n, are a collection of propositions whose conjunction results in a subnormal fuzzy subset, some conflict. One method to reduce the conflict is not to include all the propositions in fusion. Particularly, one would want to eliminate propositions that conflict strongly with most of the other propositions. In implementing such a process we must associate some measure of credibility with fusions that don't use all the information. In order to accomplish this task we use the fuzzy measure introduced by Sugeno [16, 17]. We recall if $Y = \{y_1, y_2, ..., y_n\}$ is a set of elements a fuzzy measure μ is a mapping from subsets of Y into unit interval, $\mu: 2^Y \rightarrow [0, 1]$, such that $\mu(\emptyset) = 0$, $\mu(Y) = 1$ and if A and B are ordinary subsets of Y and $A \subset B$ then $\mu(A) \leq \mu(B)$.

In our framework we shall assume $Y = \mathcal{P} = \{P_1, P_2, ..., P_n\}$, the set of all pieces of data we have. For any subset A of $\mathcal{P}$ we shall let $\mu(A)$ be the credibility we attribute to the use of the conjunction of the elements in A as the fused value. If A = $\{P_1, P_2, P_5\}$ and $\mu(A) = \alpha$, then α is the certainty we attribute to the use of just the propositions P_1, P_2 and P_5 in determining the fused information for all the sources. Since the use of only these three pieces of knowledge affords us an α degree of certainty we must qualify the results of their fusion by α, thus our qualified fused value is V *is* D *is* α - *certain* where $D = A_1 \cap A_2 \cap A_5$. Letting $\widehat{D}$ be the certainty transformation of D under α our final result is V *is* $\widehat{D}$ where $\widehat{D}(x) = D(x) \vee (1 - \alpha)$. It should be noted that if we use all the observations, A = $\mathcal{P}$, then $\mu(A) = \mu(\mathcal{P}) = 1$, and $\widehat{D} = D$.

Using these ideas we can now provide a general framework for aggregating knowledge which tries to maximize the information, specificity, of the resulting fusion. Let P_i: *V is A_i* for i = 1 to n be a collection of pieces of knowledge about V. Let μ be a fuzzy measure on the space $\mathcal{P} = \{P_1, P_2, ..., P_n\}$ as described above. Let E be any subset of $\mathcal{P}$ and let D_E be the conjunction of the propositions in E. Furthermore, let $\widehat{D_E}$ be the credibility transformation of D_E under the certainty value $\mu(E)$, $\widehat{D_E} = D_E$ *is $\mu(E)$-credible*. Our problem then becomes that of finding the subset E^* of $\mathcal{P}$ such that $Sp(\widehat{D_E}^*) = \underset{E \subset \mathcal{P}}{Max}\ [Sp(\widehat{D_E})]$. We see that our agenda here is to try to find a subset of $\mathcal{P}$ which is both credible and are not to conflicting. It is clear that this approach always results in a fused value providing at least as much information as the simple conjunction of all the datum, $Sp(\widehat{D_E}^*) \geq Sp\widehat{D}_\mathcal{P})$. It can be shown [15] that if the P_i are not conflicting the maximal information is obtained by taking the conjunction of all the pieces of information, $E^* = \mathcal{P}$, the usual intersection.

In general it is not necessary to evaluate all the possible fusions to find the most informative. The introduction of the idea of **primary subsets** helps in reducing the number of fusions we need test.. We call a subset E of set $\mathcal{P}$ a primary subset if:

1. The conjunction of the datum in E is normal, $Max_x(D_E(x)) = 1$

2. The addition of any other datum to E causes it to be non-normal.

Theorem: Assume G is a primary subset and and F is another subset of $\mathcal{P}$ such that $F \subset G$ then $E^* \neq F$.

Proof: Since $F \subset G$, $D_G \subset D_F$ and both D_G and D_F are normal thus $Sp(D_G) \geq Sp(D_F)$ furthermore since $\mu(G) \geq \mu(F)$ then $Sp(\widehat{D_G}) \geq Sp(D_F)$

This result informs us that we only need look at the subsets of datum that are primary or contain primary subsets to find the most specific fusion of the datum. We shall call these the set of viable fusions.

The result of the process of finding the most informative aggregation is very dependent on the type of fuzzy measure being used. Let us look at some of the different types of fuzzy measures we can encounter. In discussing these different measures we shall find the following definition useful. Assume μ and μ' are two fuzzy measures if $\mu(E) \geq \mu'(E)$ for all $E \subset \mathcal{P}$ we shall denote this as $\mu > \mu'$ and say that μ' is a stricter measure of certainty.

Consider the measure which we shall denote as μ_* defined as $\mu_*(\mathcal{P}) = 1$ and $\mu_*(E) = 0$ for all $E \neq \mathcal{P}$. It can be easily seen that for any other measure μ, $\mu(E) \geq \mu_*(E)$. Using this measure we allow no credibility to any aggregation that doesn't use all the observed data. At the other extreme is the measure μ^* which we define as $\mu^*(\emptyset) = 0$ and $\mu^*(E) = 1$ for all $E \neq \emptyset$, this is the most lax measure of credibility. Using this measure we allow complete credibility for any aggregation that uses at least one piece of observed data, it effectively allows almost complete discounting. Let us look at the properties of using these special measures. In the case of μ_* it can be shown that the maximal information is always attained by using a conjunction of

all the data, the optimal set is $\mathcal{P}$. In the case of μ^* if we denote $E_i = \{A_i\}$, the set consisting of just one datum, then $Sp(\widehat{D_E}*) \geq \underset{i=1 \text{ to } n}{Max} [Sp\{D_{E_i}\}]$, thus the information resulting from this type of aggregation is always at least as great as the information contained in any of the constituent datum. Furthermore, in the case of μ^* if F is any subset of constituents whose conjunction is non-conflicting, normal, then $Sp(D_E*) \geq Sp(D_F)$, we get at least as much information as we can get by combining only the non-conflicting datum.

Assume μ and μ' are two measures of credibility such that $\mu > \mu'$, it can be shown that for any definition of specificity, intersection and appropriate definition of certainty transformation the use of μ gives us a resulting piece of knowledge having at least as much information as that of μ'. An implication of this is to tell us the more lax the credibility measure the more information. It points us to the goal of trying to use the least strict credibility measure possible in aggregating our data.

Consider now the class of credibility measures called binary fuzzy measures. A credibility measure μ is called a binary measure [18] if $\mu(E) = 0$ or 1 for all E. This class of measures is useful in situations in which a subset of datum is either completely acceptable or completely unacceptable for finding the fused value. If $\mu(E) = 0$ then whatever the intersection of the datum in E, $\widehat{D_E} = X$ hence $Sp(\widehat{D_E}) = 0$. Thus all the completely unacceptable fusions will provide no information and thus can't supply the fused value. Thus the optimal subset must have measure 1.

A binary measures is completely determined by the minimal subsets. A minimal subset E of $\mathcal{P}$ is defined as one for which $\mu(E) = 1$ and the subset resulting by the removal of any element from E has a credibility measure of zero, if $F \subset E$ then $\mu(F) = 0$. If $E_1, E_2, ..., E_q$ are the collection of minimal sets then

$$\mu(F) = 1 \quad \text{if for some i, } E_i \subseteq F$$
$$\mu(F) = 0 \quad \text{if for some i, } F \subseteq E_i$$

A simple algorithm can be used to obtain the set of acceptable fusions for binary measures

    1. Set $R = \emptyset$ and S = Power set of $\mathcal{P}$

    2. Select an element in S with the smallest cardinality, denote this F

    3. Enquire the value $\mu(F)$

    4. If $\mu(F) = 0$ eliminate F from S. If $\mu(F) = 1$ remove F and all subsets containing F from S add these to R.

    5. If S is empty stop

    6. Go to step 2.

Once having the set R of subsets with measure one we can now use these to search for the one with the highest entropy. First a further pruning can be made based on the the fact that if $E \subset F$ and D_F is normal then the specificity of D_F is at least as great as D_E. The following algorithm provides the necessary pruning.

    1. Set $R = \{E/\mu(E) = 1\}$ and set $T = \emptyset$

    2.Select an element in S with the largest cardinality, denote this F

    3. Remove F from R and place it in T

4. If $\text{Max}_x(D_F(x)) = 1$ remove all subsets from R that are contained in F

5. If R is empty stop else go to step 2

The most informative subset of $\mathcal{P}$, E^* must be a member of T.

Another form of credibility measure that is useful is the additive type measure, $\mu(E) = \sum\limits_{j \in E} \mu(\{P_j\})$, $\mu(E)$ is simply the sum of credibility of the individual propositions making up E. The use of this measure only requires our obtaining the credibility of each individual piece of data.

Closely related to this is another class of credibility measures. Here we have one observation that must be included in every credible fusion, assuming this is P_1, then $\mu(F) = 0$ if $P_1 \notin F$. Furthermore we associate with each P_i a value α_i such that $\alpha_i \in [0, 1]$ and let

$$\mu(E) = \sum_{i \in E} \alpha_i \quad \text{if } P_1 \in E$$

$$\mu(E) = 0 \quad \text{if } P_i \notin E.$$

In this case P_1 is acting like any anchor observation. A generalization of this can be considered. Let G be a subset of P. We can consider a credible measure as one that has at least one of the elements in G Here then

$$\mu(E) = \sum_{i \in E} \alpha_i \quad \text{if there exists at east one element from G in E}$$

$$\mu(E) = 0 \qquad \text{otherwise.}$$

Alternatively we require that all observations in G be contained in any fusion that has non-zero credibility. here,

$$\mu(E) = \sum_{i \in E} \alpha_i \quad \text{if all elements in G are in E}$$

$$\mu(E) = 0 \qquad \text{otherwise.}$$

There exists another class of credible measures which are closely related to the OWA operators. Here we evaluate the credibility of an aggregation by the number of pieces of data included in the aggregation. In order to implement this we need a mapping from $N = \{0, 1, ..., n\}$ into the unit interval, f: $N \rightarrow I$ such that $f(0) = 0$, $f(n) = 1$ and $f(i) \geq f(j)$ for $i > j$. Using this we evaluate $\mu(E) = f(\text{Card}(E))$. Here $f(i)$ indicates the credibility we assign to any fusion of i observations.

In many situations it may be impossible to expect a complete description of the credibility measure. Therefore it becomes important to consider the formation of credibility measures from partial information. The process of forming credibility measured from partial knowledge should be guided by the following dictum:

In the face of only partial information about the credibility measure select the strictest credible measure that satisfies the partial information.

The justification for this dictum is a follows. Let $\mathcal{M}$ be the set of all credibility measures that satisfy the partial information, its clear the chosen measure should be in $\mathcal{M}$. Furthermore, recall that if μ and μ' are two credibility measures if $\mu > \mu'$ (μ' is more strict then μ) then μ' will provide a less information. Since we have no justification to select any measure then that providing the least information we pick the most strict measure in $\mathcal{M}$.

One implication of this dictum is that if we have no information about the credibility measure, all credibility measures are possible, then we use μ_*, $\mu_*(\mathcal{P}) = 1$ and $\mu(E) = 0$ for all others, that is we just allow the intersection of all the data.

As an illustration of the application of this dictum consider a situation in which all we know is that $\mu(E) = \alpha$, where E is some collection of datum. Thus the set of credibility measures which satisfies the pieces of information are all the measures for which the credibility of E is α. Using this dictum we obtain the strictest measure from this class which is

$$\mu(\mathcal{P}) = 1$$
$$\mu(F) = \alpha \quad \text{for all F s.t. } E \subseteq F \text{ and } F \neq \mathcal{P}$$
$$\mu(F) = 0 \quad \text{for all others}$$

In the case in which we know $\mu(E_1) = \alpha_1$ and $\mu(E_2) = \alpha_2$ where $\alpha_1 > \alpha_2$ then

$$\mu(\mathcal{P}) = 1$$
$$\mu(F) = \alpha_1 \quad \text{if } E_1 \subseteq F$$
$$\mu(F) = \alpha_2 \quad \text{if } E_2 \subseteq F \text{ and } E_1 \not\subseteq F$$
$$\mu(F) = 0 \quad \text{for all others}$$

6. Using Prioritization as Meta-Knowledge

Any aggregation technique that tries to avoid the loss of information that arises when conflicts exist between the data must have a mechanism based on some meta–knowledge for adjudicating between conflicts. Simply put if one source says "its a bird" and another says "its a plane" we must decide between the two or be faced with a conflict. In the preceding we described an approach which allowed us soften the requirement of fusing all the data. This approach allowed the use of only some of the data provided by assigning degrees of credibility to fusions using less then all the data. In this the meta-knowledge used was the credibilities associated with fusions, this knowledge was represented in terms of a fuzzy measure.

In this section we shall consider another approach to aggregation of data that tries to adjudicate conflicts. Here our meta-knowledge will be in the form of some kind of hierarchy or prioritization between our belief in the individual pieces of data. The effect of this prioritization is to imply that the credibility associated with a piece of lower priority data is determined by the higher priority data. Thus rather then pre assigning fixed degrees of credibility to each data in this environment the credibility of lower priority data is determined by its compatibility with higher priority data. Thus for example, if observation one has higher priority than data two and if one says "its a plane" and two says "its a bird" since they are incompatible we assign credibility zero to data two and simple conclude it is a plane. However, it two says "its a F-16" since this is compatible with data one we allow it to be considered. In this case the credibilities are dynamically changed depending upon the observations. We now more formally describe our approach.

Assume P_1: V is A and P_2: V is B are two observations on the variable V and their exists a priority in our belief of P_1 over P_2. By assigning a priority of P_1 over

P_2 we mean to indicate that the credibility associated with the information contained in P_2 will be determined by P_1, rather then being fixed. Let α indicate the degree of credibility assigned to P_2, actually it is a variable that is to be determined by the process described in the following. Let $B_\alpha = V \text{ is } B \text{ is } \alpha\text{ - credible}$ be the credibility transformed value of B, $B_\alpha(x) = S(\overline{\alpha}, B(x))$. The fusion of A and B_α is $D_\alpha = A \cap B_\alpha$, $D_\alpha(x) = T(A(x), B_\alpha(x))$. Our problem then becomes that of finding the D_α which has the highest specificity and using this as our fused value. From our definition of specificity we have $Sp(D_\alpha) = q_i - \sum_{i=2}^{n} w_i q_i$ where q_i is the ith largest of the $D_\alpha(x_j)$, here $D_\alpha(x_j) = T(A(x_j), S(\overline{\alpha}, B(x_j)))$. Our problem now becomes finding α^* such that $Sp(D_\alpha^*) = Max_{\alpha \in [0,1]} [Sp(D_\alpha)]$ Having found α^* we then have $D = D_\alpha^*$ as our fused value.

The following simple example illustrates this process.

Example: Assume $X = \{a, b, c, d\}$ and let $A = \{\frac{1}{a}, \frac{1}{b}\}$. In this example we shall use as our specificity measure $Sp(E) = q_1 - \frac{1}{3}\sum_{i=2}^{4} q_i$, all $w_j = \frac{1}{3}$.

   i. Let $B = \{\frac{1}{c}\}$. In this case $B_\alpha = \{\frac{1-\alpha}{a}, \frac{1-\alpha}{b}, \frac{1}{c}, \frac{1-\alpha}{d}\}$, $D_\alpha = A \cap B_\alpha = \{\frac{1-\alpha}{a}, \frac{1-\alpha}{b}, \frac{0}{c}, \frac{0}{d}\}$ and $Sp(D_\alpha) = 1 - \alpha - \frac{1}{3}(1 - \alpha)$. Thus $Sp(D_\alpha)$ this attains its maximum value when $\alpha = 0$. Hence the fused value is $D = \{\frac{1}{a}, \frac{1}{b}\}$. Here we note that we have completely discounted the information in B, which totally conflicted with the higher priority information in A.

   ii. Let $B = \{\frac{1}{b}, \frac{1}{c}\}$. In this case $B_\alpha = \{\frac{1-\alpha}{a}, \frac{1}{b}, \frac{1}{c}, \frac{1-\alpha}{d}\}$, $D_\alpha = A_1 \cap B_\alpha = \{\frac{1-\alpha}{a}, \frac{1}{b}, \frac{0}{c}, \frac{0}{d}\}$ and $Sp(D_\alpha) = 1 - \frac{1}{3}(1 - \alpha)$. In this case $Sp(D_\alpha)$ attains its maximum value when $\alpha = 1$ and hence our fused value is $D_\alpha^* = \{\frac{0}{a}, \frac{1}{b}, \frac{0}{c}, \frac{0}{d}\}$. Here we have completely used the information in B, which was totally compatible with higher priority information in A.

   iii. Let $B = \{\frac{0}{a}, \frac{0.6}{b}, \frac{1}{c}, \frac{0}{d}\}$. In this case $B_\alpha = \{\frac{1-\alpha}{a}, \frac{S(\overline{\alpha}, 0.6)}{b}, \frac{1}{c}, \frac{1-\alpha}{d}\}$, $D_\alpha = \{\frac{1-\alpha}{a}, \frac{S(\overline{\alpha}, 0.6)}{b}, \frac{0}{c}, \frac{0}{d}\}$. Since $1 - \alpha = S(\overline{\alpha}, 0) \leq S(\overline{\alpha}, 0.6)$ then $Sp(D_\alpha) = S(\overline{\alpha}, 0.6) - w_2(1 - \alpha)$. If we are using the product for S then

$$Sp(D_\alpha) = \overline{\alpha} + \alpha(0.6) - \frac{1}{3}(\overline{\alpha}) = \alpha(0.6) + (1 - \frac{1}{3})\overline{\alpha} = \frac{2}{3} - 0.067\alpha.$$

Here $Sp(D_\alpha)$ attains its maximum value when $\alpha = 0$ and hence our fused value is $D = \{\frac{1}{a}, \frac{1}{b}\}$.

For notational convenience we shall indicate the fusion of A and B, using the preceding methodology as $D = \text{Int}_{Sp}(A, B)$, with the understanding that the first argument is the higher priority data.

Let us look at some properties of this prioritized fusion operation. We note that this operation is not commutative, $\text{Int}_{Sp}(A, B) \neq \text{Int}_{Sp}(B, A)$. If one of the datum being fused is the whole space the results become rather simple. Consider first $\text{Int}_{Sp}(A, X)$ here $B_\alpha(x) = S(\overline{\alpha}, 1) = 1$ for all x. Thus $B_\alpha = X$ and hence $D_\alpha = A \cap X = A$ for all α, hence no opportunity exists for optimization and $\text{Int}_{Sp}(A, X) = A$. Consider now $\text{Int}_{Sp}(X, B)$ here $B_\alpha(x) = S(\overline{\alpha}, B(x))$ and $D_\alpha = X \cap B_\alpha = B_\alpha$. As we have previously shown the maximum specificity in this case occurs when $\alpha = 1$, $B_{\alpha*} = B$, hence $\text{Int}_{Sp}(X, B) = B$.

We shall now look at some of the other properties of aggregating A and B using the preceding procedure. In the following we shall assume A has priority over B, $A > B$, furthermore we shall use D^* to denote the fused value, $D^* = \text{Int}_{Sp}(A, B)$.

The first result shows that if A and B are completely non-conflicting then our fused value using the above procedure is the ordinary intersection.

Theorem: If $E = A \cap B$ and $\text{Max}_x[E(x)] = 1$ then $\text{Int}_{Sp}(A, B) = E$.

Proof: Under the premise there exists some value $\hat{x}$ such that $A(\hat{x}) = B(\hat{x}) = 1$. Consider B_α, $B_\alpha(x) = S(\overline{\alpha}, B(x))$, we can easily show that i) $B_{\alpha_1} \subseteq B_{\alpha_2}$ if $\alpha_1 > \alpha_2$ and ii) B_α is normal for all α since $B_\alpha(\hat{x}) = 1$. Consider $D_\alpha = A \cap B_\alpha$, it follows from the above that $D_{\alpha_1} \subseteq D_{\alpha_2}$ if $\alpha_1 > \alpha_2$. Since D_α is normal for all α, $D_\alpha(\hat{x}) = 1$ and $A(\hat{x}) = 1$, then from the properties of specificity $Sp(D_{\alpha_1}) \geq Sp(D_{\alpha_2})$ for all $\alpha_1 > \alpha_2$. Thus the maximal specificity occurs for $\alpha = 1$ and hence

$$D^* = \text{Int}_{Sp}(A, B) = E = A \cap B.$$

It is interesting to note that if A and B are completely conflicting, $A \cap B = \emptyset$, and $Sp(A) > 0$ then $D^* \neq A \cap B$. Since $A \cap B = \emptyset$ then $Sp(A \cap B) = 0$. If we let $\alpha = 0$ then $B_\alpha = X$ and $D_\alpha = A \cap X = A$ and hence $Sp(D_\alpha) = Sp(A) > 0$.

It can be shown that the procedure described never provides less information then the simple intersection of A and B, $Sp(\text{Int}_{Sp}(A, B)) \geq Sp(A \cap B)$, nor less information then the higher priority data, $Sp(\text{Int}_{Sp}(A, B)) \geq Sp(A)$.

Thus far we have considered only the case where we have two pieces of data to fuse. The extension to the case of multiple pieces of data having a priority relationship is straight forward. Assume P_1, $i = 1$ to n, are a collection of data, each of the form V is A_i, and furthermore assume that a priority exists among these data, $P_1 > P_2 > ... > P_n$. Our approach to this multiple case is the repeated application of the Int_{Sp} operation. Thus we first calculate

$$F_2 = \text{Int}_{Sp}(A_1, A_2)$$

then for $j = 3$ to n we calculate

$$F_j = \text{Int}_{Sp}(F_{j-1}, A_j).$$

The final value of the intersection F^* is equal to F_n. Taking advantage of the fact that $Sp(X, A) = A$ we can now express this process inductively as follows:

1. Set $F_0 = X$

2. For $j = 1$ to n calculate $F_j = Int_{Sp}(F_{j-1}, A_j)$.

In general the problem of finding D^*, $Int_{Sp}(A, B)$, is a rather complex nonlinear mathematical optimization problem as we see from recalling the procedure for finding D^*.

1. Let $B_\alpha(x) = S(\bar{\alpha}, B(x))$

2. Let $D_\alpha(x) = T(A(x), B_\alpha(x))$

3. Find the value α^* that maximizes $Sp(D_\alpha)$

4. Set $D^* = D_{\alpha}*$.

The key difficulty here is step three, the optimization of $Sp(D_\alpha)$ with respect to α. This optimization is made even more difficult by the fact that $Sp(D_\alpha)$ is a complex nonlinear function with respect to α. The non–linearity comes from two sources. The first source of non-linearity results from the use of the aggregation operators T and S used to construct D_α from A, B and α. The second source of non–linearity is introduced by the ordering operation used in the calculation of specificity.

It would be useful to find some methods for simplifying this procedure. A first approach to simplification is a selection of T, S and Sp which makes the optimization problem simpler. An appropriate selection of T and S can eliminate effects of the first source of non–linearity. Consider the selection $T(a, b) = a\, b$ and $S(a, b) = a + b - ab$. In this case

$$B_\alpha(x) = S(\bar{\alpha}, B(x)) = \bar{\alpha} + \alpha\, B(x)$$

and

$$D_\alpha(x) = T(A(x), B_\alpha(x)) = A(x) - \alpha\, A(x)\, \overline{B}(x)$$

We see the above formulation for $D_\alpha(x)$ is linear in α.

We can now formulate our optimization problem as a mathematical programming problem with respect to α. Find α to

Max: $Sp(D_\alpha)$

subject to:

$$D_\alpha(x_j) = A(x_j) - \alpha\, A(x_j) \cdot \overline{B}(x_j) \qquad j = 1, 2, ..., n$$
$$0 \le \alpha \le 1$$

We note that $A(x_j)$ and $B(x_j)$ are known fixed values for a given fusion.

Let us now consider the specificity measure. We recall if F is a fuzzy subset with membership grades $f_1 \ge f_2 \ge ... \ge f_n$ then $Sp(F) = f_1 - \sum_{j=2}^{n} w_j\, f_j$. Consider the measure where $w_j = \dfrac{1}{n-1}$. In this case $Sp(F) = \dfrac{n}{n-1}\, f_1 - \dfrac{1}{n-1}\sum_{j=1}^{n} f_j$. In our problem $F = D_\alpha$. Letting H be the largest membership grade in D_α we get

$$Sp(D_\alpha) = \frac{n}{n-1} H - \frac{1}{n-1} \left(\sum_{j=1}^{n} A(x_j) - \alpha \sum_{j=1}^{n} A(x_j) \overline{B}(x_j) \right)$$

Denoting $\sum_{j=1}^{n} A(x_j) = a$ and $b = \sum_{j=1}^{n} A(x_j)\overline{B}(x_j)$ then

$$Sp(D_\alpha) = \frac{n}{n-1} H - \frac{1}{n-1} (a - \alpha b).$$

Our problem now becomes that of finding $\alpha \in [0, 1]$ that maximizes $Sp(D_\alpha) = nH + \alpha b$. The only non-linearity left is with respect to the determination of H, the largest of the $D_\alpha(x_j)$ over j. We can now use a technique, described in [19], which uses the introduction of binary integer variables to convert this into a linear mixed integer programming problem for which many efficient codes, such as Lindo, are available.

Maximize: $nH + \alpha b$

such that:

    (1) $0 \le \alpha \le 1$ and $0 \le H \le 1$

    (2) $u_i = A(x_i) - \alpha(A(x_i) - B(x_i))$ for $i = 1$ to n

    (3) $H - u_i - Kz_i \le 0$ for $i = 1$ to n

    (4) $\sum_{i=1}^{n} z_i = n - 1$

    (5) $z_i \in \{0, 1\}$ (z_i restricted to be a binary integer variable)

In the above K is some arbitrary large number.

Let us see that this formulation solves our problem. Constraint (1) just restricts α and H to be in the unit interval. Constraint (5) restricts z_i to be binary zero/one integer variable. Constraint (4) says that only one of z_i will be zero, while the others will be one. Constraint (2) just expresses u_i as $D_\alpha(x_i)$. The key is the Constraint in (3). We note that if $z_i = 1$ this constraint is always satisfied while if $z_i = 0$ this constraint becomes $H \le u_i$. Thus this constraint along with constraint (4) implies that H must be less then or equal one of the u_i. Since our objective function increases with H, then this condition will be satisfied by having $v = Max[u_i]$.

Thus using this mathematical programming formulation we can easily obtain α^*.

Another approach to the simplification of the determination of the maximal information intersection, $Int_{Sp}(A, B)$, is to turn it into a tractable enumeration problem and perhaps accept a slightly less then optimal solution. In this approach there is no need to limit the possible operations used for S, T and Sp.

    (1) Provide a discretization of the unit interval into e_j for $j = 1$ to q where

    $0 = e_1 < e_2 < e_3 \ldots < e_q = 1$

    (2) Set $E = \{e_1, e_2, e_3, \ldots, e_q\}$

        Set $f = 0$, $g = 0$ and $i = 1$.

    (3) Let $\alpha = e_i$

    (4) Calculate

i. $B_\alpha(x_j) = S(\overline{\alpha}, B(x_j))$ for j = 1 to n

ii. $D_\alpha(x_j) = T(A(x_j), B_\alpha(x_j))$ for j = 1 to n

iii. $Sp(D_\alpha)$

(5) If $Sp(D_\alpha) > f$ then set $f = Sp(D_\alpha)$ and $g = e_i$.

(6) if e < q set i = e + 1 and go to step 3

(7) Set $\alpha^* = g$ and calculate $D^*(x_j) = T(A(x_j), B_\alpha^*(x_j))$

A third approach to simplification involves the use of a direct representation of D^* in terms of A and B without any optimization process. We recall we assumed $D_\alpha = V$ is A and V is B is α - credible in which α is the credibility of V is B. Because of the priority relationship between V is A and V is B we indicated that the credibility of V is B should be a function of its compatibility with V is A. In this approach we can consider providing some representation of the compatibility between A and B, $\alpha = Comp(A, B)$. One option is to define $\alpha = Poss[B/A] = Max_x[A(x) \wedge B(x)]$. Using this definition we see that if the intersection of A and B is normal, they are compatible, they have some solution in common, then $\alpha = 1$. On the other hand if they are completely in compatible, $\alpha = 0$. More generally, we that α is inversely related to the degree of conflict between Using this we get that $D^*(x) = A(x) \wedge (B(x) \vee (1 - Poss[B/A])) = (A(x) \wedge B(x)) \vee (A(x) \wedge (1 - Poss[B/A]))$. Other possible representations exist for the characterization of Comp(A, B) however we shall not pursue them at this point.

7. Conclusion

We considered the problem of data fusion and particularly the information resulting from the fusion of conflicting data. We first showed that the measure of specificity provides an appropriate measure for the amount of information contained in a fuzzy subset. We showed that if the data being fused is completely non-conflicting then the maximal information is obtained by taking the intersection of all the observations. When the data is conflicting the use of the intersection can result in a fused value having less information then any of its components. In order to increase the information content in this conflicting environment some meta knowledge must be introduced to adjudicate between conflicting data. Two approaches to address this problem were introduced. The first approach considered the possibility of using only a subset of the observations to construct the fused value. Central to this approach was the use of a measure of credibility assigned to subsets of observations indicating the appropriateness of using a subset of observations to calculate the fused value. The basic rational of this approach was to calculate the fused value from a subset of observations that were not to conflicting and consisted of enough of the observations to be considered a credible fusion. In this approach the meta-knowledge used was the measure of credibility. The second approach was based upon meta-knowledge in the form of a prioritization of the observations. In this approach an observation is essentially discounted if conflicts with higher priority observations.

8. References

[1]. Zadeh, L. A., "A theory of approximate reasoning," in Machine Intelligence, Vol. 9, Hayes, J., Michie, D., & Mikulich, L.I. (eds.), New York: Halstead Press, 149-194, 1979.

[2]. Yager, R. R., "Deductive approximate reasoning systems," IEEE Transactions on Knowledge and Data Engineering 3, 399-414, 1991.

[3]. Dubois, D. and Prade, H., "Fuzzy sets in approximate reasoning Part I: Inference with possibility distributions," Fuzzy Sets and Systems 40, 143-202, 1991.

[4]. Zadeh, L. A., "Fuzzy sets as a basis for a theory of possibility," Fuzzy Sets and Systems 1, 3-28, 1978.

[5]. Yager, R. R., "Entropy and specificity in a mathematical theory of evidence," Int. J. of General Systems 9, 249-260, 1983.

[6]. Yager, R. R., "Measures of specificity for possibility distributions," in Proc. of IEEE Workshop on Languages for Automation: Cognitive Aspects in Information Processing, Palma de Mallorca, Spain, 209-214, 1985.

[7]. Yager, R. R., "On the specificity of a possibility distribution," Fuzzy Sets and Systems 50, 279-292, 1992.

[8]. Yager, R. R., "Default knowledge and measures of specificity," Information Sciences 61, 1-44, 1992.

[9]. Zadeh, L. A., "Fuzzy sets and information granularity," in Advances in Fuzzy Set Theory and Applications, Gupta, M.M., Ragade, R.K. & Yager, R.R. (eds.), Amsterdam: North-Holland, 3-18, 1979.

[10]. Dubois, D. and Prade, H., Possibility Theory : An Approach to Computerized Processing of Uncertainty, Plenum Press: New York, 1988.

[11]. Zadeh, L. A., "PRUF--a meaning representation language for natural languages," International Journal of Man-Machine Studies 10, 395-460, 1978.

[12]. Yager, R. R., Ovchinnikov, S., Tong, R. and Nguyen, H., Fuzzy Sets and Applications: Selected Papers by L. A. Zadeh, John Wiley & Sons: New York, 1987.

[13]. Yager, R. R., "Approximate reasoning as a basis for rule based expert systems," IEEE Trans. on Systems, Man and Cybernetics 14, 636-643, 1984.

[14]. Dubois, D. and Prade, H., "Fuzzy sets in approximate reasoning Part 2: logical approaches," Fuzzy Sets 40, 203-244, 1991.

[15]. Yager, R. R., "Conflict resolution in the fusion of fuzzy knowledge via information maximization," International Journal of General Systems, (To Appear).

[16]. Sugeno, M., "Theory of fuzzy integrals and its application," Doctoral Thesis, Tokyo Institute of Technology, 1974.

[17]. Sugeno, M., "Fuzzy measures and fuzzy integrals: a survey," in Fuzzy Automata and Decision Process, Gupta, M.M., Saridis, G.N. & Gaines, B.R. (eds.), Amsterdam: North-Holland Pub, 89-102, 1977.

[18]. Yager, R. R., "A general approach to criteria aggregation using fuzzy measures," International Journal of Man-Machine Studies 38, 187-213, 1993.

[19]. Yager, R. R., "Constrained OWA aggregation," Fuzzy Sets and Systems 81, 89-101, 1996.

Social Choice under Fuzziness: A Perspective

Hannu Nurmi[1] and Janusz Kacprzyk[2]

[1] Department of Political Science
University of Turku
FIN-20014 Turku, Finland
Email: hnurmi@utu.fi
[2] Systems Research Institute
Polish Academy of Sciences
ul. Newelska 6
01–447 Warsaw, Poland
Email: kacprzyk@ibspan.waw.pl

D71
D81

Summary. The mainstream of social choice (group decision making) theory takes as its point of departure the assumption that each individual is endowed with a connected and transitive binary relation of weak preference over the set of decision alternatives (options, variants, ...). The theory focuses on social choice correspondences (functions) which map the individual preference relations to the set of social choices (alternatives). In social choice (group decision making) theory under fuzziness the starting point is the concept of an individual fuzzy preference relation. Moreover, a fuzzy majority may also be included. The aim is to find plausible aggregation methods using fuzzy preference relations, and possibly a fuzzy majority. First, we will show how the introduction of fuzzy preference relations may provide means for a way out of basic incompatibility results and paradoxes in social choice. Moreover, we will deal with ways of solving compound majority paradoxes using fuzzy preference relations. Then, taking into account the perspective adopted, we will sketch some known definitions of social choice solution concepts under fuzzy preference relations and fuzzy majority, and present three basic approaches: (1) one based on first aggregating the individual preference relations into collective preference relations and then defining various solutions, i.e. subsets of alternatives called social choices, (2) one based on defining solutions directly from individual fuzzy preference relations, and (3) one based on fuzzy tournaments.

1 Introduction

Social choice theory has a long albeit discontinuous history. Marquis de Condorcet and Jean-Charles de Borda – two late 18-th century theorists – are usually named as the founding fathers of the theory (see [13]). Early pioneers can however be found already in the Middle Ages (see [45]). Indeed, when tracing the history of a theory which is so closely related to practice as the theory of group (social) choice is to voting, one is faced with the problem of determining when a particular author is elaborating a theory itself rather than pondering upon an application problem. Anyway, the justification of regarding Borda and Condorcet as social choice theorists is that they started from specific assumptions and set out to prove results pertaining to the general properties of group decision methods.

The modern axiomatic social choice theory has become notorious for its negative results. The earliest of them, the famous Arrow [3] impossibility theorem, gave rise to a whole *genre* of results showing that various intuitively plausible properties of social choice methods are incompatible (see [40]). These results are based on the assumption that the individual members of a group are endowed with a connected and transitive preference relation over pairs of decision alternatives (options, variants, ...).

In this article we will replace this assumption with two other ones, i.e. those of an individual fuzzy preference relation and of an individual fuzzy tournament. We will show how the above helps overcome main paradoxes and incompatibility results of the theory. Moreover, we will show that the inclusion of a fuzzy majority amplifies the above.

Our analysis will concern more fundamental issues than just the derivation of new solution concepts for social choice (group decision making) under fuzziness which is more often pursued in the literature (for more details on these, see, e.g, [27], [28], [29], [30], [31], [32], [34], [35], [50], [67], etc.)

The perspective adopted in this paper is less often considered in the literature, and among more relevant papers along this line of reasoning one should certainly site [64]; see also [51], [56], [57].

The organization of the article is the following. First, we present the classic paradoxes of Borda and Condorcet. Second, we proceed to the notation and definitions. Third, we outline the two best-known incompatibility results of modern social choice theory. Fourth, we discuss another class of paradoxes, i.e. those related to compound majorities. This class of paradoxes has received relative little attention in the literature although its importance to real world voting bodies cannot be denied. Fifth, we discuss some solution concepts based on fuzzy preference relations and fuzzy majorities. Finally, the fuzzy tournaments are focused upon.

2 Some problems of social choice

The basic setting that the social choice theory (which is practically equated here with group decision making) focuses upon is as follows. A group consisting of individuals has to make a decision concerning a set of alternatives. In some formulations of the problem the group has to determine its collective preference ranking of the alternatives. More often, however, the task is to find a set of alternatives (or a single alternative) which is *collectively* (i.e. by the group as a whole) regarded as best. We shall start with two classic versions of such a collective choice problem.

2.1   Paradoxes of the founding fathers

In 1770 Jean-Charles de Borda appeared in front of the French Academy of Sciences and presented the following problem. Suppose that a group of 9 individuals is to make a choice from three candidates for an office, A, B and C. Suppose that the members have somewhat different views of the candidates, namely 4 members ranking them in the order (i.e. from the best to the worst) ABC, 3 in the order BCA and 2 in the order CBA. The views of the group can thus be depicted as in Table 2.1.

Table 1. Borda's paradox

members 1-4	members 5-7	members 8,9
A	B	C
B	C	B
C	A	A

Borda observed that should the plurality voting method be employed, then A would get 4 votes, B – 3 votes and C – 2 votes, so that A would win. In Borda's opinion A would be, however, a bad choice. To wit, in pairwise comparison with B, A would be defeated by 5 votes to 4. Similarly, in pairwise comparison with C, A would loose by 5 votes to 4.

To avoid the possibility of electing a candidate that in pairwise comparisons would be regarded worse than any other available candidate by a majority of voters, Borda proposed a system nowadays called the *Borda count* (see, e.g., [17]). In this system the voters give points to alternatives so that the alternative ranked first receives $k-1$ points, the alternatives ranked second $k-2$ points, ..., the alternative ranked last receives 0 points from the voter in question. The points given to an alternative by each voter are then summed up which yields the Borda count of the alternative. The alternative with the largest Borda count is declared the winner (for a discussion of the properties of the Borda count, see [21]).

Borda provided therefore a solution to a problem of considerable importance. His contemporary Marquis de Condorcet later pointed out that the Borda count is not an entirely faultless system, i.e. it may happen that an alternative that defeats all the others in pairwise comparisons – known in modern times as the Condorcet winner – is not necessarily chosen by the Borda count.

Condorcet's paradox, however, is related to the following situation (Table 2.1). Here three groups of voters consider the alternatives A, B and C in pairs according to a fixed agenda. Assuming that the groups are of equal size or that any two of them constitute a majority of voters, one is led to the conclusion that regardless of which alternative one picks as the winner, there always exists a majority of voters preferring some other alternative to it.

Table 2. Condorcet's paradox

Group I	Group II	Group III
A	B	C
B	C	A
C	A	B

These two paradoxes started a research tradition which somewhat discontinuously has led to modern social choice theory (see [13], [63]). We now turn to the basic notation and definitions of the theory.

3 Notation and basic definitions

The following notation and definitions are standard (see, e.g., [48], [61]). We consider the set N of n voters and a set X of k alternatives (options, candidates, policies, . . .). Each voter $i \in N$ is endowed with a complete and transitive preference relation R_i over X. The set of all possible transitive and complete preference relations of voter i is W_i. An n-tuple of individual preference relations is called a preference profile and denoted by R^N.

We have then the following basic definitions.

Definition 1. A *social choice function* (SCF, for brevity) is a function F from the set of preference profiles to X.

The set of all preference profiles involving N is denoted by W^N.

Definition 2. A *social choice correspondence* (SCC, for brevity), is a function from W^N to 2^X, the power set of X (the family of all subsets of X including X and $\emptyset$).

Thus, a SCF always gives a single alternative (the winner), while SCCs may produce ties between several alternatives.

Definition 3. A *social welfare function* (SWF, for brevity) is a function f from W^N to the set of complete and transitive preference relations over X.

Let now F be a SCF and $R^N \in W^N$. Then, we have the following definition.

Definition 4. The *matrix form game associated with F and R^N* is denoted by $g(f, R^N)$ where the strategy set of each $i \in N$ is W_i, f is the outcome function, and R_i is i's preference relation over the outcome set X.

In other words, the strategies of voters are their reported preferences over the decision alternatives.

Definition 5. An *equilibrium point* of $g(f, R^N)$ is a profile $T^N \in W^N$ if for all $i \in N$: $f(T^N)R_i f(T^{N-\{i\}}, R_i')$, for all $R_i' \in W_i$. Here $T^{N-\{i\}}$ denotes the profile of $n - 1$ preference relations which is obtained from T^N by deleting i's preference relation.

This is the best-known equilibrium notion, the so-called *Nash equilibrium*. It means that in an equilibrium point no voter regrets for having voted in the way he or she did, provided that the others stick to their strategies.

Definition 6. A *strong equilibrium point*, in turn, is a $T^N \in W^N$ if for any coalition S of s voters and for any s-tuple of strategies L^S of the members of S, there exists a voter $j \in S$ who regards $f(T^N)$ at least as good an outcome as $f(T^{N-S}, L^S)$.

Definition 7. If for any $R^N \in W^N$, R^N is an equilibrium point in $g(f, R^N)$, then F is *individually non-manipulable* or *strategy- proof*.

In individually non-manipulable viting systems, it is never beneficial to an individual not to report his or her true preference relation, provided that the others do.

Definition 8. An SCF F is called *coalitionally strategy-proof* if for any $R^N \in W^N$ the strategy R^N is a strong equilibrium point.

Clearly if an SCF is coalitionally strategy-proof, and it is also individually strategy-proof. What is less obvious, however, is that the converse is also true (see, e.g., [26], Lemma 5.3).

Definition 9. Given the set N of players, a *simple game* is defined as $G = (N, V)$ where V is the set of winning coalitions.

We now define a *core* $C(G, X, R^N)$ of a simple game G with the help of a binary *dominance relation*, dom. Given a profile $R^N \in W^N$ and any $x, y \in X$, $x \operatorname{dom}(R^N)y$ if there is a coalition $K \in V$ such that x is strictly preferred to y by all members of K.

Definition 10. The *core* $C(G, X, R^N)$ consists of alternatives not dominated by any other alternatives, i.e. of non-dominated alternatives.

3.1 Some incompatibility results

The best-known result in the modern social choice theory is Arrow's impossibility theorem (cf., e.g., [3], [40]). It states that unrestricted domain, independence of irrelevant alternatives, Pareto condition and non-dictatorship are properties that cannot all characterize any social welfare function.

Definition 11. The function f has *unrestricted domain* iff it is defined for the entire Cartesian product.

Definition 12. The function f is *independent of irrelevant alternatives* iff the social preference relation over any two alternatives x and y depends on the individual preference relations regarding x and y only.

Definition 13. The *Pareto condition* is satisfied iff xP_iy for all individuals i implies that xRy. Here P_i denotes the asymmetric part of R_i.

Definition 14. The *Non-dictatorship condition* is satisfied when there is no individual i such that xRy iff xR_iy, for all $x, y \in X$.

The above incompatibility result has generated a rich literature in which the result and its relevance has been discussed (see, e.g., [40]).

We now proceed to another result which has also been viewed as having fatal implications for democracy. Gibbard–Satterthwaite's theorem deals with SCFs ([22], [65]). It states that all universal and non-trivial SCFs are either manipulable or dictatorial.

Definition 15. An SCF is *universal* iff its domain is unrestricted.

Definition 16. An SCF is *non-trivial* iff for any $x \in X$ there is a preference n-tuple such that the value of the function is x.

Definition 17. An SCF h is *manipulable by individual i in situation* (X, S^N), where S^N is a fixed preference profile of n individuals, iff $h(X, S^N) = y$ and $h(X, T^N) = x$ with xP_iy, and T^N can be obtained from S^N by changing the i's preference relation.

Definition 18. An SCF h is *manipulable* iff there is a situation (X, S^N) and an individual j such that j can manipulate h in (X, S^N).

Therefore, Gibbard and Satterthwaite's theorem states that for all non-dictatorial, universal and non-trivial SCFs a situation (X, R^N) exists where R^N is not an equilibrium point.

Condorcet's voting paradox is the best-known paradox in the theory of voting. Of somewhat more recent origin are paradoxes related to combining majorities. The earliest of these paradoxes bears the name of Moise Ostrogorski [60].

3.2 Compound majority paradoxes

Ostrogorski's paradox pertains to situations in which parties competing for electoral support are characterized by stands taken on various issues. Consider Table 3.2 discussed by Daudt and Rae [16] (see also [12], [44], [62]). In this example there are two parties X and Y and voters are grouped into four groups A, B, C and D. The three first groups comprise 20% of the electorate each, while group D consists of 40% of the electorate. The entries in the table indicate which party is considered better by the voters represented by the

Table 3. Ostrogorski's paradox

group	issue 1	issue 2	issue 3	party supported
A (20%)	X	X	Y	X
B (20%)	X	Y	X	X
C (20%)	Y	X	X	X
D (40%)	Y	Y	Y	Y

row on the issue represented by the column. Thus, e.g., the voters in group A consider X better than Y on issue 1.

Now if the party choice of a voter is determined on the basis of the party regarded better in most issues (assuming that the issues are of equal importance), then the voters in A, B and C vote for X, whereas the voters in D vote for Y. Thus, 60% of the voters choose X. However, considering the issues one at a time, one immediately observes that on each issue party Y is supported by 60% of the voters. Clearly, it makes a huge difference whether the issues are voted upon one at a time or simultaneously as party platform.

Anscombe's [2] paradox belongs to the compound majority paradoxes as well. It appears to be closely related to Ostrogorski's paradox. It consists of the observation that a majority of voters may be in a minority on a majority of issues to be voted upon. Table 3.2 reproduces Wagner's [68] example of the paradox. Assuming that issues are decided by simple majority, a majority of

Table 4. Anscombe's paradox

voters	issue 1	issue 2	issue 3
voter 1	yes	yes	no
voter 2	no	no	no
voter 3	no	yes	yes
voter 4	yes	no	yes
voter 5	yes	no	yes

voters, i.e. voters 1–3, are on the losing side in two issues out of three: voter 1 is in the minority on issues 2 and 3, voter 2 in issues 1 and 3, voter 3 in issues 1 and 2.

In countries where consultative non-binding referenda are being resorted to, a particular problem of some importance may be encountered, namely that of deciding which one is more authoritative: the referendum outcome or the parliamentary voting outcome. To wit, it may happen that the majority of voters favours an opinion and the majority of the representatives its negation. This problem has certain similarities with Ostrogorski's paradox.

Table 5. Paradox of representation

opinions	MPs of A	MPs of B		total vote
	1–6	7,8	9	
"yes"	5	11	12	64
"no"	6	0	0	36

Consider again an example. Let us assume for the sake of illustration that the parliament consists of 9 members (MPs) and that there are 100 voters. Assume, moreover, that the support for each elected member is roughly the same, i.e. 11 votes for 8 members and 12 votes for 1 member. Let this last named member be a party B representative. Party A has 6 out of 9 or 2/3 of the parliament seats, while party B has 3 out of 9 or 1/3 of the seats. Suppose that the support of the parties corresponds to the seat distribution, i.e. 2/3 of the electorate supports party A and 1/3 party B (see Table 3.2).

Let now a referendum be called in which the voters are asked to answer either "yes" or "no" to a question. The distribution of votes in both parliamentary elections and the referendum is indicated in the above table. Clearly "yes" wins the referendum receiving 64 votes out of 100.

Suppose, however, that the same issue is being subjected to a parliamentary vote. Then, assuming that the MPs know the distribution of opinions of their own supporters, it is plausible to predict that they vote in accordance with what they think is the opinion of the majority of their supporters. Thus, the MPs of party A would vote for "no" and the MPs of party B would vote for "yes". Obviously, "no" wins by a handsome margin 6 to 3. What is therefore the right outcome?

These are some of the problems discussed in social choice theory where the point of departure, as was pointed out above, is the assumption that the individuals have connected and transitive preference relations over the set of alternatives. We now proceed to approach these problems by replacing these assumptions with "softer" ones.

4   Avoiding the incompatibility results

In probabilistic voting (cf. [24], [25], [53]) the point of departure is that we know probabilities that individuals assign to various alternatives. These probabilities play an analogous role to the individual preference relations in the standard theory of collective choice. It is natural to interpret them so that the more likely an individual is to vote for an alternative, the more desirable he considers it.

Consider again a finite alternative set X with k elements and denote by q_{ij} the probability that individual i votes for alternative j, for $i = 1,\ldots,n$ and $j = 1,\ldots,k$. We assume that, for each i, $\Sigma_{j=1,\ldots,k} q_{ij} = 1$ and $q_{ij} \geq 0$. We call

$p = (p_1, \ldots, p_n)$ the probability vector of the collectivity or group N. There are many ways of arriving at this vector as, e.g., the average rule: $p_j = s_j/n$ where s_j is the sum of probabilities given to alternative j $(j = 1, \ldots, k)$.

It can easily be seen that this remarkably simple rule satisfies all Arrow's conditions when the latter are modified to fit into the probabilistic framework (see [24], [25]). These are the following in the probabilistic framework.

Definition 19. *Collective rationality:* the collective preference relation over X induced by the average rule is complete, reflexive and transitive.

Definition 20. *Citizen's sovereignty:* for any probability vector p of the group, there exists an n-tuple of individual probabilities that results in p when the average rule is applied.

Definition 21. *Symmetry:* permutation of individuals does not affect the outcome.

Definition 22. *Preservation of unanimity:* if every individual assigns a higher choice probability to alternative i than to alternative j, then so does the collectivity.

Definition 23. rm *Pareto principle:* if alternative i Pareto dominates alternative j, then the collectivity assigns a higher choice probability to i than to j.

Definition 24. *Certainty principle:* the collectivity chooses alternative i with certainty, i.e. with probability 1, iff all individuals choose i with probability 1.

Definition 25. *Independence of irrelevant alternatives:* the choice probability or alternative i depends only on the choice probabilities that the individuals assign to i.

Definition 26. *Non-dictatorship:* no proper subset of individual choice probabilities determines the collective choice probability vector completely.

All these conditions are satisfied by the average rule. First, the collective choice probability vector, which can be interpreted as a collective preference relation, produces clearly a connected and transitive relation over the set of alternatives. Second, an example of individual choice probabilities that guarantee the citizen's sovereignty is one in which all individuals have an identical probability vector over the alternatives that coincides with the collective choice probability vector p. Third, when computing the averages of probability values, it obviously makes no difference in which order the probabilities are summed up. Thus, the symmetry is guaranteed. Fourth, unanimity is preserved since the average of higher probability numbers is obviously larger than the average of smaller probability numbers. Fifth, the Pareto principle is satisfied since if every individual except one is indifferent between i and j, i.e. assigns an equal choice probability to them, and one individual assigns to i a higher choice probability than to j, then also the collective choice probability of i is larger than that of j. Sixth, since the individual choice probabilities have the maximum value of 1, the only way in which their average value is 1 is when they are all equal to 1. Seventh, the collective choice probability of i depends on the individual choice probabilities of i being the average of the latter. Eight, because the outcome of the average rule is determined by all individual choice probabilities, no individual can alone determine the outcome.

The crux of the above way to avoid Arrow's result is thus to assume that the individuals assign choice probabilities to alternatives. Obviously, this is a more stringent assumption than that of connected and transitive preference relations in the sense that the latter assumption implies the former, while the converse does not hold. In other words, the individual choice probabilities can be mapped into connected and transitive preference relations, but any connected and transitive preference relation is consistent with an infinite number of choice probability vectors. In a way the choice probability vector induces a preference relation.

The way out of Gibbard-Satterthwaite theorem suggested by Barbera does not presuppose individual choice probabilities ([5]). Instead, the individual preference ranking assumption is the point of departure. A ranking of alternative set X is a binary connected, asymmetric and transitive relation. We now define a measure over X as a function which assigns a non-negative number to each alternative in X. We denote the measure of $x \in X$ by $m(x)$. The weight of the measure m is $\Sigma_{x \in X} m(x)$.

A *scheme* is a function that assigns to each profile of strict preferences a measure with a fixed weight. In the following the schemes are denoted by f. A special case of measures is one in which the weight equals 1. These are called *lotteries*. Barbera calls schemes with weight 1, i.e. lotteries, *decision schemes*. The decision schemes thus tell us, given the preference profile, what is the probability of various alternatives being chosen. Hence, the output of the decision process is the same as in the case of probabilistic voting.

Three classes of decision schemes are of particular importance:

1. point voting schemes,
2. supporting size schemes, and
3. simple schemes,

and they are defined below.

Definition 27. The *point voting schemes* are representable by positional scoring vectors $(a_1, \ldots, a_k)$ where $a_1 \geq \cdots \geq a_k \geq 0$ and the probability that alternative x is chosen in a given profile is determined by $f(x) = \Sigma_{i \in N} a_{r(i,x)}$. Here $r(i, x)$ denotes the rank of alternative x in the individual i's preference ordering.

The choice probability is then determined so that an alternative is given a score a_i every time a voter ranks it to the i'th rank. Clearly, in the Borda count $a_i = k - i$. Since we are dealing with decision schemes, the scoring vectors must be defined so that the sum of scores equals 1.

Definition 28. The *supporting size schemes* are characterized by supporting size scoring vectors $(b_n, \ldots, b_0)$ such that: (a) $b_n \geq \cdots \geq b_0 \geq 0$, (b) there exists a number K such that $b_j + b_{n-j} = K$, for each $j \leq n/2$, and (c) in any fixed profile $f(x) = \Sigma_{y \in X - \{y\}} b_{s(x,y)}$. Here $s(x,y)$ denotes the number of individuals who prefer x to y in the profile.

In decision schemes the scoring vectors have to be calibrated so that $p = (p(x_1), \ldots, p(x_k))$ determined on the basis of f is a probability vector.

Definition 29. The *simple schemes* are characterized by numbers $q \geq 0$ and $s \geq 0$ such that $f(x) = \Sigma_{y \in X - \{x\}} \Sigma_{i \in N} q v_{xy}^i + k$. Here $v_{xy}^i = 1$ if $x P_i y$ and $v_{xy}^i = 0$ if $y P_i x$.

Thus, the score of x is computed so that for all other alternatives y one counts the number individuals preferring x to y, multiplies this number by q and adds k to the result obtained.

Barbera [5] demonstrates that the set of simple decision schemes is the interesection of point voting and supporting size decision schemes. From this one immediately observes that there are decision schemes which allow for multiple representations.

The first way out of the Gibbard–Satterthwaite theorem is opened by the following theorem by Barbera [5]: a decision scheme is anonymous, neutral and non-manipulable iff it is a probability mixture of a point voting and supporting size decision scheme.

A probability mixture of decision schemes for a fixed profile is defined as

$$f(x) = c_1 f_1(x) + \cdots + c_t f_t(x)$$

where $c_i \geq 0$, for $i = 1, \ldots, t$ and $\Sigma_i c_i = 1$. The proof of this theorem rests partly on Gibbard's result [22]. Since both point voting and supporting size decision schemes exist, one can thus find strategy-proof decision schemes as well.

One can do somewhat better, though, by characterizing the three types of decision schemes. With regard to the points voting schemes Barbera proves the following [5]: a decision scheme is a point voting one iff it is anonymous, neutral, strategy-proof and satisfies a condition called individual-independence. This condition is defined as follows. Consider four preference profiles P, P', $P*$, and $P * *$ such that P' is obtained from P by changing the individual i's preference order from P_i to P_i' and $P * *$ is obtained from $P*$ by changing the i's preference order from P_i* to $P_i * *$. For any alternative x we define now the probability gain imputable to i when the profile changes from P to P' as follows: $D(x, , P') = f(x, P') - f(x, P)$. And similarly for $P*$ and $P**$. Suppose that $P_i = P_i*$ and $P'_i = P_i**$. The scheme f is individual-independent iff for the above four profiles, for any $i \in N$ and for any $x \in X$, $D(x, P, P') = D(x, P*, P**)$. Intuitively, a scheme is alternative- independent iff the individual i's change of mind in an identical way in any two profiles, *ceteris paribus*, produces the same probability gain for any alternative.

This characterization of point voting schemes thus enables us to find methods that are do not give individuals incentives for strategic misrepresentation of preferences. Barbera [5] gives a similar characterization to supporting size decision schemes.

Another independence condition is now called for, i.e. the alternative independence. Consider two preference profiles P and P' that are related to each other as, for a fixed pair of alternatives x and y:

1. for all individuals i: either (a) x is immediately above y in the i's preference order or (b) y is immediately above x in the i's preference order,
2. for all individuals i, if (a) is the case, then either $P_i = P'_i$ or P'_i is obtained from P_i by exchanging y and x, or if (b) is the case, then either $P_i = P'_i$ or P'_i is obtained from P_i by exchanging x and y, and
3. for all indiviuals i and another alternatives z, the rank of z is the same in P and P'.

Definition 30. A scheme f is *alternative-independent* iff $C(x, y, P, P') = C(x, y, P*, P**)$ when P and P', on the one hand, and $P*$ and $P**$, on the other hand, are related to each other according to (1)–(3) given above, and, moreover, for all individuals i: xP_iy iff $xP_i * y$ and xP'_iy iff $xP_i * *y$; $C(x, y, P, P') = f(x, P') - f(x, P)$ denotes the probability gain of x which is due to y when P is changed to P'.

Barbera's [5] characterization of supporting size decision schemes can now be stated: a decision scheme is a supporting size one iff it is anonymous, neutral, strategy-proof and alternative-independent. Finally, simple decision schemes are neutral, anonymous, strategy-proof, alternative-independent and individual-independent. Conversely, all decision schemes having the five last mentioned properties are equivalent to simple decision schemes.

We thus have two ways of constructing strategy-proof decision schemes: point voting schemes and supporting size schemes. Any probability mixture of them will do as well. So, of course, will a scheme that is an intersection of the two basic schemes, i.e. a simple scheme.

The preceding ways out of the Arrow and Gibbard–Satterthwaite results make use of opinion aggregation procedures that produce probability distributions over the alternatives. In contexts where the same decision making body considers problems of equal importance many times in a sequence, one could with some justification resort to random mechanisms in making the actual choices. Thus, one could ascertain that right outcomes are reached in expected values at least. On the other hand, in non-repetitive decision contexts where one alternative has to be chosen, the resort to a random mechanism may be more difficult to justify.

Things get more manageable if one can do with fuzzy sets as decision outcomes. Then one could simply interpret the probabilities assigned to various alternatives as membership degrees with respect to the collective goal set. After all, each alternative has a probability value in the $[0, 1]$ interval. This could obviously be regarded as a membership degree. But are there any circumstances in which fuzzy sets will suffice as decision outcomes? Surely. At least such situations in which several lower level bodies separately consider alternatives in order to submit their opinions for aggregation on another (typically higher) organizational level could fit to this type of output requirement. What we then are confronted with is a fuzzy set aggregation problem which is equivalent to the problem of aggregating fuzzy individual goal sets or subjective choice probabilities.

Intriligator's result ([24], [25]), which shows a way out of thr Arrow theorem, rests on the assumption of individual choice probabilities. In nonrepetitive choice situations the notion of individual choice probability is not intuitively obvious. Rather than assuming that a person preferring x to y makes occasionally a mistake which accounts for a non-zero probability of y being chosen from $\{x, y\}$, one could assume that underlying the choice probability is a fuzzy preference relation [53].

We obtain the fuzzy preference relation from individual i's utility function $U_i(x)$ as follows. First of all, it is well-known from axiomatic decision theory that the existence of a connected and transitive preference relation over the set X of alternatives guarantees the existence of a utility function U_i that represents the preferences (see, e.g., [23]).

Thus, if such a preference relation can be assumed, it implies the existence of a utility function. Next, we define

$$f_{jl} = g_i(x_j, x_l)$$

for all x_j and x_l in X so that:

1. $g_i(x_j, x_l) = 0.5$ if $U_i(x_j) = U_i(x_l)$,
2. g_i is monotone increasing function of $U_i(x_j)$, and
3. g_i is monotone decreasing function of $U_i(x_l)$.

The probability that individual i votes for alternative x_j can be related to the fuzzy preference relation f_{jk} of i as follows:

(i) if $f_{jk} > 0.5$, then it is not the case that $q_{ik} > q_{ij}$,
(ii) if $f_{jk} < 0.5$, then it is not the case $q_{ij} > q_{ik}$, and
(iii) if $f_{jk} = 0.5$, then $q_{ij} = q_{ik}$.

Thus, the fuzzy preference relation f_{jk} generates a probabilistic voting vector.

If, instead of individual preference relation, we are given a fuzzy individual choice function $h_i(x_j)$ for all x_j in X, we can also generate a probabilistic voting vector. Here h_i is the membership function indicating the degree in which x_j satisfies individual i's goals. Let H_i denote the sum of membership degrees of all elements of X in i's goal set. Then $q_{ij} = h_i(x_j)/H_i$ gives us the desired probabilistic voting vector.

We thus have methods that enable us to generate probabilistic voting if the individuals have either connected and transitive individual weak preference relations or fuzzy individual choice functions. Probabilistic voting, in turn, is a way of avoiding some negative results of social choice theory.

Let us now turn to the compound majority paradoxes to determine if the theory of fuzzy sets can provide solutions to them.

Consider again Table 3.2 and assume that instead of voting for X and Y on each issue, the individuals would indicate the degree to which X and Y satisfy their goal sets with respect to each issue. We thus obtain the result as in Table 4. The first subscript of the entries refers to the issue and the

Table 6. Example of fuzzy goal sets

group	issue 1	issue 2	issue 3
A (20%)	a_{1x}, a_{1y}	a_{2x}, a_{2y}	a_{3x}, a_{3y}
B (20%)	b_{1x}, b_{1y}	b_{2x}, b_{2y}	b_{3x}, b_{3y}
C (20%)	c_{1x}, c_{1y}	c_{2x}, c_{2y}	c_{3x}, c_{3y}
D (40%)	d_{1x}, d_{1y}	d_{2x}, d_{2y}	d_{3x}, d_{3y}

second to the party. For example, b_{2y} indicates the degree to which party Y satisfies group B's goals on issue 2. Each group i can now be characterized by an ordered pair $(i(x), i(y))$ where $i = A, B, C, D$ and $i(x)$ $(i(y)$, respectively) denotes the (weighted or unweighted) sum of goal satisfaction scores of party X $(Y$, respectively) in i's goal sets. Similarly, each issue j can be characterized by a pair $(j(x), j(y))$ where $j(x)$ $(j(y)$, respectively) denotes the sum of the goal satisfaction values assigned by the groups to party X $(Y$, respectively) on issue j.

Let $I(x) = \Sigma_i i(x)$ and $I(y) = \Sigma_i i(y)$, for $i = A, B, C, D$. Similarly, let $J(x) = \Sigma_j j(x)$ and $J(y) = \Sigma_j j(y)$, for $j = 1, 2, 3$. Clearly, $I(x) = J(x)$ and $I(y) = J(y)$. Thus, Ostrogorski's paradox can be avoided. However, there is a price to paid for this, namely what we end up with is a distribution of sums of goal set satisfaction values over the alternatives. What to do with them?

The most obvious way to proceed is to resort to probabilistic decision rule, i.e. to define first $p(x) = I(x)/(I(x) + I(y))$ and $p(y) = I(y)/(I(x) + I(y))$, and then to employ a random mechanism with two outcomes o_1, o_2 with probabilities $p(x), p(y)$.

Anscombe's paradox and the paradox of representation can be handled in an analogous way, i.e. by allowing the voters to express their opinions in the form of membership degrees. The results are then aggregate membership degree distributions over the alternatives and, thus, probabilistic mechanisms can be resorted in the determination of the alternative to be chosen (in cases where membership degree distributions are not adequate).

Having discussed ways of avoiding various incompatibility results of the social choice theory, we now turn to group choice situations involving fuzzy relations at the outset. The problem focused upon is that of finding plausible solutions – that is, sets of intuitively best alternatives – in those situations.

5   Solutions based on fuzzy social preference relation

Bezdek *et al.* ([10], [11]) discuss the problem of finding the set of undominated alternatives or other stable outcomes given a collective fuzzy preference ordering over the alternative set; see also [50].

Consider a nonfuzzy set X and a subset M_n of n-dimensional real space V_n defined as follows

$$M_n = \{R \in V_n \mid 0 \leq r_{ij} \leq 1; r_{ii} = 0, \forall i; r_{ij} + r_{ji} = 1, \forall i \neq j\}$$

The elements of M_n are interpreted as the degrees of individual or group preference for s_i over s_j, with $r_{ij} = 1$ indicating the maximum preference of s_i over s_j, $r_{ij} = 0.5$ indicating indifference between the two, and $r_{ij} = 0$ indicating a maximum preference of s_j over s_i. Moreover, each value of r_{ij} in the open interval $(0.5, 1)$ indicates the intensity of preference of s_i over s_j, the intensity varying from "mild" to "strong".

We now define a couple of solution concepts for voting games with fuzzy collective preference relation.

Definition 31. The set S_α of α-*consensus winners* is defined as:

$$s_i \in S_\alpha \text{ iff } \forall s_i \neq s_j : r_{ij} \geq \alpha,$$

with $0.5 < \alpha \leq 1$

Whenever S_α is nonempty, it is a singleton, but it does not always exist. Thus, it may be useful to find other solution concepts that specify a nonempty alternative sets even when S_α is empty. One possible candidate is a straightforward extension of Kramer's minimax set ([41]). We call it a set of *minimax consensus winners*, denote it by S_M and define as follows.

Definition 32. Let $\bar{r}_j = max_i r_{ij}$ and $\bar{r} = min_j max_i r_{ij}$. Then $s_i \in S_M$ (the set of minimax consensus winners) iff $\bar{r}_i = \bar{r}$.

Clearly S_M is always nonempty, but not necessarily a singleton. As a solution set it has the same interpretation as Kramer's minimax set: it consists of those alternatives which, when confronted with their toughest competitors, fare best, i.e. win by the largest score (if $\bar{r} \leq 0.5$) or lose by the smallest one (if $\bar{r} > 0.5$).

These solution concepts are based on the social preference relation matrix. Other ones can be obtained in several ways. For instance, one may start from a preference profile over a set of alternatives and construct the $[r_{ij}]$ matrix as follows:

$$r_{ij} = \begin{cases} \frac{1}{m}\Sigma_{k=1}^m a_{ij}^k & \text{for } i \neq j \\ r_{ij} = 0 & \text{for } i = j \end{cases}$$

where $a_{ij}^k = 1$ if s_i is strictly preferred to s_j by voter k, and $a_{ij}^k = 0$ otherwise. For the properties of the $[r_{ij}]$ we refer the reader to [66] (see also, e.g., [6], [14], [15]).

There is nothing "fuzzy" in the above solutions. As the method of constructing the social preference relation matrix suggests, the starting point can just a be the ordinary preference profile as well.

We now turn to solution concepts which utilize fuzzy preference relations as essential ingredients in the definition of solution concepts.

6 Solutions based on individual fuzzy preferences

Let us first consider solution concepts that do not require any preference aggregation at all. One of the best solution concepts is that of a core or a set of undominated alternatives. Suppose that the decision rule (required majority) be r.

Definition 33. An alternative $s_i \in X$ belongs to the *core* iff there is no other alternative $y \in X$ that defeats x by the required majority r.

We can extend the notion of a core to cover fuzzy individual preference relations by defining a *the fuzzy α-core* as follows:

Definition 34. An alternative $s_i \in X$ belongs to the *fuzzy α- core* X_α iff there exists no other alternative $s_j \in X$ such that $r_{ij} > \alpha$ for at least r individuals.

It is easy to see that if the nonfuzzy core is nonempty, so is X_α for some $\alpha \in (0,1]$. In other words, $\exists \alpha \in (0,1]$: core $\subset X_\alpha$. Moreover, for any two values $\alpha_1, \alpha_2 \in (0,1]$ such that $\alpha_1 < \alpha_2$, we have:

$$X_{\alpha_1} \subseteq X_{\alpha_2}$$

The intuitive interpretation of the fuzzy α-core is obvious: an alternative is a member of X_α iff a sufficient majority of voters does not feel strongly enough against it.

Another nonfuzzy solution concept with much intuitive appeal is a minimax set (see [41]). In a nonfuzzy setting it is defined as follows.

Definition 35. For each $x, y \in X$ denote the number of individuals preferring x to y by $n(x,y)$. Then define

$$v(x) = max_y n(x,y)$$

and

$$n* = min_x v(x)$$

Now the minimax set is

$$Q(n*) = \{x \mid v(x) = n*\}$$

Thus, $Q(n*)$ consists of those alternatives that in pairwise comparison with any other alternative are defeated by no more than $n*$ votes. Obviously, if $n* < m/2$, where m is the number of individuals, then $Q(n*)$ is singleton and $x \in Q(n*)$ is the core if the simple majority rule is being applied.

Analogously, we can define a *the minimax degree set* $Q(\beta)$ as follows. Given $s_i, s_j \in X$ and let, for individuals $k = 1, \ldots, m$:

$$v_D^k(x_j) = max_i r_{ij}$$

We now define

$$v_D(x_j) = max_k v_D^k(x_j)$$

Let $min_j v_D(x_j) = \beta$. Then

$$Q(\beta) = \{x_j \mid v_D(x_j) = \beta\}$$

For properties of the minimax degree set, we refer to [50].

Another concept that is analogous to the nonfuzzy mimimax set is a *minimax opposition set*. Let n_{ij} be the number of those individuals for whom $r_{ij} > r_{ji}$ and let $v_f = max_i n_{ij}$. Denote by $\bar{v}_f$ the minimum of $v_f(x_j)$ with respect to j, i.e.

$$\bar{v}_f = min_j v_f(x_j)$$

Then: $Q(v_f) = \{x_j \mid v_f(x_j) = \bar{v}_f\}$.

But, clearly, $Q(v_f) = Q(n*)$ since $r_{ij} > r_{ji}$ implies that the individual prefers alternative x_i to x_j. Similarly, the preference of x_i over x_j implies that $r_{ij} > r_{ji}$. Consequently, the minimax opposition set does not take into account the intensity of preferences as expressed in the individual preference relation matrices.

A more general solution concept, the *α-minimax set* denoted $Q^\alpha(v_f^\alpha)$, is defined as follows. Let $n_\alpha(x_i, x_j)$ be the number of individuals for whom $r_{ij} \leq \alpha$ (with $0 \leq \alpha < 0.5$) for some value of $\alpha \in (0, 1]$. We now define $\forall x_i \in X : v_f^\alpha(x_i) = max_j n_\alpha(x_i, x_j)$ and $\bar{v}_f^\alpha = min_i v_f^\alpha(x_i)$. Then

$$Q^\alpha(v_f^\alpha) = \{x_i \mid v_f^\alpha(x_i) = \bar{v}_f^\alpha\}$$

It can be shown that $Q^\alpha(v_f^\alpha) \subseteq Q(n*)$ (see [50]).

7   Fuzzy tournaments

One purpose of studying fuzzy tournaments is to overcome the difficulties inherent in the use of conventional solution concepts, namely the fact that the latter tend to produce too large solution sets and are therefore not decisive enough. Another purpose of our discussion is to apply analogues of the nonfuzzy solutions to contexts where the opinions of individuals can be represented by more general constructs than just connected and transitive preference relations (cf., e.g., [39]).

Let us take a look at a few solution concepts of nonfuzzy tournaments; for more details and a more extensive coverage, see Nurmi and Kacprzyk's paper [58].

Definition 36. Given the alternative set X, a tournament P on X is a complete and asymmetric relation on X.

In the context of group decision making P can be viewed as a strict preference relation. When X is of small cardinality, P can be expressed as a matrix $[p_{ij}], p_{ij} \in \{0, 1\}$ so that $p_{ij} = 1$ if the alternative represented by row i is preferred to that represented by column j, and $p_{ij} = 0$ if the alternative represented by column j is preferred to that represented by row i.

Suppose that each individual has a complete, transitive and asymmetric preference relation over X, and that the number of individuals is odd. Then a tournament can be constructed through pairwise comparisons of alternatives. In the ensuing tournament alternative s_i is preferred to s_j iff the number of individuals preferreing the former to the latter is larger than the number of individual preferring s_j to s_i.

Perhaps the best-known solution concept of tournaments is the Condorcet winner.

Definition 37. The *Condorcet winner* is an alternative which is preferred to all other alternatives by a majority.

The main problem with this solution concept is that it does not always exist.

Definition 38. The *Copeland winning set* UC_C consists of those alternatives that have the largest number of 1s in their corresponding rows in the tournament matrix.

In other words, the Copeland winners defeat more alternatives than any other alternatives do.

Definition 39. The uncovered set is defined by means of a binary relation of covering. An alternative s_i *covers* another alternative s_j iff s_i defeats s_j and everything that s_j defeats. The *uncovered set* consists of those alternatives that are covered by no alternatives (see [46], [47]).

Definition 40. The *Banks set* is the set of end-points of Banks chains. Starting from any alternative s_i the *Banks chain* is constructed as follows. First one looks for an alternative that defeats s_i. Suppose that such an alternative exists and is s_j (if one does not exist, then of course s_i is the Condorcet winner). Next one looks for another alternative that defeats both s_i and s_j, etc. Eventually, no alternative can be found that would defeat all previous ones in the chain starting from s_i. The last alternative which defeats all previous ones is the end-point of the Banks chain starting from s_i. The Banks set is then the set of all those end points (see [4]).

The following relationships hold between the above mentioned solutions (cf. [49], [55]):

- all solutions converge to the Condorcet winner when one exists,
- the uncovered set includes the Copeland winning set and the Banks set,
- when X contains less than 7 elements, the uncovered set and the Banks set coincide, and
- when the cardinality of X exceeds 12, the Banks set and the Copeland winning set may be distinct; however, they both always belong to the uncovered set.

Given a group N of n individuals, a collective fuzzy tournament $F = [r_{ij}]$ can be obtained through pairwise comparisons of alternatives so that

$$r_{ij} = \frac{card\{k \in N \mid s_i P_k s_j\}}{n}$$

where P_k is a nonfuzzy tournament representing the preferences of individual k.

Let us now define a *strong fuzzy covering relation* $C_S \subset X \times X$ as follows

$$\forall i, j, l \in \{1, \dots, m\} : s_i C_S s_j \Leftrightarrow r_{il} \geq r_{jl} \& r_{ij} > r_{ji}$$

Clearly, the strong fuzzy covering relation implies the nonfuzzy covering relation, but not *vice versa*. The set of C_S-undominated alternatives is denoted by UC_S.

Definition 41. The *weak fuzzy covering relation* $C_W \subset X \times X$ is defined as follows:

$$\forall s_i, s_j \in X :$$
$$s_i C_W s_j \Leftrightarrow r_{ij} > r_{ji}$$
$$\& card\{s_l \in X : r_{il} > r_{jl}\} \geq card\{s_p \in X : r_{jp} > r_{ip}\}$$

Obviously, $s_i C_S s_j$ implies $s_i C_W s_j$, but not conversely. Thus, the set of C_W-undominated alternatives, UC_W, is always a subset of UC_S. Moreover, the Copeland winning set is always included in UC_S, but not necessarily in UC_W (see [58]).

If one is looking for a solution that is a plausible subset of the uncovered set, then UC_W is not appropriate since it is possible that UC_C is not always a subset of the uncovered set, let alone the Banks set.

Another solution concept, the α-ucovered set, is based on the individual fuzzy preference tournament matrices. One first defines the fuzzy domination relation D and an α-covering relation $C_\alpha \subseteq X \times X$ as follows.

Definition 42. $s_i D s_j$ iff at least 50% of the individuals prefer s_i to s_j to a degree of at least 0.5.

Definition 43. If $s_i C_\alpha s_j$, then $s_i D s_j$ and $s_i D_\alpha s_k$, for all $s_k \in X$ for which $s_j D_\alpha s_k$.

Definition 44. The α-uncovered set consist of those alternatives that are not α-covered by any other alternative.

An obvious candidate for a plausible solution concept for fuzzy tournaments is an α-uncovered set with the smallest value of α.

Other fuzzy solution concepts analogous to their nonfuzzy counterparts can be defined (see [58]). For example, the α-*Banks set* can constructed by imposing the restriction that the majority of voters prefer the next alternative to the previous one in the Banks chain with intensity of at least α.

All the preceding solutions are based on nonfuzzy majorities exemplified by "at least 50%", "at least 2/3", etc. Fuzzy solutions have, however, been constructed in a way that makes the notion of majority itself fuzzy as exemplified by "most", "almost all", "much more than a half", etc. (see, e.g., various papers by Kacprzyk, Fedrizzi and Nurmi [27], [28], [29], [30], [31], [32], [34], [35]). While these solutions are clearly applicable whenever fuzzy membership degrees are given to various linguistic quantifiers, nothing general can be said about their "sizes" in comparison to their related nonfuzzy solutions.

8 Concluding remarks

The social choice theory is riddled with many paradoxes, incompatibilities and anomalies. Some of them are crucially dependent on the specific assumptions concerning the structure of individual opinions. In particular, the individuals are assumed to be endowed with connected and transitive preference relations over the set of alternatives. The theory focuses upon collective decision making procedures which are typically modeled as choice functions. Replacing this focus and the assumption concerning preferences with the focus on probabilistic voting mechanisms and with the assumption that the voters be endowed with fuzzy preference relations or fuzzy goal sets does away with many of the paradoxical results. In the preceding we have given an overview of the work that has been done along these lines. Moreover, we sketched related issues concerned with the determination of social choice (group decision making) solutions under fuzzy preference relations (including fuzzy tournaments) and a fuzzy majority.

References

1. Aizerman, M.A. (1985). New problems in the general choice theory, Social Choice and Welfare 2, 235-282.
2. Anscombe, G.E.M. (1976). On frustration of the majority by fulfilment of the majority's will. Analysis, 36, 161-168.
3. Arrow, K.J. (1963). Social choice and individual values, 2nd edition, Wiley, New York.
4. Banks, J.S. (1985). Sophisticated voting outcomes and agenda control. Social Choice and Welfare, 6, 295-306.
5. Barbera, S. (1979). Majority and positional voting in a probabilistic framework. Review of Economic Studies, XLVI, 379-389.
6. Barrett, C.R. and Pattanaik, P.K. (1990). Aggregation of fuzzy preferences. In J. Kacprzyk and M. Fedrizzi, (Eds.): Multiperson Decision Making Models using Fuzzy Sets and Possibility Theory, Kluwer, Dordrecht, pp. 155-162.
7. Barrett, C.R., Pattanaik, P.K. and Salles, M. (1986). On the structure of fuzzy social welfare functions. Fuzzy Sets and Systems, 19, 1-10.
8. Barrett, C.R., Pattanaik, P.K. and Salles, M. (1990). On choosing rationally when preferences are fuzzy. Fuzzy Sets and Systems, 34, 197-212.
9. Barrett, C.R., Pattanaik, P.K. and Salles, M. (1992). Rationality and aggregation of preferences in an ordinally fuzzy framework. Fuzzy Sets and Systems, 49, 9-13.
10. Bezdek, J.C., Spillman, B. and Spillman, R. (1978). A fuzzy relation space for group decision theory. Fuzzy Sets and Systems, 1, 255-268.
11. Bezdek, J.C., Spillman, B. and Spillman, R. (1979). Fuzzy relation spaces for group decision theory. Fuzzy Sets and Systems, 2, 5-14.
12. Bezembinder, Th. and Van Acker, P. (1985). The Ostrogorski paradox and its relation to nontransitive choice. Journal of Mathematical Sociology, 11, 131-158.
13. Black, D. (1958). Theory of committees and elections, Cambridge University Press, Cambridge.
14. Blin, J.M. (1974). Fuzzy relations in group decision theory, J. of Cybernetics 4, 17-22.
15. Blin, J.M. and Whinston, A.P. (1973). Fuzzy sets and social choice. J. of Cybernetics 4, 17-22.
16. Daudt, H. and Rae, D. (1978). Social contract and the limits of majority rule. In Birnbaum, P., Lively, J. and Parry, G. eds., Democracy, Consensus and Social Contract, SAGE Publications, London.
17. DeGrazia, A. (1953). Mathematical derivation of an election system. Isis 44, 42-51.

18. Fedrizzi, M., Kacprzyk, J. and Nurmi, H. (1993). How different are social choice functions: a rough sets approach. In Eklund, P. and Mattila, J. eds. Fuzziness in Finland 1993. Abo Akademi, Reports on Computer Science & Mathematics, Ser. B, No 15, Turku.

19. Fedrizzi, M., Kacprzyk, J. and Nurmi, H. (1993). Consensus degrees under fuzzy majorities and fuzzy preferences using OWA (ordered weighted average) operators, Control and Cybernetics, 22, 71–80.

20. Fedrizzi, M., Kacprzyk, J. and Nurmi, H. (1996). How different are social choice functions: a rough sets approach, Quality and Quantity, 30, 87–99.

21. Fishburn, P.C. (1974). Paradoxes of voting. American Political Science Review, 68, 537- 546.

22. Gibbard, A. (1973). Manipulation of schemes that mix voting with chance. Econometrica, 45, 665-681.

23. Harsanyi, J.C.(1977). Rational behavior and bargaining equilibrium in games and social situations, Cambridge University Press, Cambridge.

24. Intriligator, M.D. (1973). A probabilistic model of social choice. Review of Economic Studies, 40, 553-560.

25. Intriligator, M.D. (1982). Probabilistic models of choice. Mathematical Social Sciences, 2, 157-166.

26. Ishikawa, S. and Nakamura, K. (1979). The strategy-proof social choice functions. Journal of Mathematical Economics, 6, 283-295.

27. Kacprzyk, J. (1985). Group decision-making with a fuzzy majority via linguistic quantifiers. Part I: A consensory-like pooling; Part II: A competitive-like pooling, Cybernetics and Systems: an Int. J., 16, 119–129 (Part I), 131–144 (Part II).

28. Kacprzyk, J. (1986). Group decision making with a fuzzy linguistic majority. Fuzzy Sets and Systems, 18, 105-118.

29. Kacprzyk, J. (1987). On some fuzzy cores and 'soft' consensus measures in group decision making. In Bezdek, J.C., ed., The Analysis of Fuzzy Information. CRC Press, Boca Raton, FL.

30. Kacprzyk, J. and Fedrizzi, M. (1986). 'Soft' consensus measures for monitoring real consensus reaching processes under fuzzy preferences, Control and Cybernetics, 15, 309–323.

31. Kacprzyk, J. and Fedrizzi, M. (1988). A 'soft' measure of consensus in the setting of partial (fuzzy) preferences, European Journal of Operational Research, 34, 315–325.

32. Kacprzyk, J. and Fedrizzi, M. (1989). A 'human-consistent' degree of consensus based on fuzzy logic with linguistic quantifiers, Mathematical Social Sciences, 18, 275–290.

33. Kacprzyk, J. and Fedrizzi,M., Eds. (1990). Multiperson Decision Making Models Using Fuzzy Sets and Possibility Theory, Kluwer, Dordrecht.

34. Kacprzyk, J., Fedrizzi, M. and Nurmi, H. (1992). Group decision making and consensus under fuzzy preferences and fuzzy majority, Fuzzy Sets and Systems, 49, 21–31.

35. Kacprzyk, J. and Nurmi, H. (1989). Linguistic quantifiers and fuzzy majorities for more realistic and human-consistent group decision making. In Evans, G., Karwowski, W. and Wilhelm, M., eds., Fuzzy Methodologies for Industrial and Systems Engineering. Elsevier, Amsterdam.

36. Kacprzyk, J. and Nurmi, H. (1998). Group decision making under fuzziness. In. Słowiński, R., ed., Fuzzy Sets in Decision Analysis, Operations Research and Statistics, Kluwer, Boston, pp. 103 - 136.

37. Kacprzyk, J., Nurmi, H. and Fedrizzi, M., Eds. (1996). Consensus under Fuzziness, Kluwer, Boston.

38. Kacprzyk, J., Nurmi, H. and Fedrizzi, M. (1999). Group decision making and a measure of consensus under fuzzy preferences and a fuzzy linguistic majority. In L.A. Zadeh and J. Kacprzyk, eds., Computing with Words in Information/Intelligent Systems 2. Applications. Physica-Verlag, Heidelberg and New York, pp. 243 - 269.

39. Kacprzyk, J. and Roubens, M., Eds. (1988). Non-Conventional Preference Relations in Group Decision Making. Springer, Berlin.

40. Kelly, J.S. (1978). Arrow Impossibility Theorems, Academic Press, New York.

41. Kramer, G.H. (1977). A dynamical model of political equilibrium. Journal of Economic Theory, 16, 310-334.

42. Kuzmin, V.B. and Ovchinnikov, S.V. (1980a). Group decisions I: In arbitrary spaces of fuzzy binary relations, Fuzzy Sets and Systems, 4, 53–62.

43. Kuzmin, V.B. and Ovchinnikov, S.V. (1980b). Design of group decisions II: In spaces of partial order fuzzy relations, Fuzzy Sets and Systems, 4, 153–165.

44. Lagerspetz, E. (1995). Paradoxes and representation. Electoral Studies, forthcoming.

45. McLean, I. and Urken, A.B., Eds. (1995). Classics of social choice, The University of Michigan Press, Ann Arbor.

46. Miller, N.R. (1977). Graph-theoretical approaches to the theory of voting. American Journal of Political Science, 21, 769-803.

47. Miller, N.R. (1980). A new solution set for tournaments and majority voting. American Journal of Political Science, 24, 68-96.

48. Moulin, H. (1983). The Strategy of Social Choice, North-Holland, Amsterdam.

49. Moulin, H. (1986). Choosing from a tournament. Social Choice and Welfare, 3, 271-291.

50. Nurmi, H. (1981). Approaches to collective decision making with fuzzy preference relations. Fuzzy Sets and Systems, 6, 249-259.

51. Nurmi, H. (1982). Imprecise notions in individual and group decision theory: resolution of Allais paradox and related problems, Stochastica, VI, 283–303.

52. Nurmi, H. (1983). Voting procedures: a summary analysis, British Journal of Political Science, 13, 181–208.

53. Nurmi, H. (1984). Probabilistic voting. Political Methodology, 10, 81-95.

54. Nurmi, H. (1987). Comparing Voting Systems, Reidel, Dordrecht.

55. Nurmi, H. (1988a). Banks, Borda and Copeland: a comparison of some solution concepts in finite voting games. In Sainsbury, D. ed., Democracy, Sate and Justice, Almqvist and Wiksell, Stockholm.

56. Nurmi, H. (1988b). Assumptions on individual preferences in the theory of voting procedures. In J. Kacprzyk and M. Roubens (Eds.): Non-Conventional Preference Relations in Decision Making, Springer-Verlag, Heidelberg, pp. 142–155.

57. Nurmi, H., Fedrizzi, M. and Kacprzyk, J. (1990). Vague notions in the theory of voting. In J. Kacprzyk and M. Fedrizzi (Eds.): Multiperson Decision Making Models Using Fuzzy Sets and Possibility Theory, Kluwer, Dordrecht, pp. 43–52.

58. Nurmi, H. and Kacprzyk, J. (1991). On fuzzy tournaments and their solution concepts in group decision making, European Journal of Operational Research, 51, 223-232.
59. Nurmi, H., Kacprzyk, J. and Fedrizzi, M. (1996). Probabilistic, fuzzy and rough concepts in social choice, European Jornal of Operational Research, 95, 264 - 277.
60. Ostrogorski, M. (1903). La Démocratie et l'Organisation des Partis Politiques. Calmann-Levy, Paris (2 vols.).
61. Peleg, B. (1984). Game-Theoretic Analysis of Voting in Committees. Cambridge University Press, Cambridge.
62. Rae, D. and Daudt,H. (1976). The Ostrogorski paradox: a peculiarity of compound majority decision. European Journal of Political Research, 4, 391-398.
63. Riker, W.H. (1961). Voting and summation of preferences. American Political Science Review, 55, 900-911.
64. Salles, M. (1996). Fuzzy utility. In S. Barbera, P.J. Hammond and C. Seidl (Eds.): Handbook of Utility Theory. Kluwer, Boston (forthcoming).
65. Satterthwaite, M.A. (1975). Strategy-proofness and Arrow's conditions. Journal of Economic Theory, 10, 187-217.
66. Skala, H.J. (1978). Arrow's impossibility theorem: some new aspects. In Gottinger, H.W. and Leinfellner, W., eds. Decision Theory and Social Ethics, D. Reidel, Dordrecht.
67. Tanino, T. (1990). On group decision making under fuzzy preferences. In J. Kacprzyk and M. Fedrizzi (Eds.): Multiperson Decision Making Models Using Fuzzy Sets and Possibility Theory, Kluwer, Dordrecht, pp. 172–185.
68. Wagner, C. (1983). Anscombe's paradox and the rule of three-fourths. Theory and Decision, 15, 303-308.

FUZZY EXTENSION OF THE ROUGH SET APPROACH TO MULTICRITERIA AND MULTIATTRIBUTE SORTING

Salvatore Greco[1], Benedetto Matarazzo[1], Roman Slowinski[2]

[1]Faculty of Economics, University of Catania, Corso Italia, 55,
  95129 Catania, Italy

[2]Institute of Computing Science, Poznan University of Technology,
  60-965 Poznan, Poland

Abstract: We consider a sorting (classification) problem in the presence of multiple attributes and criteria, called MA&C sorting problem. It concerns an assignment of some actions to some pre-defined and preference-ordered decision classes. The actions are described by a finite set of attributes and criteria. Both, attributes and criteria take values from corresponding domains, however, the domains of attributes are not preference-ordered, while the domains of criteria (scales) are totally ordered by preference relations. In order to construct a comprehensive preference model that could be used to support the sorting task, we are considering a preferential information of the decision maker (DM) in the form of assignment examples, i.e. exemplary assignments of some reference actions to the decision classes. The preference model being inferred from these examples is a set of "*if..., then...*" decision rules. The rules are derived from rough approximations of decision classes made up of reference actions. They satisfy conditions of completeness and dominance, and manage with possible ambiguity (inconsistencies) in the set of examples. Our idea of rough approximations involves two relations together: similarity, being a generalization of classic indiscernibility relation defined on attributes, and dominance relation defined on criteria. In this paper, we propose a fuzzy extension of the rough set approach to MA&C sorting problem.

Keywords: rough sets, fuzzy sets, multiple criteria and attributes, sorting problem, similarity, dominance, decision rules

1 Introduction

The rough sets theory has been proposed by Z. Pawlak (1982, 1991) to deal with inconsistency problems following from information granulation. It operates on an information table composed of a set U of objects (actions) described by a set Q of attributes. Its basic notions are: indiscernibility relation on U, lower and upper approximation of a subset or a partition of U, dependence and reduction of attributes from Q, and decision rules derived from lower approximations and boundaries of subsets identified with decision classes. The original rough sets idea has proved to be particularly useful in the analysis of multiattribute classification problems; however, it was failing when attributes whose domains are preference ordered (criteria) had to be taken into account. In order to deal with problems of multicriteria decision making (MCDM), like sorting, choice or ranking, a number of methodological changes to the original rough sets theory were necessary (Greco, Matarazzo and Slowinski, 1999a). The main change is the substitution of the indiscernibility relation by a dominance relation (crisp or fuzzy), that permits approximation of ordered sets in multicriteria sorting. In order to approximate preference relations in multicriteria choice and ranking problems, another change is necessary: substitution of the information table by a pairwise comparison table, where each row corresponds to a pair of objects described by binary relations on particular criteria. In all those MCDM problems, the new rough set approach ends with a set of decision rules, playing the role of a comprehensive preference model. It is more general than the classical functional or relational model and it is more understandable for the users because of its natural syntax. A fuzzy extension of the rough approximation by dominance relation has already been proposed by the authors in (Greco, Matarazzo and Slowinski, 1999a and 1999b).

In this paper we propose a further fuzzy extension of the rough approximation by dominance and similarity relations used together. A crisp case of this kind of rough approximation has been characterized in (Greco, Matarazzo and Slowinski, 1998c). The paper is organized as follows. Next section presents a comparison of rough sets theory and fuzzy sets theory. Section three illustrates the motivations for approximation by joint use of dominance and similarity relations. Section four introduces rough approximation by fuzzy dominance and similarity relations. Section five deals with rule induction. Section six presents a didactic example. Conclusions are grouped in the last section.

2 Rough sets and fuzzy sets theory

A number of relations exist between the rough sets theory and other mathematical theories dealing with particular types of vagueness or, more generally, with "imperfect" data. Let us point out the particularly fruitful complementarity of fuzzy sets theory and rough sets theory, which has been acknowledged by a large number of studies (see e.g. Dubois and Prade, 1990, 1992; Pawlak, 1985; Slowinski, 1995; Yao, 1996; Slowinski and Stefanowski, 1994 and 1996). Indeed, both theories deal with different types of imperfect information that can be encountered together.

As to fuzzy sets, they deal with a type of vagueness arising when the boundaries of a class of objects are not sharply defined. Informally, a fuzzy set may be regarded as a class of objects with gradual progression from non-membership to membership. An object is characterized by a grade of membership intermediate between zero (non-membership) and one (full membership). Three different semantics can be associated with the use of fuzzy sets (Dubois, Prade and Yager, 1997):

- a first semantics expressing closeness, proximity, similarity and the like; under this semantics, objects with membership one are viewed as prototypical (referent) objects of the fuzzy set, while the other membership grades estimate the closeness of objects (subjects) to the prototypical ones,

- a second semantics expressing an incomplete or vague state of information under the form of possibility distributions; this view of fuzzy sets enables imprecise or uncertain information to be processed,

- a third semantics expressing preferences between pairs of objects; the gradedness introduced by the use of fuzzy sets refines the classic crisp preference structures.

In many situations it is required to consider more than one semantics at a time. In the following, when using fuzzy sets in conjunction with rough sets, we will precise the type of semantics considered.

As to rough sets, they deal with a type of vagueness arising when a partition of objects into classes is ambiguous for the reason of limited discernibility of objects by the language of their description (attribute values).

It is clear that the two types of vagueness are not exclusive and can appear together in real world decision problems. This motivates the fuzzy extensions of the rough set approach.

3 Rough approximation by dominance relations

As pointed out by Greco, Matarazzo and Slowinski (1998a), the original rough set approach cannot extract all the essential knowledge contained in the decision table of multicriteria sorting problems, i.e. problems of assigning a set of actions described by a set of criteria to one of pre-defined and ordered classes. Notwithstanding, in many real problems it is important to consider the *ordinal properties* of the considered criteria as well as preference-ordered decision classes.

For example, in bankruptcy risk evaluation, if the debt index (total debt/total activity) of firm A has a modest value, while the same index of firm B has a significant value, then, within the rough set approach, the two firms are merely discernible, but no preference is given to one of them with reference to the attribute "debt ratio". In reality, from the point of view of the bankruptcy risk evaluation, it would be advisable to consider firm A better than firm B, and not simply different (discernible). Therefore, the attribute "debt ratio" is a criterion. Let us observe that the rough set approach based on the use of indiscernibility or similarity relations is not able to capture the specific kind of inconsistency which may occur when in the decision table there is at least one criterion. For instance, in the bankruptcy risk evaluation, which is a sorting problem, if firm A is better than B with respect to all the considered criteria (e.g. debt ratio, return on equity, etc.) but firm A is assigned to a class of higher risk than B, then there is an inconsistency which cannot be captured by the original rough set approach, because these firms are discernible. In order to detect this inconsistency, the rough approximation should handle the ordinal properties of criteria. This can be made by replacing the indiscernibility or similarity relation by the dominance relation, which is a very natural concept within multicriteria decision analysis.

On the basis of these considerations, Greco, Matarazzo and Slowinski (1998a) have proposed a new rough set approach to multicriteria sorting problems based on dominance relation. Let also mention that it is sometimes reasonable to consider both criteria and attributes (without ordered domains) in sorting problems. More precisely, a rough set approximation based on a binary relation which is in a part dominance (with respect to considered criteria) and in a part indiscernibility (with respect to considered attributes) has been proposed (Greco, Matarazzo and Slowinski 1998b). After that, a more general binary relation which is in a part dominance, in a part indiscernibility and in a part similarity has been considered (Greco, Matarazzo and Slowinski, 1998c).

4 Approximations by means of fuzzy dominance relations

Let us remember that, formally, by an *information table* we understand the 4-tuple S=<U,Q,V,f>, where U is a finite set of objects, Q is a finite set of *attributes*, $V = \bigcup_{q \in Q} V_q$ and V_q is a domain of the attribute q, and f:U×Q→V is a total function such that f(x,q)∈ V_q for every q∈Q, x∈U, called an *information function* (see Pawlak, 1991).

Furthermore, an information table can be seen as *decision table* assuming that the set of attributes Q=C∪D and C∩D=∅, where set C contains so-called *condition attributes*, and D, *decision attributes*.

In this section we refine the concept of rough approximation based on dominance and similarity by introducing gradedness through the use of fuzzy sets in the sense of the third semantics, according to the typology given in section 2.

In this section we will use the notion of criterion only when the preferential ordering of the attribute domain will be important in a given context. Therefore, we divide the set C of condition attributes in two disjoint subsets:

- the subset of criteria, denoted by $C^>$; the domains of criteria are ordered according to (let say, increasing) preference,

- the set of nominal or qualitative attributes, denoted by $C^\sim$; the domains of attributes are not preference-ordered.

In the crisp case, for each q∈$C^>$ there exists an outranking relation S_q on U while for each q∈$C^\sim$ there exists a similarity relation R_q on U. For each q∈$C^>$ and for x,y∈U, "xS_qy" means "x is at least as good as y with respect to criterion q" and S_q is supposed to be a complete preorder, i.e. strongly complete and transitive. Moreover, for each q∈$C^\sim$ and for x,y∈U, "xR_qy" means "x is similar to y with respect to attribute q" and R_q is supposed to be reflexive only. If relation R_q is also symmetric, it is called tolerance relation. In the folllowing, for each P⊆C we denote by $P^>$ the set of criteria contained in C, i.e. $P^>=P \cap C^>$, and by $P^\sim$ the set of attributes which are not criteria contained in C, i.e. $P^\sim=P \cap C^\sim$.

Let us consider now the fuzzy case. Let S_q be a fuzzy outranking relation on U with respect to criterion q∈$C^>$, i.e. S_q:U×U→[0,1], such that S_q(x,y) represents the credibility of the proposition "x is at least as good as y with respect to criterion q". Moreover, let R_q be a fuzzy similarity relation with respect to the attribute q∈$C^\sim$, i.e. R_q:U×U→[0,1], such that R_q(x,y) represents the credibility of the proposition "x is similar to y with respect to attribute q".

We assume that S_q is a fuzzy partial T-preorder, i.e. that it is reflexive ($S_q(x,x)=1$ for each $x \in U$) and T-transitive ($T(S_q(x,y),S_q(y,z)) \leq S_q(x,z)$, for each $x,y,z \in U$) (see Fodor and Roubens, 1995). We assume, moreover, that similarity relation R_q is reflexive. However, for simplicity, we suppose that it is also symmetric (i.e. for each $x,y \in U$, $R_q(x,y)=R_q(y,x)$); this means that, strictly speaking, R_q is a tolerance relation.

Using the fuzzy outranking relation S_q, $q \in C^>$, and the fuzzy similarity relation $R_q(x,y)$, $q \in C^\sim$, a *fuzzy P-dominance relation* on U (denoted by $D_P(x,y)$) can be defined for each $P \subseteq C$ as follows:

$$D_P(x,y)= T\left(\underset{q \in P^>}{T} \left(S_q(x,y)\right), \underset{q \in P^\sim}{T} \left(R_q(x,y)\right)\right).$$

Given $(x,y) \in U \times U$, $D_P(x,y)$ represents the credibility of the proposition "x outranks y with respect to each criterion q from $P^>$ and x is similar to y with respect to each attribute from $P^\sim$". If the attributes in P are all criteria (i.e. $P^>=P$), then $D_P(x,y)$ represents the credibility of the proposition "x outranks y with respect to each criterion q from P" or, more synthetically, "x P-dominates y". For simplicity we shall use this expression also when $P^> \neq P$.

Now, let $Cl=\{Cl_t, t \in M\}$, $M=\{1,...,n\}$, be a set of fuzzy decision classes in U, such that for each $x \in U$, $Cl_t(x)$ represents the membership function of x to Cl_t. We suppose that the classes of Cl are ordered according to increasing preference, i.e. for all $r,s \in T$, such that $r>s$, the elements of Cl_r are comprehensively better than the elements of Cl_s. For example, in a problem of bankruptcy risk evaluation, Cl_1 is a set of unacceptable risk firms, Cl_2 is a set of high risk firms, Cl_3 is a set of medium risk firms, and so on.

On the basis of the membership functions of the fuzzy class Cl_t, we can define fuzzy membership functions of two other sets:

1) the upward cumulative fuzzy set $Cl_t^\geq$, whose membership function $Cl_t^\geq(x)$ represents the credibility of the proposition "x belongs at least to class Cl_t",

$$Cl_t^\geq(x)= \begin{cases} 1 & \text{if } \exists s \in M : Cl_s(x) > 0 \text{ and } s > t \\ Cl_t(x) & \text{otherwise} \end{cases}$$

2) the downward cumulative fuzzy set $Cl_t^\leq$, whose membership function $Cl_t^\leq(x)$ represents the credibility of the proposition "x belongs at most to class Cl_t",

$$Cl_t^\leq(x)= \begin{cases} 1 & \text{if } \exists s \in M : Cl_s(x) > 0 \text{ and } s < t \\ Cl_t(x) & \text{otherwise} \end{cases}$$

The P-lower and the P-upper approximations of $Cl_t^\geq$ with respect to $P \subseteq C$ are fuzzy sets in U, whose membership functions (denoted by $\underline{P}[Cl_t^\geq(x)]$ and $\overline{P}[Cl_t^\geq(x)]$, respectively) are defined as:

$$\underline{P}[Cl_t^\geq(x)] = \underset{y \in U}{T} (T^*(N(D_P(y,x)), Cl_t^\geq(y))),$$

$$\overline{P}[Cl_t^\geq(x)] = \underset{y \in U}{T^*} (T(D_P(x,y), Cl_t^\geq(y))).$$

$\underline{P}[Cl_t^\geq(x)]$ represents the credibility of the proposition "for all $y \in U$, y does not P-dominate x and/or y belongs to $Cl_t^\geq$", while $\overline{P}[Cl_t^\geq(x)]$ represents the credibility of the proposition "there is at least one $y \in U$ P-dominated by x which belongs to $Cl_t^\geq$".

Intuitively, $\underline{P}[Cl_t^\geq(x)]$ represents the credibility that x belongs certainly to $Cl_t^\geq$, while $\overline{P}[Cl_t^\geq(x)]$ represents the credibility that x belongs possibly to $Cl_t^\geq$, taking into account the information provided by P.

The P-lower and P-upper approximations of $Cl_t^\leq$ with respect to $P \subseteq C$ (denoted by $\underline{P}[Cl_t^\leq(x)]$ and $\overline{P}[Cl_t^\leq(x)]$, respectively) can be defined, analogously, as:

$$\underline{P}[Cl_t^\leq(x)] = \underset{y \in U}{T} (T^*(N(D_P(x,y)), Cl_t^\leq(y))),$$

$$\overline{P}[Cl_t^\leq(x)] = \underset{y \in U}{T^*} (T(D_P(y,x), Cl_t^\leq(y))).$$

$\underline{P}[Cl_t^\leq(x)]$ represents the credibility of the proposition "for all $y \in U$, x does not P-dominate y and/or y belongs to $Cl_t^\leq$", while $\overline{P}[Cl_t^\leq(x)]$ represents the credibility of the proposition "there is at least one $y \in U$ P-dominating x which belongs to $Cl_t^\leq$".

$\underline{P}[Cl_t^\leq(x)]$ and $\overline{P}[Cl_t^\leq(x)]$ have an intuitive interpretation analogous to that of $\underline{P}[Cl_t^\geq(x)]$ and $\overline{P}[Cl_t^\geq(x)]$.

Let us remark that using the T^*-implication, denoted by $I_{\overrightarrow{T^*,N}}$, it is possible to rewrite the definitions of $\underline{P}[Cl_t^\geq(x)]$, $\overline{P}[Cl_t^\geq(x)]$, $\underline{P}[Cl_t^\leq(x)]$ and $\overline{P}[Cl_t^\leq(x)]$ in the following way:

$$\underline{P}[Cl_t^\geq(x)] = \underset{y \in U}{T} (I_{\overrightarrow{T^*,N}} (D_P(y,x), Cl_t^\geq(y))),$$

$$\overline{P}[Cl_t^{\geq}(x)] = \underset{y\in U}{T^*}\,(N(\,I_{T^*,N}^{\rightarrow}\,(D_P(x,y),\,N(\,Cl_t^{\geq}(y)))))\,,$$

$$\underline{P}[Cl_t^{\leq}(x)] = \underset{y\in U}{T}\,(I_{T^*,N}^{\rightarrow}\,(D_P(x,y),\,Cl_t^{\leq}(y)))\,,$$

$$\overline{P}[Cl_t^{\leq}(x)] = \underset{y\in U}{T^*}\,(N(\,I_{T^*,N}^{\rightarrow}\,(D_P(y,x),\,N(Cl_t^{\leq}(y)))))\,.$$

The following definitions are necessary to introduce the next results. A strict negation is a strictly decreasing continuous function $N:[0,1]\rightarrow[0,1]$ satisfying $N(0)=1$, $N(1)=0$. (T, T^*, N) is a De Morgan triplet iff $N(T^*(x,y))=T(N(x),N(y))$, where N is a strict negation. A negation N is involutive iff for all $x\in[0,1]$, $N(N(x))=x$.

Theorem 1 The following results hold:

1) $\underline{P}[Cl_t^{\geq}(x)] \leq Cl_t^{\geq}(x) \leq \overline{P}[Cl_t^{\geq}(x)]$, for each $x\in U$ and for each $t\in M$,

2) $\underline{P}[Cl_t^{\leq}(x)] \leq Cl_t^{\leq}(x) \leq \overline{P}[Cl_t^{\leq}(x)]$, for each $x\in U$ and for each $t\in M$,

3) for (T, T^*, N) being a De Morgan triplet, if negation N is involutive, and $N(Cl_t^{\geq}(x))=Cl_{t-1}^{\leq}(x)$ for each $x\in U$ and $t=2,\ldots,n$, then

   3.1) $\underline{P}[Cl_t^{\geq}(x)] = N(\overline{P}[Cl_{t-1}^{\leq}(x)]$, $t=2,\ldots n$,

   3.2) $\underline{P}[Cl_t^{\leq}(x)] = N(\overline{P}[Cl_{t+1}^{\geq}(x)])$, $t=1,\ldots,n-1$,

   3.3) $\overline{P}[Cl_t^{\geq}(x)] = N(\underline{P}[Cl_{t-1}^{\leq}(x)])$, $t=2,\ldots n$,

   3.4) $\overline{P}[Cl_t^{\leq}(x)] = N(\underline{P}[Cl_{t+1}^{\geq}(x)])$, $t=1,\ldots,n-1$,

4) given $R\subseteq P$, for each $x\in U$ and for each $t\in M$,

   4.1) $\underline{P}[Cl_t^{\geq}(x)] \geq \underline{R}[Cl_t^{\geq}(x)]$,

   4.2) $\underline{P}[Cl_t^{\leq}(x)] \geq \underline{R}[Cl_t^{\leq}(x)]$,

   4.3) $\overline{P}[Cl_t^{\geq}(x)] \leq \overline{R}[Cl_t^{\geq}(x)]$,

   4.4) $\overline{P}[Cl_t^{\leq}(x)] \leq \overline{R}[Cl_t^{\leq}(x)]$.

Proof. Given a T-norm T, for each $a,b\in[0,1]$, such that $T(a,b)\leq\min(a,b)$, we have:

$$\underline{P}[Cl_t^{\geq}(x)] = \underset{y\in U}{T}\,(T^*(N(D_P(y,x)),\,Cl_t^{\geq}(y)))\leq$$

$$\leq \min_{y\in U} (T^*(N(D_P(y,x)), Cl_t^{\geq}(y))) \leq$$

$$\leq T^*(N(D_P(x,x)), Cl_t^{\geq}(x)).$$

Furthermore, remembering that for each $x\in U$, $D_P(x,x)=1$, and for each $a\in[0,1]$, $T^*(0,a)=a$, we have

$$T^*(N(D_P(x,x)), Cl_t^{\geq}(x)) = T^*(N(1), Cl_t^{\geq}(x)) = T^*(0, Cl_t^{\geq}(x)) = Cl_t^{\geq}(x).$$

Thus we proved that $\underline{P}[Cl_t^{\geq}(x)] \leq Cl_t^{\geq}(x)$.

Given a T-conorm T^*, for each $a,b\in[0,1]$, such that $T^*(a,b)\geq\max(a,b)$, we have

$$\overline{P}[Cl_t^{\geq}(x)] = T^*_{y\in U}(T(D_P(x,y), Cl_t^{\geq}(y)))\geq$$

$$\geq \max_{y\in U}(T(D_P(x,y), Cl_t^{\geq}(y))) \geq$$

$$\geq T(D_P(x,x), Cl_t^{\geq}(x)).$$

Furthermore, remembering again that for each $x\in U$, $D_P(x,x)=1$, and for each $a\in[0,1]$, $T(1,a)=a$, we have

$$T(D_P(x,x), Cl_t^{\geq}(x)) = T(1, Cl_t^{\geq}(x)) = Cl_t^{\geq}(x).$$

Thus we proved that $\overline{P}[Cl_t^{\geq}(x)]\geq Cl_t^{\geq}(x)$. The statement 2) can be proved analogously.

With respect to 3.1), we have

$$\underline{P}[Cl_t^{\geq}(x)] = T_{y\in U}(T^*(N(D_P(y,x)), Cl_t^{\geq}(y))) =$$

$$=N(\ T^*_{y\in U}(N(T^*(N(D_P(y,x)), Cl_t^{\geq}(y)))))=$$

$$=N(\ T^*_{y\in U}(T(D_P(y,x), N(Cl_t^{\geq}(y)))))=$$

$$=N(\ T^*_{y\in U}(T(D_P(y,x), Cl_{t-1}^{\leq}(y)))) = N(\overline{P}[Cl_{t-1}^{\leq}(x)]).$$

Analogous proof can be given for 3.2) - 3.4).

With respect to 4.1), since $R\subseteq P$, we have

$$D_R(x,y) = T_{q\in R}(S_q(x,y)) \geq T_{q\in P}(S_q(x,y)) = D_P(x,y).$$

Therefore, for the monotonicity property of T, T^* and N, we obtain

$$\underline{P}[Cl_t^\geq(x)] = \underset{y\in U}{T} (T^*(N(D_P(y,x)), Cl_t^\geq(y))) \leq$$

$$\leq \underset{y\in U}{T} (T^*(N(D_R(y,x)), Cl_t^\geq(y))) \leq \underline{R}[Cl_t^\geq(x)]$$

thus proving 4.1). The proof of 4.2) and 4.3) is analogous.

Results 1) to 4) of Theorem 1 are fuzzy counterparts of the following properties characteristic for the crisp rough set approach: 1) (inclusion property) says that $Cl_t^\geq$ includes its P-lower approximation and is included in its P-upper approximation; 2) is the same inclusion property but with respect to $Cl_t^\leq$; 3) (complementarity property) says that the P-lower (P-upper) approximation of $Cl_t^\geq$ is the complement of the P-upper (P-lower) approximation of its complementary set $Cl_{t-1}^\leq$ (analogous property holds for $Cl_t^\leq$); 4) (monotonicity property) says that, using larger sets of attributes, it is possible to obtain more accurate approximations of $Cl_t^\geq$: thus, while in the crisp case the lower approximation becomes greater (precisely - not smaller) and the upper approximation becomes smaller (not greater), in the fuzzy case the membership degree of the lower approximation increases (does not decrease) and the membership degree of the upper approximation decreases (does not increase) when the set of attributes becomes larger.

5 Rule induction

Using the fuzzy dominance relation one is able to induce decision rules from a decision table. In the following we consider the following decision rules

1) *certain decision rules of type* $D_\geq$, which have the following form:

"*if* $f(x,q_1)$ is at least as good as r_{q1} *and* $f(x,q_2)$ is at least as good as r_{q2} *and* ... *and* $f(x,q_p)$ is at least as good as r_{qp} *and* $f(x,q_{p+1})$ is similar to r_{qp+1} *and* $f(x,q_{p+2})$ is similar to r_{qp+2} *and* ... *and* $f(x,q_e)$ is similar to r_{qe}, *then* x *belongs to* $Cl_t^\geq$ ",

where $\{q_1,q_2,...,q_p\}\subseteq C^>$, $\{q_1,q_2,...,q_p\}\subseteq C^\sim$, $(r_{q1},r_{q2},...,r_{qp})\in V_{q1}\times V_{q2}\times...\times V_{qp}$ and $t\in M$;

2) *possible decision rules of type* $D_\geq$, which have the following form:

"*if* $f(x,q_1)$ is at least as good as r_{q1} *and* $f(x,q_2)$ is at least as good as r_{q2} *and* ... *and* $f(x,q_p)$ is at least as good as r_{qp} *and* $f(x,q_{p+1})$ is similar to r_{qp+1} *and* $f(x,q_{p+2})$ is similar to r_{qp+2} *and* ... *and* $f(x,q_e)$ is similar to r_{qe}, *then* x *could belong to* $Cl_t^\geq$ ",

where $\{q_1,q_2,...,q_p\}\subseteq C^>$, $\{q_1,q_2,...,q_p\}\subseteq C^\sim$, $(r_{q1},r_{q2},...,r_{qp})\in V_{q1}\times V_{q2}\times...\times V_{qp}$ and $t\in M$;

3) **certain** decision rules of type $D_\leq$, which have the following form:

"*if* $f(x,q_1)$ is at most as good as r_{q1} *and* $f(x,q_2)$ is at most as good as r_{q2} *and* ... *and* $f(x,q_p)$ is at most as good as r_{qp} *and* $f(x,q_{p+1})$ is similar to r_{qp+1} *and* $f(x,q_{p+2})$ is similar to r_{qp+2} *and* ... *and* $f(x,q_e)$ is similar to r_{qe}, *then* x *belongs* to $Cl_t^\leq$ ",

where $\{q_1,q_2,...,q_p\} \subseteq C^>$, $\{q_1,q_2,...,q_p\} \subseteq C^\sim$, $(r_{q1},r_{q2},...,r_{qp}) \in V_{q1} \times V_{q2} \times ... \times V_{qp}$ and $t \in M$;

4) **possible** decision rules of type $D_\leq$, which have the following form:

"*if* $f(x,q_1)$ is at most as good as r_{q1} *and* $f(x,q_2)$ is at most as good as r_{q2} *and* ... *and* $f(x,q_p)$ is at most as good as r_{qp} *and* $f(x,q_{p+1})$ is similar to r_{qp+1} *and* $f(x,q_{p+2})$ is similar to r_{qp+2} *and* ... *and* $f(x,q_e)$ is similar to r_{qe}, *then* x *could belong* to $Cl_t^\leq$ ",

where $\{q_1,q_2,...,q_p\} \subseteq C^>$, $\{q_1,q_2,...,q_p\} \subseteq C^\sim$, $(r_{q1},r_{q2},...,r_{qp}) \in V_{q1} \times V_{q2} \times ... \times V_{qp}$ and $t \in M$.

With each decision rule r there is associated a **credibility** $\chi(r)$.

A statement r: "*if* $f(x,q_1)$ is at least as good as r_{q1} *and* $f(x,q_2)$ is at least as good as r_{q2} *and* ... *and* $f(x,q_p)$ is at least as good as r_{qp} *and* $f(x,q_{p+1})$ is similar to r_{qp+1} *and* $f(x,q_{p+2})$ is similar to r_{qp+2} *and* ... *and* $f(x,q_e)$ is similar to r_{qe}, *then* x *belongs* to $Cl_t^\geq$ ", is accepted as a certain decision rule of type $D_\geq$ with a credibility equal to $\chi(r)$ if there is at least one $w \in U$ such that $f(w,q_1)=r_{q1}$ and $f(w,q_2)=r_{q2}$ and ... and $f(w,q_e)=r_{qe}$, and $\underline{P}[Cl_t^\geq(w)] = \chi(r) > 0$, where $P=\{q_1,...,q_e\}$, $P^>=\{q_1,...,q_p\}$, $P^\sim=\{q_{p+1},...,q_e\}$.

A statement r: "*if* $f(x,q_1)$ is at least as good as r_{q1} *and* $f(x,q_2)$ is at least as good as r_{q2} *and* ... *and* $f(x,q_p)$ is at least as good as r_{qp} *and* $f(x,q_{p+1})$ is similar to r_{qp+1} *and* $f(x,q_{p+2})$ is similar to r_{qp+2} *and* ... *and* $f(x,q_e)$ is similar to r_{qe}, *then* x *could belong* to $Cl_t^\geq$ ", is accepted as a possible decision rule of type $D_\geq$ with a credibility equal to $\chi(r)$ if there is at least one $w \in U$ such that $f(w,q_1)=r_{q1}$ and $f(w,q_2)=r_{q2}$ and ... and $f(w,q_e)=r_{qe}$, and $\overline{P}[Cl_t^\geq(w)] = \overline{C}[Cl_t^\geq(w)] = \chi(r) \geq 0$, where $P=\{q_1,...,q_e\}$, $P^>=\{q_1,...,q_p\}$, $P^\sim=\{q_{p+1},...,q_e\}$.

A statement r: "*if* $f(x,q_1)$ is at most as good as r_{q1} *and* $f(x,q_2)$ is at most as good as r_{q2} *and* ... *and* $f(x,q_p)$ is at most as good as r_{qp} *and* $f(x,q_{p+1})$ is similar to r_{qp+1} *and* $f(x,q_{p+2})$ is similar to r_{qp+2} *and* ... *and* $f(x,q_e)$ is similar to r_{qe}, *then* x *belongs* to $Cl_t^\leq$ ", is accepted as a certain decision rule of type $D_\leq$ with a credibility equal to $\chi(r)$ if there is at least one $w \in U$ such that $f(w,q_1)=r_{q1}$ and $f(w,q_2)=r_{q2}$ and ... and $f(w,q_e)=r_{qe}$, and $\underline{P}[Cl_t^\leq(w)] = \chi(r) > 0$, where $P=\{q_1,...,q_e\}$, $P^>=\{q_1,...,q_p\}$, $P^\sim=\{q_{p+1},...,q_e\}$.

A statement r: "*if* $f(x,q_1)$ is at most as good as r_{q1} *and* $f(x,q_2)$ is at most as good as r_{q2} *and* ... *and* $f(x,q_p)$ is at most as good as r_{qp} *and* $f(x,q_{p+1})$ is similar to r_{qp+1} *and* $f(x,q_{p+2})$ is similar to r_{qp+2} *and* ... *and* $f(x,q_e)$ is similar to r_{qe}, *then* x *could belong* to

$Cl_t^{\leq}$", is accepted as a possible decision rule of type $D_{\leq}$ with a credibility equal to $\chi(r)$ if there is at least one $w \in U$ such that $f(w,q_1)=r_{q1}$ and $f(w,q_2)=r_{q2}$ and ... and $f(w,q_e)=r_{qe}$, and $\bar{P}[Cl_t^{\leq}(w)] = \bar{C}[Cl_t^{\leq}(w)] = \chi(r) \geq 0$, where $P=\{q_1,...,q_e\}$, $P^{>}=\{q_1,...,q_p\}$, $P^{\sim}=\{q_{p+1},...,q_e\}$.

The different calculation of credibility for certain and possible decision rules comes from point 4 of Theorem 1. It says that the credibility of membership of object $x \in U$ to the upper approximation of $Cl_t^{\geq}$ or $Cl_t^{\leq}$, $t \in M$, does not increase (usually decreases) when considering larger sets of attributes. In consequence, considering smaller sets of attributes there is the possibility of overestimating the credibility of membership of object $x \in U$ to the upper approximation of $Cl_t^{\geq}$ or $Cl_t^{\leq}$.

Therefore, a possible decision rule built on object $w \in U$ belonging to P-upper approximation of cumulative classes should have no greater credibility than the credibility of the possible decision rule built on the same object $w \in U$ belonging to P-upper approximation of the same cumulative classes, where $P \subset C$.

A certain decision rule r of type $D_{\geq}$, "*if* $f(x,q_1)$ is at least as good as r_{q1} *and* $f(x,q_2)$ is at least as good as r_{q2} *and* ... *and* $f(x,q_p)$ is at least as good as r_{qp} *and* $f(x,q_{p+1})$ is similar to r_{qp+1} *and* $f(x,q_{p+2})$ is similar to r_{qp+2} *and* ... *and* $f(x,q_e)$ is similar to r_{qe}, *then* x *belongs* to $Cl_t^{\geq}$ ", whose credibility is equal to $\chi(r)$, is called ***minimal*** if there is no other certain decision rule s: "*if* $f(x,h_1)$ is at least as good as s_{h1} *and* $f(x,h_2)$ is at least as good as s_{h2} *and* ... *and* $f(x,h_p)$ is at least as good as s_{hp} *and* $f(x,h_{k+1})$ is similar to s_{hk+1} *and* $f(x,h_{k+2})$ is similar to s_{hk+2} *and* ... *and* $f(x,h_g)$ is similar to s_g, *then* x *belongs* to $Cl_v^{\geq}$ ", whose credibility is $\chi(s)$, such that $\{h_1,...,h_k,h_{k+1},...,h_g\} \subseteq \{q_1,..., q_e\}$, r_{h1} is at least as good as s_{h1}, r_{h2} is at least as good as $s_{h2},...$, r_{hk} is at least as good as s_{hk}, $r_{hk+1}=s_{hk+1},..., r_{hg}=s_{hg}$, $v \geq t$, and $\chi(s) \geq \chi(r)$.

One can define analogously the minimality condition for possible decision rules of type $D_{\geq}$ and for certain and possible decision rules of type $D_{\leq}$. In other words, by a minimal decision rule we understand such an implication that there is no implication of at least the same credibility with an antecedent of at least the same weakness and a consequent of at least the same strength.

6 An example

In Table 1, four firms are described by means of three attribute:

1) q_1 - net worth,

2) q_2 - growth rate of sales (%),

3) q_3 - return on equity (%).

Let us observe that the domain of attribute q_1 is not preference-ordered: firm x having a greater net worth than firm y is not necessarily better because it could be less profitable. On the contrary, the domains of attributes q_2 and q_3 are ordered according to increasing preference because, in general: firm x having a growth rate of sales greater than firm y is preferred to y, and firm x having a return on equity greater than firm y is also preferred to y. Therefore attributes q_2 and q_3 are criteria.

Using rough sets analysis we want to explain the return on equity (q_3) using information about net worth (q_1) and growth rate of sales (q_2). Therefore, return on equity is the decision attribute and net worth and return on equity are two condition attributes.

Table 1. Information table

Firm	q_1	q_2	q_3
F1	1550	8	17
F2	1450	5	14.5
F3	1050	4	15.5
F4	950	3.5	14.5

The information contained in Table 1 has been analysed first using the crisp rough set approach based on joint use of dominance and indiscernibility (see Greco, Matarazzo and Slowinski, 1998b). The domain of the attribute net worth has been divided (discretized) into three subintervals:

- if $f(x,q_1) \leq 1000$, then firm x has a **low** net worth (code 1),

- if $1000 < f(x,q_1) \leq 1500$, then firm x has a **medium** net worth (code 2),

- if $f(x,q_1) > 1500$, then firm x has a **high** net worth (code 3).

Also the domain of return on equity has been divided into two preference-ordered classes as follows:

- if $f(x, q_3) \leq 15$, then firm x is **not-highly** profitable (code Cl_1),

- if $f(x, q_3) > 15$, then firm x is **highly** profitable (code Cl_2).

The attribute growth rate of sales has not been discretized. The coded decision table is presented in Table 2.

Table 2. Coded decision table

Firm	q_1	q_2	q_3
F1	3	8	Cl_2
F2	2	5	Cl_1
F3	2	4	Cl_2
F4	1	3.5	Cl_1

Using the rough set approach based on joint use of dominance and indiscernibility, we approximate the class $Cl_1^\leq$ of (at most) non-highly profitable firms and the class $Cl_2^\geq$ of (at least) highly profitable firms. Since only two classes are considered, in this particular case we have $Cl_1^\leq = Cl_1$ and $Cl_2^\geq = Cl_2$.

Let us remember the interpretation of rough approximations of a set $X \subseteq U$, taking into account the information provided by a subset of attributes $P \subseteq C$:

- P-lower approximation, denoted by $\underline{P}(X)$, represents the set of objects belonging certainly to X,

- P-upper approximation, denoted by $\overline{P}(X)$, represents the set of objects belonging possibly to X,

- P-boundary, denoted by $Bn_C(X)$, is the set difference between $\overline{P}(X)$ and $\underline{P}(X)$, and represents the set of ambiguous objects.

The C-lower approximations, the C-upper approximations and the C-boundaries of the classes $Cl_1^\leq$ and $Cl_2^\geq$ are, respectively, as follows: $\underline{C}(Cl_1^\leq) = \{F4\}$, $\overline{C}(Cl_1^\leq) = \{F2,F3,F4\}$, $Bn_C(Cl_1^\leq) = \{F2,F3\}$, $\underline{C}(Cl_2^\geq) = \{F1\}$, $\overline{C}(Cl_2^\geq) = \{F1,F2,F3\}$, $Bn_C(Cl_1^\leq) = \{F2,F3\}$.

Let us remark that firms F2 and F3 are ambiguous and belong to the boundary, because firm F2 dominates firm F3 (because F2 and F3 have both a medium net worth, so they are indiscernible with respect to q_1, but F2 has a growth rate of sales greater than F3), however, F3 is a highly profitable firm and F3 is not.

The following minimal set of decision rules can be obtained from the considered decision table (within parentheses there are objects supporting the corresponding rule):

1) if $f(x,q_1)=1$, then $x \in Cl_1^{\leq}$

   (F4)

[i.e. if the net worth of the firm is low, then the firm is (at most) non highly profitable]

2) if $f(x,q_1)=3$, then $x \in Cl_2^{\geq}$

   (F1)

[i.e. if the net worth of the firm is high, then the firm is (at least) highly profitable]

3) if $4 \leq f(x,q_2) \leq 5$, then $x \in Cl_1 \cup Cl_2$ (F2, F3)

[i.e. if the growth rate of sales is between 4% and 5%, then the firm is non-highly profitable or highly profitable, and there is not enough information to make an assignment to exactly one class].

It is clear that the result of the crisp rough set approach based on indiscernibility and dominance is not completely satisfactory. The assignment of F2 to the highly profitable class is inconsistent with the assignment of F3 to the non-highly profitable class, because F2 is dominated by F3. However, this dominance is based on the indiscernibility of F2 and F3 with respect to net worth. Indeed, according to the adopted discretization, the net worth of F2 and F3 belong to the same medium subinterval of net worth. In fact, their original values are on the opposite ends of this subinterval and, intuitively, they should not be considered indiscernible. Moreover, the assignment of F4 to non-highly profitable class is not considered inconsistent with the assignment of F3 to highly profitable class, altough F4 is very similar to F3 on both condition attributes.

We will show that the rough set approach based on joint use of similarity and dominance (see Greco, Matarazzo and Slowinski 1998c) is better adapted to the analysis of this case. With respect to net worth, a similarity relation R has been defined on the sets of firms such that x and y are similar if the difference between the two net worth scores is smaller than 150; more formally:

$$xRy \text{ iff } |f(x,q_2) - f(y,q_2)| \leq 150.$$

Using this definition of similarity we approximate again the classes $Cl_1^{\leq}$ and $Cl_2^{\geq}$. The C-lower approximations, the C-upper approximations and the C-boundaries of the classes $Cl_1^{\leq}$ and $Cl_2^{\geq}$ are, respectively, as follows: $\underline{C}(Cl_1^{\leq})=\varnothing$, $\overline{C}(Cl_1^{\leq})=\{F3,F4\}$, $Bn_C(Cl_1^{\leq})=\{F3,F4\}$, $\underline{C}(Cl_2^{\geq})=\{F1\}$, $\overline{C}(Cl_2^{\geq})=\{F1,F3,F4\}$,

$Bn_C(Cl_1^{\leq})=\{F3,F4\}$.

The following minimal set of decision rules can be obtained from the considered decision table (within parentheses there are objects supporting the corresponding rule):

1) if $f(x,q_1)$ is similar to 1450 and $f(x,q_2) \leq 5$, then $x \in Cl_1^{\leq}$

   (F2)

   [i.e. if the net worth of the firm is similar to 1450 and the growth rate of sales is at most 5%, then the firm is (at most) non-highly profitable]

2) if $f(x,q_1) \geq 8$, then $x \in Cl_2^{\geq}$

   (F1)

   [i.e. if the growth rate of sales is at least 8%, then the firm is (at least) highly profitable]

3) if $f(x,q_1)$ is similar to 950 and $3.5 \leq f(x,q_2) \leq 4$, then $x \in Cl_1 \cup Cl_2$ (F2, F3)

   [i.e. if the net worth of the firm is similar to 950 and the growth rate of sales is between 3.5% and 4%, then the firm is non-highly profitable or highly profitable, and there is not enough information to make an assignment to exactly one class].

Let us remark that now the assignment of F4 to a highly profitable class is inconsistent with the assignment of F3 to the non-highly profitable class, because F3 dominates F4. In fact, F3 dominates F4 because F3 is similar to F4 with respect to net worth and F3 has a greater rate of sales than F4. On the other hand, the assignment of F2 is no more inconsistent with another firm: using similarity instead of indiscernibility, F2 does not dominate F3. Therefore, F2 belongs to the lower approximation of the non-highly profitable class, which is concordant with intuition.

The obtained results are now more convincing, nevertheless, not completely. For example, the assignment of F2, F3, and F4 to two different classes is rather questionable, because the return on equity (q_3) of these three firms is quite close to the threshold separating the two classes. Moreover, due to the adopted definition of similarity, F3 and F4 are considered "fully" similar with respect to net worth, however there is a non-negligible difference between the two firms. Perhaps, it would be better to say that they are similar to a certain degree. Analogous arguments hold for F1 and F2. Moreover, although F4 has a growth rate of sales worse than F3, the difference is not high and thus it is not completely false that F4 has a growth rate of sales as good as F3. To deal with all these problems of graded relations, fuzzy set approach can be useful.

A fuzzy similarity relation for the attribute q_1 can be defined as follows:

$$R_{q1}(x,y) = \begin{cases} 0 & , \quad \text{if } |f(x,q_1)-f(y,q_1)| > 200 \\ 1 & , \quad \text{if } f(x,q_1) = f(x,q_2) \\ \text{linear} & , \qquad \text{otherwise} \end{cases}$$

It can be interpreted as follows: the similarity is full if the two net worth values are the same ($R_{q1}(x,y)=1$); there is no similarity at all if the difference between the net worth values of the firms is greater than 200 ($R_{q1}(x,y)=0$); in between, there is a zone of partial similarity ($0<R_{q1}(x,y)<1$).

A fuzzy outranking relation with a degree of credibility between zero (completely false) and 1 (completely true) can be defined for criterion q_2, as follows:

$$S_{q2}(x,y) = \begin{cases} 0 & , \quad \text{if } f(y,q_2)-f(x,q_2) > 2 \\ 1 & , \quad \text{if } f(x,q_2) \geq f(y,q_2) \\ \text{linear} & , \qquad \text{otherwise} \end{cases}$$

It can be interpreted as follows: if the return on sales of a firm x is 2% or more smaller than that of firm y, then x is definitely not as good as y; if the return on sales of a firm x is equal to or greater than that of firm y, then x is definitely as good as y; in between, the outranking relation is partially true.

Finally, according to the decision criterion q_3, the firms are assigned to two fuzzy preference-ordered classes: Cl_1="non-highly profitable firms", and Cl_2="highly profitable firms". The membership functions of these fuzzy classes are defined as follows:

$$Cl_1(x) = \begin{cases} 1 & , \quad \text{if } f(x,q_3) < 14\% \\ 0 & , \quad \text{if } f(x,q_3) > 16\% \\ \text{linear} & , \qquad \text{otherwise} \end{cases}$$

and

$$Cl_2(x) = \begin{cases} 0 & , \quad \text{if } f(x,q_3) < 14\% \\ 1 & , \quad \text{if } f(x,q_3) > 16\% \\ \text{linear} & , \qquad \text{otherwise} \end{cases}$$

Table 3 presents C-lower and C-upper approximations of fuzzy decision classes, obtained by means of fuzzy dominance defined on $C=\{q_1,q_2\}$.

Table 3. Rough approximations by fuzzy dominance

Firm	$\underline{C}[Cl_1^{\leq}(x)]$	$\overline{C}[Cl_1^{\leq}(x)]$	$\underline{C}[Cl_2^{\geq}(x)]$	$\overline{C}[Cl_2^{\geq}(x)]$
F1	0	0	1	1
F2	0.75	0.75	0.25	0.25
F3	0.25	0.5	0.5	0.75
F4	0.5	0.75	0.25	0.5

The following minimal and certain decision rules were obtained from the decision table presented in Table 3 (each rule is followed by its credibility degree):

1) if the net worth is similar to 1550, then the firm is highly profitable
(credibility=0.5)

2) if the net worth is similar to 1450, then the firm is highly profitable
(credibility=0.25)

3) if the net worth is similar to 1050, then the firm is highly profitable
(credibility=0.5)

4) if the net worth is similar to 950, then the firm is highly profitable
(credibility=0.25)

5) if the net worth is similar to 1450, then the firm is non-highly profitable
(credibility=0.5)

6) if the net worth is similar to 1050, then the firm is non-highly profitable
(credibility=0.25)

7) if the net worth is similar to 950, then the firm is non-highly profitable
(credibility=0.5)

8) if the growth rate of sales is at least 8%, then the firm is highly profitable
(credibility=1)

9) if the growth rate of sales is at least 3.5%, then the firm is highly profitable
(credibility=0.25)

10) if the net worth is similar to 1450 and the growth rate of sales is at most 5%, then the firm is non-highly profitable
(credibility=0.75)

Furthermore, the following minimal and possible decision rules were obtained from the decision table presented in Table 3:

1) if the net worth is similar to 1050, then the firm could be highly profitable
(credibility=0.75)

2) if the net worth is similar to 950, then the firm could be highly profitable
(credibility=0.5)

3) if the net worth is similar to 1050, then the firm could be non-highly profitable
(credibility=0.5)

4) if the net worth is similar to 950, then the firm could be non-highly profitable
(credibility=0.75)

5) if the growth rate of sales is at least 4%, then the firm could be highly profitable
(credibility=0.75)

6) if the growth rate of sales is at most 5%, then the firm could be non-highly profitable
(credibility=0.75)

7) if the growth rate of sales is at most 3.5%, then the firm could be non-highly profitable
(credibility=0.75)

7 Conclusion

We introduced and characterized fuzzy rough approximation using fuzzy dominance and similarity relations considered jointly. This extensions of the rough set methodology permits to deal with sorting problems where multiple attributes and criteria are used together to describe the objects. We proved that our extension of the rough approximation into the fuzzy context maintains the same desirable properties of the crisp rough approximation of decision classes. A simple example served to illustrate advantage of the proposed extension.

Acknowledgement

The research of the first two authors has been supported by the Italian Ministry of University and Scientific Research (MURST). The third author wishes to acknowledge financial support from State Committee for Scientific Research, KBN.

References

Dubois, D. and H. Prade. 1990. "Rough fuzzy sets and fuzzy rough sets". *Int. J. of General Systems* **17**, 191-200.

Dubois, D. and H. Prade. 1992. "Putting rough sets and fuzzy sets together". [In]: R. Slowinski (ed.) *Intelligent Decision Support, Handbook of Applications and Advances of the Rough Sets Theory*. Kluwer, Dordrecht, pp. 203-233.

Dubois, D., H. Prade, and R.R. Yager. 1997. "A manifesto: Fuzzy information engineering". [In]: D. Dubois, H. Prade, R.R. Yager (eds.) *Fuzzy Information Engineering*. Wiley, New York, pp. 1-8.

Fodor, J., and M. Roubens. 1994. *"Fuzzy Preference Modelling and Multicriteria Decision Support"*. Kluwer, Dordrecht.

Greco, S., B. Matarazzo and R. Slowinski. 1996. "Rough approximation of preference relation by dominance relations". *ICS Research Report* 16/96, Warsaw University of Technology and *European Journal of Operational Research* **117** (1999) 63-83.

Greco, S., B. Matarazzo and R. Slowinski. 1998a. "A new rough set approach to evaluation of bankruptcy risk". [In]: C. Zopounidis (ed.) *Operational Tools in the Management of Financial Risk*. Kluwer, Dordrecht, pp. 121-136.

Greco, S., B. Matarazzo and R. Slowinski. 1998b. "A new rough set approach to multicriteria and multiattribute classification". [In]: L. Polkowski, A. Skowron (eds.) *Proceedings of the First International Conference on Rough sets and Current Trends in Computing (RSTCTC '98)*, Warsaw, June 22-26, 1998; Springer-Verlag, Berlin, pp. 60-67.

Greco, S., B. Matarazzo and R. Slowinski. 1998c. "On joint use of indiscernibility, similarity and dominance in rough approximation of decision classes". *Research Report* RA-012/98, Poznan University of Technology, Poznan. Also in: D. K. Despotis, C. Zopounidis (eds.) *Proc. 5th International Conference of the Decision Sciences Institute*, Athens, Greece, 4-7 July 1999, pp. 1380-1382.

Greco, S., B. Matarazzo and R. Slowinski. 1999a. "The use of rough sets and fuzzy sets in MCDM". [In]: T. Gal, T. Stewart and T. Hanne (eds.) *Advances in Multiple Criteria Decision Making*. Chapter 14, Kluwer, Dordrecht, pp. 14.1-14.59.

Greco, S., B. Matarazzo and R. Slowinski. 1999b. "Fuzzy dominance as basis for rough approximations". [In]: *Proc. 4th Meeting of the EURO WG on Fuzzy Sets and 2nd Internat. Conf. on Soft and Intelligent Computing, EUROFUSE-SIC '99*. Budapest, May 25-28, 1999, pp. 273-278.

Pawlak, Z. 1982. "Rough sets". *International Journal of Information & Computer Sciences* **11**, 341-356.

Pawlak, Z. 1991. *"Rough Sets. Theoretical Aspects of Reasoning about Data"*. Kluwer, Dordrecht.

Pawlak, Z. 1985. "Rough sets and fuzzy sets". *Fuzzy Sets and Systems* **17**, 99-102.

Slowinski, R. 1995. "Rough set processing of fuzzy information". [In]: T.Y. Lin, A. Wildberger (eds.) *Soft Computing: Rough Sets, Fuzzy Logic, Neural Networks, Uncertainty Management, Knowledge Discovery*. Simulation Councils, Inc., San Diego, CA, pp. 142-145.

Slowinski, R. and J. Stefanowski. 1994. "Handling various types of uncertainty in the rough set approach". [In]: W. P. Ziarko (ed.) *Rough Sets, Fuzzy Sets and Knowledge Discovery*, Springer-Verlag, London, pp. 366-376.

Slowinski, R. and J. Stefanowski. 1996. "Rough set reasoning about uncertain data". *Fundamenta Informaticae* **27**, 229-243.

Yao, Y. 1996. "Combination of rough sets and fuzzy sets based on α-level sets". [In]: T. Y. Lin, N. Cercone (eds.) *Rough Sets and Data Mining*. Kluwer, Boston, pp. 301-321.

Behavioral Analysis of Aggregation in Multicriteria Decision Aid

Jean-Luc Marichal

D 8 I

Department of Management, FEGSS
University of Liège
Boulevard du Rectorat 7 - B31
4000 Liege, Belgium
E-mail: jl.marichal@ulg.ac.be

Summary. The most often used operator to aggregate criteria in decision making problems is the classical weighted arithmetic mean. In many problems however, the criteria considered interact, and a substitute to the weighted arithmetic mean has to be adopted. It was shown that, under rather natural conditions, the discrete Choquet integral is an adequate aggregation operator that extends the weighted arithmetic mean by taking into consideration of the interaction among criteria. However, since this operator is constructed from coefficients (weights) whose meaning is not always very clear for the decision maker, it is useful to define from these coefficients some indices that offer a better understanding of the behavioral properties of the aggregation. We present and discuss the following indices: the global importance of criteria, the interaction among criteria, the influence of the criteria on the aggregation, the tolerance of the decision maker, and the dispersion of the weights on the criteria.

1   Introduction

Let us consider a finite set of *alternatives* $A = \{a, b, c, \ldots\}$ and a finite set of *criteria* $N = \{1, \ldots, n\}$ in a multicriteria decision making problem. Each alternative $a \in A$ is associated with a *profile* $x^a = (x_1^a, \ldots, x_n^a) \in \mathbb{R}^n$, where, for any $i \in N$, x_i^a represents the partial score of a related to criterion i. We assume that all the partial scores are defined according to the same interval scale, that is, they are defined up to the same positive linear transformation. Particularly, this will enable us to embed the scale in the unit interval $[0, 1]$.

From the profile of any alternative $a \in A$, one can compute a global score $M(x^a)$ by means of an aggregation operator $M : \mathbb{R}^n \to \mathbb{R}$ which takes into account the weights of importance of the criteria. Once the global scores are computed, they can be used to rank the alternatives or select an alternative that best satisfies the given criteria.

Until recently, the most often used aggregation operators were the weighted arithmetic means, that is, operators of the form

$$M_\omega(x) = \sum_{i=1}^n \omega_i \, x_i,$$

with $\sum_i \omega_i = 1$ and $\omega_i \geq 0$ for all $i \in N$. However, since these operators are not able to model in any understandable way an interaction among criteria, they can be used only in the presence of independent criteria. They are not appropriate for the aggregation of interacting criteria.

In order to have a flexible representation of complex interaction phenomena between criteria (e.g. positive or negative synergy between some criteria), it is useful to substitute to the weight vector ω a non-additive set function on N to define a weight not only on each criterion, but also on each subset of criteria. For this purpose the concept of *fuzzy measure* [23] has been introduced.

Now, a suitable aggregation operator, which generalizes the weighted arithmetic mean, is the discrete Choquet integral, whose use was proposed by many authors (see e.g. [6] and the references there). Of course, the large flexibility of this aggregation operator is due to the use of a fuzzy measure, which makes it possible to model interaction phenomena existing among criteria. However, the meaning of the values of such a fuzzy measure is not always clear for the decision maker. These values, which represent the importance of each combination of criteria, do not give immediately the global importance of the criteria nor the degree of interaction among them.

In fact, from a given fuzzy measure, it is possible to derive some indices or parameters that describe the behavior of the fuzzy measure or, equivalently, that of the Choquet integral that is used to aggregate the criteria. Alternatively, when the fuzzy measure is not completely known, such indices can help the decision maker to assess it. This corresponds to the inverse problem of identifying the weights from parametric specifications on criteria, see [14].

The aim of this paper is to present the following behavioral indices: the global importance of criteria, the interaction among criteria, the influence of the criteria on the aggregation, the tolerance of the decision maker, and the dispersion of the fuzzy measure.

The outline of this paper is as follows. In Section 2 we recall the definition of the discrete Choquet integral and some of its particular cases. Sections 3, 4, and 5 are respectively devoted to the importance indices, interaction indices, and influence indices. Sections 6 and 7 deal with the tolerance of the decision maker by means of the concepts of conjunction and disjunction degrees as well as the veto and favor indices. Section 8 introduces a generalization of the Shannon entropy to measure the dispersion of a fuzzy measure. Finally, in Section 9 we present a practical example demonstrating the use of the parameters presented in this paper.

In order to avoid an heavy notation, cardinality of subsets $S, T, \ldots$ will be denoted whenever possible by the corresponding lower case letters $s, t, \ldots$, otherwise by the standard notation $|S|, |T|, \ldots$. Moreover, we will often omit braces for singletons, e.g., writing $a(i)$, $N \setminus i$ instead of $a(\{i\})$, $N \setminus \{i\}$. Also, for pairs, we will often write ij instead of $\{i, j\}$, as for example $a(ij)$.

For any subset $S \subseteq N$, e_S will denote the characteristic vector of S in $\{0, 1\}^n$, i.e., the vector of $\{0, 1\}^n$ whose i-th component is 1 if and only if $i \in S$.

Finally, $\wedge$ and $\vee$ will denote the minimum and maximum operations, respectively.

2 The Choquet integral and its particular cases

The use of the Choquet integral has been proposed by many authors as an adequate substitute to the weighted arithmetic mean to aggregate interacting criteria, see e.g. [6,12]. In the weighted arithmetic mean model, each criterion $i \in N$ is given a weight $\omega_i \in [0, 1]$ representing the importance of this criterion in the decision. In the Choquet integral model, where criteria can be dependent, a fuzzy measure [23] is used to define a weight on each combination of criteria, thus making it possible to model the interaction existing among criteria.

Definition 1. A fuzzy measure on N is a set function $v : 2^N \to [0, 1]$ satisfying the following conditions:
  $i)$ $v(\emptyset) = 0, v(N) = 1$,
  $ii)$ $S \subseteq T \Rightarrow v(S) \leq v(T)$.

The set of all fuzzy measures on N will be denoted by $\mathcal{F}_N$ as we continue. Moreover, for any fuzzy measure v on N and any permutation π on N, πv will denote the fuzzy measure on N defined by $\pi v(\pi(S)) = v(S)$ for all $S \subseteq N$, where $\pi(S) = \{\pi(i) \mid i \in S\}$.

For any $S \subseteq N$, $v(S)$ can be interpreted as the weight of importance of the combination S of criteria, or better, its importance or power to make the decision alone (without the remaining criteria).

The concept of Choquet integral was first introduced in capacity theory [1]. Its use as a (fuzzy) integral with respect to a fuzzy measure was then proposed by Murofushi and Sugeno [17,18].

Definition 2. Let $v \in \mathcal{F}_N$. The Choquet integral of $x : N \to \mathbb{R}$ with respect to v is defined by

$$\mathcal{C}_v(x) := \sum_{i=1}^{n} x_{(i)} [v(A_{(i)}) - v(A_{(i+1)})],$$

where $(\cdot)$ indicates a permutation on N such that $x_{(1)} \leq \ldots \leq x_{(n)}$. Also $A_{(i)} = \{(i), \ldots, (n)\}$, and $A_{(n+1)} = \emptyset$.

Thus defined, the Choquet integral has very good properties for aggregation (see e.g. Grabisch [6]). For instance, it is continuous, non decreasing, comprised between min and max, stable under the same transformations of interval scales in the sense of the theory of measurement, and coincides with the weighted arithmetic mean (discrete Lebesgue integral) as soon as the fuzzy measure is additive. Moreover, in [11,12] the author proposed an axiomatic characterization of the class of all the Choquet integrals with n arguments. The statement is the following.

Theorem 1. *The operators* $M_v : \mathbb{R}^n \to \mathbb{R}$ $(v \in \mathcal{F}_N)$ *are*

- *linear w.r.t. the fuzzy measure, that is, there exist 2^n functions $f_T : \mathbb{R}^n \to \mathbb{R}$ $(T \subseteq N)$, such that*

$$M_v = \sum_{T \subseteq N} v(T)\, f_T, \qquad v \in F_N.$$

- *non decreasing in each argument,*
- *stable for the admissible positive linear transformations, that is,*

$$M_v(r\, x + s\, e_N) = r\, M_v(x) + s$$

for all $x \in \mathbb{R}^n$, $r > 0$, $s \in \mathbb{R}$.
- *properly weighted by v, that is,*

$$M_v(e_S) = v(S), \qquad S \subseteq N,\ v \in F_N,$$

if and only if $M_v = C_v$ for all $v \in \mathcal{F}_N$.

The axioms presented in the previous characterization are natural enough in the context of multicriteria decision making. The first one is proposed to keep the aggregation model as simple as possible. The second axiom says that increasing a partial score along any criterion cannot decrease the global score. The third axiom only demands that the aggregated value is stable with respect to any change of scale. Finally, assuming that the partial score scale is embedded in $[0, 1]$, the fourth axiom suggests that the weight of importance of any subset S of criteria is defined as the global evaluation of the alternative that completely satisfies criteria S and totally fails to satisfy the others.

The fourth axiom is fundamental. It gives an appropriate definition of the weights of subsets of criteria, interpreting them as global evaluation of particular profiles.

Now, the Möbius transform of a given fuzzy measure $v \in \mathcal{F}_N$ is a set function $a : 2^N \to \mathbb{R}$ defined by

$$a(S) = \sum_{T \subseteq S} (-1)^{s-t}\, v(T), \qquad S \subseteq N.$$

The transformation is invertible and we have (see e.g. [19])

$$v(S) = \sum_{T \subseteq S} a(T), \qquad S \subseteq N.$$

The Möbius transform enables us to express some functions of v in a simpler form. For example, the Choquet integral is written [12]

$$\mathcal{C}_v(x) = \sum_{T \subseteq N} a(T) \bigwedge_{i \in T} x_i, \qquad x \in \mathbb{R}^n.$$

We now present some subclasses of Choquet integrals. Any vector $\omega \in [0,1]^n$ such that $\sum_i \omega_i = 1$ will be called a *weight vector* as we continue.

2.1 The weighted arithmetic mean

Definition 3. For any weight vector $\omega \in [0,1]^n$, the weighted arithmetic mean operator WAM_ω associated to ω is defined by

$$\mathrm{WAM}_\omega(x) = \sum_{i=1}^n \omega_i\, x_i.$$

We can easily see that WAM_ω is a Choquet integral $\mathcal{C}_v$ with respect to an additive fuzzy measure:

$$v(S) = \sum_{i \in S} \omega_i, \qquad S \subseteq N.$$

The corresponding Möbius representation is given by

$$\begin{cases} a(i) = \omega_i, & \forall i \in N, \\ a(S) = 0, & \forall S \subseteq N \text{ such that } s \geq 2. \end{cases}$$

Conversely, the weights associated to WAM_ω are given by

$$\omega_i = v(i) = a(i), \qquad i \in N.$$

The class of weighted arithmetic mean WAM_ω includes two important special cases, namely:

- the arithmetic mean

$$\mathrm{AM}(x) = \frac{1}{n} \sum_{i=1}^n x_i,$$

when $\omega_i = 1/n$ for all $i \in N$. In this case, we have $v(S) = s/n$ for all $S \subseteq N$ and $a(i) = 1/n$ for all $i \in N$.
- the k-th projection

$$\mathrm{P}_k(x) = x_k,$$

when $\omega_k = 1$ for some $k \in N$. In this case, we have $v(S) = 1$ if $S \ni k$ and 0 otherwise. Moreover, we have $a(i) = 1$ if $i = k$ and 0 otherwise.

2.2 The ordered weighted averaging operator

Yager [25] defined in 1988 the ordered weighted averaging operators (OWA) as follows.

Definition 4. For any weight vector $\omega \in [0,1]^n$, the ordered weighted averaging operator OWA_ω associated to ω is defined by

$$\mathrm{OWA}_\omega(x) = \sum_{i=1}^{n} \omega_i\, x_{(i)}$$

with the usual convention that $x_{(1)} \leq \cdots \leq x_{(n)}$.

The following result, due to Grabisch [5], shows that any OWA operator is a Choquet integral w.r.t. a fuzzy measure that depends only on the cardinality of subsets.

Proposition 1. Let $v \in \mathcal{F}_N$. Then the following assertions are equivalent.
  i) For any $S, S' \subseteq N$ such that $|S| = |S'|$, we have $v(S) = v(S')$.
  ii) There exists a weight vector ω such that $C_v = \mathrm{OWA}_\omega$.
  iii) C_v is a symmetric function.

The fuzzy measure v associated to OWA_ω is given by

$$v(S) = \sum_{i=n-s+1}^{n} \omega_i, \qquad S \subseteq N,\ S \neq \emptyset,$$

and its Möbius representation by [7, Theorem 1]

$$a(S) = \sum_{j=0}^{s-1} \binom{s-1}{j}(-1)^{s-1-j}\,\omega_{n-j}, \qquad S \subseteq N,\ S \neq \emptyset.$$

Conversely, the weights associated to OWA_ω are given by

$$\omega_{n-s} = v(S \cup i) - v(S) = \sum_{T \subseteq S} a(T \cup i), \qquad i \in N,\ S \subseteq N \setminus i.$$

The class of ordered weighted averaging operators OWA_ω includes some important special cases, namely:

- the arithmetic mean AM when $\omega_i = 1/n$ for all $i \in N$.
- the k-th order statistic
$$OS_k(x) = x_{(k)},$$

when $\omega_k = 1$ for some $k \in N$. In this case, we have

$$v(S) = \begin{cases} 1 & \text{if } s \geq n-k+1, \\ 0 & \text{otherwise,} \end{cases}$$

$$a(S) = \begin{cases} (-1)^{s-n+k-1}\binom{s-1}{n-k} & \text{if } s \geq n-k+1, \\ 0 & \text{otherwise.} \end{cases}$$

- the min operator

$$\min(x) = \min_{i \in N} x_i,$$

when $\omega_1 = 1$. In this case, we have $v(S) = a(S) = 1$ if $S = N$ and 0 otherwise.

- the max operator

$$\max(x) = \max_{i \in N} x_i,$$

when $\omega_n = 1$. In this case, we have $v(S) = 1$ and $a(S) = (-1)^{s+1}$ for all $S \neq \emptyset$.

2.3 The partial minimum and maximum operators

Definition 5. For any non-empty subset $T \subseteq N$, the partial minimum operator $\min_T$ and the partial maximum operator $\max_T$, associated to T, are respectively defined by

$$\min_T(x) = \min_{i \in T} x_i,$$
$$\max_T(x) = \min_{i \in T} x_i.$$

For the operator $\min_T$, we have

$$v(S) = \begin{cases} 1, & \text{if } S \supseteq T, \\ 0, & \text{else,} \end{cases}$$

$$a(S) = \begin{cases} 1, & \text{if } S = T, \\ 0, & \text{else.} \end{cases}$$

For the operator $\max_T$, we have

$$v(S) = \begin{cases} 1, & \text{if } S \cap T \neq \emptyset, \\ 0, & \text{else,} \end{cases}$$

$$a(S) = \begin{cases} (-1)^{s+1}, & \text{if } \emptyset \neq S \subseteq T, \\ 0, & \text{else.} \end{cases}$$

3 Importance indices

The overall importance of a criterion $i \in N$ into a decision problem is not solely determined by the number $v(i)$, but also by all $v(T)$ such that $T \ni i$. Indeed, we may have $v(i) = 0$, suggesting that element i is unimportant, but it may happen that for many subsets $T \subseteq N \setminus i$, $v(T \cup i)$ is much greater than $v(T)$, suggesting that i is actually an important element in the decision.

Shapley [22] has proposed in 1953 a definition of a coefficient of importance, based on a set of reasonable axioms. The *importance index* or *Shapley value* of criterion i with respect to v is defined by:

$$\phi(v, i) := \sum_{T \subseteq N \setminus i} \frac{(n - t - 1)! \, t!}{n!} [v(T \cup i) - v(T)]. \tag{1}$$

The Shapley value is a fundamental concept in game theory expressing a power index. Its use in multicriteria decision making was proposed in 1992 by Murofushi [15].

Thus defined, it can be interpreted as a weighted average value of the marginal contribution $v(T \cup i) - v(T)$ of element i alone in all combinations. To make this clearer, it is informative to rewrite the index as follows:

$$\phi(v, i) = \frac{1}{n} \sum_{t=0}^{n-1} \frac{1}{\binom{n-1}{t}} \sum_{\substack{T \subseteq N \setminus i \\ |T| = t}} [v(T \cup i) - v(T)].$$

Thus, the average value of $v(T \cup i) - v(T)$ is computed first over all the subsets of the same size t and then over all the possible sizes.

It is worth noting that the Shapley value fulfills the following properties:

$$\phi(v, i) \geq 0, \qquad i \in N,$$

and

$$\sum_{i=1}^{n} \phi(v, i) = 1.$$

Note also that, when v is additive, we clearly have $v(T \cup i) - v(T) = v(i)$ for all $i \in N$ and all $T \subseteq N \setminus i$, and hence

$$\phi(v, i) = v(i), \qquad i \in N. \tag{2}$$

If v is non-additive then some criteria are dependent and (2) generally does not hold anymore. This shows that it is reasonable to search for a coefficient of overall importance for each criterion.

In terms of the Möbius representation, the Shapley value takes a very simple form [22]:

$$\phi(v, i) = \sum_{T \ni i} \frac{1}{t} a(T).$$

The best known axiomatic supporting the Shapley value is given in the following theorem, see e.g. [22].

Theorem 2. *The numbers* $\psi(v, i)$ $(i \in N, v \in \mathcal{F}_N)$:

- *are linear w.r.t. the fuzzy measure, that is, there exist real constants p_T^i $(T \subseteq N)$ such that*

$$\psi(v, i) = \sum_{T \subseteq N} p_T^i \, v(T), \qquad i \in N, v \in \mathcal{F}_N.$$

- *are symmetric, that is, for any permutation π on N, we have*

$$\psi(v, i) = \psi(\pi v, \pi(i)), \qquad i \in N, v \in \mathcal{F}_N.$$

- *fulfill the "null criterion" axiom, that is, for any $i \in N$ and any $v \in \mathcal{F}_N$,*

$$v(T \cup i) = v(T) \quad \forall T \subseteq N \setminus i \quad \Rightarrow \quad \psi(v, i) = 0.$$

- *fulfill the "efficiency" axiom, that is,*

$$\sum_{i=1}^{n} \psi(v, i) = 1, \qquad v \in \mathcal{F}_N.$$

if and only if $\psi(v, i) = \phi(v, i)$ for all $i \in N$ and all $v \in \mathcal{F}_N$.

Let us comment on the axioms presented in this characterization. As for the Choquet integral (cf. Theorem 1), we ask the importance indices to be linear w.r.t. the corresponding fuzzy measure. Next, the symmetry axiom demands that the indices are independent of the name (label) given to each criterion. The third axiom, which is quite natural, says that when a criterion does not contribute in the decision problem then it has a zero global importance. The last axiom naturally acts as a normalization property.

Fuzzy measure v	$\phi(v, i)$
v_{WAM_ω}	ω_i
v_{OWA_ω}	$1/n$
$v_{\min_T}$	$\begin{cases} 1/t & \text{if } i \in T \\ 0 & \text{otherwise} \end{cases}$
$v_{\max_T}$	$\begin{cases} 1/t & \text{if } i \in T \\ 0 & \text{otherwise} \end{cases}$

Table 1. Importance indices for various fuzzy measures

Table 1 gives the importance indices for fuzzy measures corresponding to particular Choquet integrals.

4 Interaction indices

Another interesting concept is that of *interaction* among criteria. We have seen that when the fuzzy measure is not additive then some criteria interact. Of course, it would be interesting to appraise the degree of interaction among any subset of criteria.

Consider first a pair $\{i, j\} \subseteq N$ of criteria. It may happen that $v(i)$ and $v(j)$ are small and at the same time $v(ij)$ is large. Clearly, the number $\phi(v, i)$ merely measures the average contribution that criterion i brings to all possible combinations, but it does not explain why criterion i may have a large importance. In other words, it gives no information on the interaction phenomena existing among criteria.

Suppose that i and j are positively correlated or competitive (resp. negatively correlated or complementary). Then the marginal contribution of j to every combination of criteria that contains i should be strictly less than (resp. greater than) the marginal contribution of j to the same combination when i is excluded. Thus, depending on whether the correlation between i and j is positive or negative, the expression

$$v(T \cup ij) - v(T \cup i) - v(T \cup j) + v(T)$$

is ≤ 0 or ≥ 0 for all $T \subseteq N \setminus ij$, respectively. We call this expression the marginal interaction between i and j, conditioned to the presence of elements of the combination $T \subseteq N \setminus ij$. Now, an interaction index for $\{i, j\}$ is given by an average value of this marginal interaction. Murofushi and Soneda [16] proposed in 1993 to calculate this average value as for the Shapley value. Setting

$$(\Delta_{ij} v)(T) := v(T \cup ij) - v(T \cup i) - v(T \cup j) + v(T),$$

the *interaction index* of criteria i and j related to v is then defined by

$$I(v, ij) := \sum_{T \subseteq N \setminus ij} \frac{(n - t - 2)! \, t!}{(n - 1)!} (\Delta_{ij} v)(T).$$

We immediately see that this index is negative as soon as i and j are positively correlated or competitive. Similarly, it is positive when i and j are negatively correlated or complementary. Moreover, it has been shown in [8] that $I(v, ij) \in [-1, 1]$ for all $i, j \in N$.

The interaction index among a combination S of criteria was introduced by Grabisch [8] as a natural extension of the case $s = 2$. It was also axiomatized very recently by Grabisch and Roubens [10]. The *interaction index* of S ($s \geq 2$) related to v, is defined by

$$I(v, S) := \sum_{T \subseteq N \setminus S} \frac{(n - t - s)! \, t!}{(n - s + 1)!} (\Delta_S v)(T),$$

where

$$(\Delta_S v)(T) := \sum_{L \subseteq S} (-1)^{s-l} v(L \cup T).$$

In terms of the Möbius representation, it is written [8]

$$I(v, S) = \sum_{T \supseteq S} \frac{1}{t - s + 1} a(T), \qquad S \subseteq N. \tag{3}$$

Viewed as a set function, it coincides on singletons with the Shapley value (1). Moreover, it was proved in [9] that the transformation (3) is invertible and its inverse is written:

$$a(S) = \sum_{T \supseteq S} B_{t-s} I(v, T), \qquad S \subseteq N,$$

where B_n is the n-th Bernoulli number, that is, the n-th element of the numerical sequence $\{B_n\}_{n \in \mathbb{N}}$ defined recursively by

$$\begin{cases} B_0 = 1, \\ \sum_{k=0}^{n} \binom{n+1}{k} B_k = 0, \qquad n \in \mathbb{N} \setminus \{0\}. \end{cases}$$

Table 2 gives the interaction indices for fuzzy measures corresponding to particular Choquet integrals, see [7,12]. For v_{OS_k}, we have used the convention that $\binom{p}{q} = 0$ whenever $p < q$ or $q < 0$.

5 Influence indices

In Section 3 we have presented the concept of overall importance of each criterion. Now, it would be natural to appraise the global importance (or influence) of any combination of criteria on the aggregation process.

In [13] the author proposed the following definition of the influence of criteria on the Choquet integral. Given a subset $S \subseteq N$ of criteria, the influence of S on C_v is defined as the average amplitude of the range of C_v that criteria S may control when assigning partial scores to the criteria not in S at random.

Definition 6. The *influence of* $S \subseteq N$ *on* $C_v : [0,1]^n \to \mathbb{R}$ is defined by

$$I(C_v, S) := \int_0^1 \cdots \int_0^1 \left[\lim_{\substack{x_j \to 1 \\ j \in S}} C_v(x) - \lim_{\substack{x_j \to 0 \\ j \in S}} C_v(x) \right] dx_{i_1} \cdots dx_{i_{n-s}},$$

where $N \setminus S = \{i_1, \ldots, i_{n-s}\}$.

Fuzzy measure v	$I(v,S)$ for $s \geq 2$
$v\mathrm{WAM}_\omega$	0
$v\mathrm{OWA}_\omega$	$\dfrac{1}{n-s+1} \displaystyle\sum_{j=0}^{s-2} \binom{s-2}{j}(-1)^{s-j}\left(\omega_{s-j-1}-\omega_{n-j}\right)$
$v\mathrm{OS}_k$	$\dfrac{(-1)^{k+1}}{n-s+1}\left[\binom{s-2}{n-k}(-1)^{n-s}+\binom{s-2}{s-k-1}\right]$
$v_{\min_T}$	$\begin{cases}\dfrac{1}{t-s+1} & \text{if } T \supseteq S \\[2mm] 0 & \text{otherwise}\end{cases}$
$v_{\max_T}$	$\begin{cases}\dfrac{(-1)^{s+1}}{t-s+1} & \text{if } T \supseteq S \\[2mm] 0 & \text{otherwise}\end{cases}$

Table 2. Interaction indices for various fuzzy measures

¿From this definition, the following formulas can be obtained [13]:

$$I(\mathcal{C}_v, S) = \sum_{T \subseteq N \setminus S} \frac{(n-t-s)!\,t!}{(n-s+1)!}\left[v(T \cup S)-v(T)\right], \qquad S \subseteq N, \qquad (4)$$

$$I(\mathcal{C}_v, S) = \sum_{\substack{T \subseteq N \\ T \cap S \neq \emptyset}} a(T)\,\frac{1}{|T \setminus S|+1}, \qquad S \subseteq N. \qquad (5)$$

Moreover, we clearly have $I(\mathcal{C}_v, S) \in [0,1]$ for all $S \subseteq N$, and we can see that the closer $I(\mathcal{C}_v, S)$ is to 1, the more the subset S has influence on the aggregation.

As for the interaction index, the influence index coincides on singletons with the Shapley value (1). However, the transformations (4) and (5), although they are linear, are not invertible.

Table 3 gives the influence indices for particular Choquet integrals, see [13].

Choquet integral $\mathcal{C}_v$	$I(\mathcal{C}_v, S)$
WAM$_\omega$	$\displaystyle\sum_{i \in S} \omega_i$
OWA$_\omega$	$\displaystyle\sum_{i=1}^{n} \omega_i \, \frac{i \wedge s \wedge (n-i+1) \wedge (n-s+1)}{n-s+1}$
OS$_k$	$\displaystyle\frac{k \wedge s \wedge (n-k+1) \wedge (n-s+1)}{n-s+1}$
min$_T$	$\begin{cases} \dfrac{1}{\lvert T \setminus S \rvert + 1} & \text{if } T \cap S \neq \emptyset \\ 0 & \text{otherwise} \end{cases}$
max$_T$	$\begin{cases} \dfrac{1}{\lvert T \setminus S \rvert + 1} & \text{if } T \cap S \neq \emptyset \\ 0 & \text{otherwise} \end{cases}$

Table 3. Influence indices for various Choquet integrals

6 Conjunction and disjunction degrees

Consider the cube $[0,1]^n$ as a probability space with uniform distribution. Then the expected value of $\mathcal{C}_v(x)$, that is,

$$\mathrm{E}(\mathcal{C}_v) = \int_{[0,1]^n} \mathcal{C}_v(x)\, dx, \qquad (6)$$

represents the *average value* of the Choquet integral $\mathcal{C}_v$ over $[0,1]^n$. This expression gives the average position of $\mathcal{C}_v$ within the interval $[0,1]$.

Since the Choquet integral is always internal to the set of its arguments, that is

$$\min x_i \leq \mathcal{C}_v(x) \leq \max x_i, \qquad x \in [0,1]^n,$$

from (6) it follows that

$$\mathrm{E}(\min) \leq \mathrm{E}(\mathcal{C}_v) \leq \mathrm{E}(\max), \qquad v \in \mathcal{F}_N.$$

The relative position of $\mathrm{E}(\mathcal{C}_v)$ with respect to the lower bound of the interval $[\mathrm{E}(\min), \mathrm{E}(\max)]$ is called the conjunction degree or the degree of andness of $\mathcal{C}_v$. It represents the degree to which the average value of $\mathcal{C}_v$ is close to that of min.

Definition 7. The degree of andness of $\mathcal{C}_v$ is defined by

$$\text{andness}(\mathcal{C}_v) := \frac{\text{E(max)} - \text{E}(\mathcal{C}_v)}{\text{E(max)} - \text{E(min)}}.$$

Similarly, the relative position of $\text{E}(\mathcal{C}_v)$ with respect to E(max) is called the disjunction degree or the degree of orness of $\mathcal{C}_v$.

Definition 8. The degree of orness of $\mathcal{C}_v$, is defined by

$$\text{orness}(\mathcal{C}_v) := \frac{\text{E}(\mathcal{C}_v) - \text{E(min)}}{\text{E(max)} - \text{E(min)}}.$$

An immediate consequence of these definitions is that

$$\text{andness}(\mathcal{C}_v) + \text{orness}(\mathcal{C}_v) = 1.$$

Moreover, we have $\text{andness}(\mathcal{C}_v), \text{orness}(\mathcal{C}_v) \in [0, 1]$.

These two concepts have been introduced as early as 1974 by Dujmović [3,4] in the particular case of power means. Here we have adapted his definitions to the Choquet integral.

The degree of orness is a measure of the tolerance of the decision maker. Indeed, tolerant decision makers can accept that only *some* criteria are satisfied. This corresponds to a disjunctive behavior ($\text{orness}(\mathcal{C}_v) > 0.5$), whose extreme example is max. On the other hand, intolerant decision makers demand that *most* criteria are satisfied. This corresponds to a conjunctive behavior ($\text{orness}(\mathcal{C}_v) < 0.5$), whose extreme example is min. When $\text{orness}(\mathcal{C}_v) = 0.5$ the decision maker is medium (neither tolerant nor intolerant).

Using the identity

$$\int_{[0,1]^n} \bigwedge_{i \in S} x_i \, dx = \frac{1}{s+1}, \qquad S \subseteq N,$$

(see [9]) and the expression of $\mathcal{C}_v$ in terms of the Möbius representation, we have the following result.

Proposition 2. *For any $v \in \mathcal{F}_N$, we have*

$$\text{orness}(\mathcal{C}_v) = \frac{1}{n-1} \sum_{T \subseteq N} \frac{n-t}{t+1} a(T),$$

where a is the Möbius representation of v.

In terms of the fuzzy measure v the degree of orness takes the following form, see [11].

Proposition 3. *For any $v \in \mathcal{F}_N$, we have*

$$\text{orness}(\mathcal{C}_v) = \frac{1}{n-1} \sum_{T \subsetneq N} \frac{(n-t)!\, t!}{n!}\, v(T),$$

that is,

$$\text{orness}(\mathcal{C}_v) = \frac{1}{n-1} \sum_{t=1}^{n-1} \frac{1}{\binom{n}{t}} \sum_{\substack{T \subsetneq N \\ |T|=t}} v(T). \tag{7}$$

Corollary 1. *Let $v \in \mathcal{F}_N$. Then*

$$\text{orness}(\mathcal{C}_v) = 0 \;\Leftrightarrow\; \mathcal{C}_v = \min$$
$$\text{orness}(\mathcal{C}_v) = 1 \;\Leftrightarrow\; \mathcal{C}_v = \max$$

The concept of orness was defined independently by Yager [25] in the particular case of OWA operators, see also Yager [26]. His definition is based on the use of the so-called regular increasing monotone quantifiers, that is, increasing functions $Q : [0,1] \to [0,1]$, with $Q(0) = 0$ and $Q(1) = 1$, which represent linguistic quantifiers such as *all*, *most*, *many*, *at least k*. For any $k \in N$, $Q(k/n)$ indicates the lowest global evaluation of an alternative that fully satisfies k criteria:

$$Q(k/n) = \text{OWA}_\omega\big(e_{\{1,\dots,k\}}\big) = \sum_{i=1}^{k} \omega_{n-i+1}.$$

Yager then defined

$$\text{orness}(\text{OWA}_\omega) = \frac{1}{n-1} \sum_{k=1}^{n-1} Q(k/n) = \frac{1}{n-1} \sum_{k=1}^{n} (k-1)\, \omega_k.$$

These definitions can be adapted to the more general case of the Choquet integrals. The average value of the lowest global evaluation over all the alternatives that fully satisfy k criteria is given by

$$Q(k/n) = \frac{1}{\binom{n}{k}} \sum_{\substack{K \subseteq N \\ |K|=k}} \mathcal{C}_v(e_K), \qquad k \in N.$$

The orness of $\mathcal{C}_v$ can then be defined by

$$\text{orness}(\mathcal{C}_v) = \frac{1}{n-1} \sum_{k=1}^{n-1} Q(k/n),$$

and we retrieve (7).

Choquet integral $\mathcal{C}_v$	andness$(\mathcal{C}_v)$	orness$(\mathcal{C}_v)$
WAM$_\omega$	$\dfrac{1}{2}$	$\dfrac{1}{2}$
OWA$_\omega$	$\dfrac{1}{n-1}\displaystyle\sum_{i=1}^{n}(n-i)\,\omega_i$	$\dfrac{1}{n-1}\displaystyle\sum_{i=1}^{n}(i-1)\,\omega_i$
OS$_k$	$\dfrac{n-k}{n-1}$	$\dfrac{k-1}{n-1}$
min$_T$	$\dfrac{n\,t-1}{(n-1)(t+1)}$	$\dfrac{n-t}{(n-1)(t+1)}$
max$_T$	$\dfrac{n-t}{(n-1)(t+1)}$	$\dfrac{n\,t-1}{(n-1)(t+1)}$

Table 4. Degrees of andness and orness for various Choquet integrals

Table 4 gives the degrees of andness and orness for particular Choquet integrals.

It can also be interesting to appraise the dispersion of $\mathcal{C}_v$ around its average value by calculating its variance, that is,

$$\sigma^2(\mathcal{C}_v) = \int_{[0,1]^n} \left[\mathcal{C}_v(x) - \mathrm{E}(\mathcal{C}_v)\right]^2 dx.$$

In terms of the Möbius representation, this expression is written

$$\sigma^2(\mathcal{C}_v) = \sum_{S,T\subseteq N} a(S)\,a(T) \frac{s+t-|S\cup T|}{(s+1)(t+1)(|S\cup T|+2)}.$$

For example,

$$\sigma^2(\mathrm{WAM}_\omega) = \frac{1}{12}\sum_{i=1}^{n}\omega_i^2,$$

$$\sigma^2(\mathrm{min}_T) = \frac{t}{(t+1)^2\,(t+2)},$$

$$\sigma^2(\mathrm{max}_T) = \frac{t}{(t+1)^2\,(t+2)}.$$

7 Veto and favor effects

An interesting behavioral phenomenon in aggregation is the veto effect, and its counterpart, the favor effect. A criterion $k \in N$ is said to be a *veto* or a *blocker* for C_v if its non satisfaction entails necessarily a low global score. Formally, k is a veto for C_v if

$$C_v(x) \leq x_k, \qquad x \in [0,1]^n. \tag{8}$$

Similarly, the criterion k is a *favor* or a *pusher* for C_v if its satisfaction entails necessarily a high global score:

$$C_v(x) \geq x_k, \qquad x \in [0,1]^n. \tag{9}$$

The concepts of veto and favor were already proposed by Dubois and Koning [2] in the context of social choice functions, where "favor" was called "dictator".

A consequence of the definition is that no aggregation operator can model simultaneously a veto on a criterion and a favor on another one. Indeed it is not possible to have

$$x_i \leq C_v(x) \leq x_j \quad \text{for all } x \in [0,1]^n.$$

Note that if the decision maker considers that a given criterion must absolutely be satisfied (veto criterion), then he/she is conjunctive oriented. Indeed, by (8) we have orness$(C_v) \leq 0.5$, which is sufficient. Similarly, if the decision maker considers that a given criterion is sufficient to be satisfied (favor criteria) then he/she is disjunctive oriented. By (9) we have orness$(C_v) \geq 0.5$.

The following two results can be easily proved [11].

Proposition 4. *Let $k \in N$ and $v \in \mathcal{F}_N$. Then the following assertions are equivalent:*
i) k is a veto for C_v
ii) $v(T) = 0$ whenever $T \not\ni k$ (or, equivalently, $v(N \setminus k) = 0$)
iii) $\exists \lambda \in [0,1[$ such that $\forall x \in [0,1]^n$, with $x_k \leq \lambda$, we have $C_v(x) \leq \lambda$

Proposition 5. *Let $k \in N$ and $v \in \mathcal{F}_N$. Then the following assertions are equivalent:*
i) k is a favor for C_v
ii) $v(T) = 1$ whenever $T \ni k$ (or, equivalently, $v(k) = 1$)
iii) $\exists \lambda \in]0,1]$ such that $\forall x \in [0,1]^n$, with $x_k \geq \lambda$, we have $C_v(x) \geq \lambda$

It seems reasonable to define indices that measure the degree of veto or favor of a given criterion. A natural definition of a degree of veto (resp. favor) consists in considering the probability

$$\Pr[C_v(x) \leq x_k] \qquad (\text{resp. } \Pr[C_v(x) \geq x_k])$$

where $x \in [0,1]^n$ is a multi-dimensional random variable uniformly distributed. Unfortunately, such an index does not depend always continuously on v. For example, one can easily show [11] that

$$\Pr[\mathrm{WAM}_\omega(x) \le x_k] = \begin{cases} 1, & \text{if } \omega_k = 1, \\ 1/2, & \text{otherwise.} \end{cases}$$

As for power and interaction indices, we search for veto and favor indices which are linear with respect to the fuzzy measure. In [11] the author introduced the following indices, based on an axiomatic characterization:

$$\mathrm{veto}(\mathcal{C}_v, i) := 1 - \frac{1}{n-1} \sum_{T \subseteq N \setminus i} \frac{(n-t-1)!\,t!}{(n-1)!}\, v(T), \qquad i \in N,$$

$$\mathrm{favor}(\mathcal{C}_v, i) := \frac{1}{n-1} \sum_{T \subseteq N \setminus i} \frac{(n-t-1)!\,t!}{(n-1)!}\, v(T \cup i) - \frac{1}{n-1}, \qquad i \in N.$$

In terms of the Möbius representation of v, these indices are written:

$$\mathrm{veto}(\mathcal{C}_v, i) = 1 - \frac{n}{n-1} \sum_{T \subseteq N \setminus i} \frac{1}{t+1}\, a(T), \qquad i \in N,$$

$$\mathrm{favor}(\mathcal{C}_v, i) = \frac{n}{n-1} \sum_{T \subseteq N \setminus i} \frac{1}{t+1}\, [a(T \cup i) + a(T)] - \frac{1}{n-1}, \qquad i \in N,$$

The axiomatic that supports these indices is given in the following result.

Theorem 3. *The numbers $\psi(\mathcal{C}_v, i)$ $(i \in N, v \in \mathcal{F}_N)$:*

- *are linear w.r.t. the fuzzy measure, that is, there exist real constants p_T^i $(T \subseteq N)$ such that*

$$\psi(\mathcal{C}_v, i) = \sum_{T \subseteq N} p_T^i\, v(T), \qquad i \in N, v \in \mathcal{F}_N.$$

- *are symmetric, that is, for any permutation π on N, we have*

$$\psi(\mathcal{C}_v, i) = \psi(\mathcal{C}_{\pi v}, \pi(i)), \qquad i \in N, v \in \mathcal{F}_N.$$

- *fulfill the "boundary" axiom, that is, for any $T \subseteq N$, $T \ne \emptyset$, and any $i \in T$, we have*

$$\psi(\min_T, i) = 1, \quad (\textit{resp. } \psi(\max_T, i) = 1)$$

- *fulfill the "normalization" axiom, that is, for any $v \in \mathcal{F}_N$,*

$$\psi(\mathcal{C}_v, i) = \psi(\mathcal{C}_v, j) \quad \forall i, j \in N$$

$$\Downarrow$$

$$\psi(\mathcal{C}_v, i) = \mathrm{andness}(\mathcal{C}_v) \quad (\textit{resp. } \mathrm{orness}(\mathcal{C}_v)) \quad \forall i \in N.$$

if and only if $\psi(\mathcal{C}_v, i) = \text{veto}(\mathcal{C}_v, i)$ *(resp.* $\text{favor}(\mathcal{C}_v, i)$*) for all* $i \in N$ *and all* $v \in \mathcal{F}_N$.

Let us comment on the axioms presented in this characterization. As for the importance indices, we ask the veto and favor indices to be linear w.r.t. the fuzzy measure and symmetric. Next, the boundary axiom is motivated by the observation that any $i \in T$ is a veto (resp. favor) criterion for $\min_T$ (resp. $\max_T$). Finally, the normalization axiom says that if the degree of veto (resp. favor) does not depend on criteria, then it identifies with the degree of intolerance (resp. tolerance) of the decision maker.

It is easy to observe that $\text{veto}(\mathcal{C}_v, i), \text{favor}(\mathcal{C}_v, i) \in [0, 1]$. Furthermore, we have, for any $v \in \mathcal{F}_N$,

$$\frac{1}{n} \sum_{i=1}^{n} \text{veto}(\mathcal{C}_v, i) = \text{andness}(\mathcal{C}_v),$$

$$\frac{1}{n} \sum_{i=1}^{n} \text{favor}(\mathcal{C}_v, i) = \text{orness}(\mathcal{C}_v),$$

$$\text{veto}(\mathcal{C}_v, i) + \text{favor}(\mathcal{C}_v, i) = 1 + \frac{n\,\phi(v, i) - 1}{n - 1}, \qquad i \in N.$$

Thus defined, we see that $\text{veto}(\mathcal{C}_v, i)$ is more or less the degree to which the decision maker demands that criterion i is satisfied. Similarly, $\text{favor}(\mathcal{C}_v, i)$ is the degree to which the decision maker considers that a good score along criterion i is sufficient to be satisfied.

Table 5 gives the veto and favor indices for particular Choquet integrals.

8 Measure of dispersion

Consider the weighted arithmetic mean (WAM) as an aggregation operator. It is clear that, in such an aggregation process, the use of the information contained in the arguments $x_1, \ldots, x_n$ strongly depends upon the weight vector ω. For example, consider two weighted arithmetic means with weights vectors of the form

$$(1, 0, \ldots, 0) \quad \text{and} \quad (1/n, \ldots, 1/n),$$

respectively. We note that these operators are quite different in the sense that the first one focuses the total weight on only one argument (projection on the first argument) whereas the second one distributes the total weight among all the arguments evenly (arithmetic mean).

In order to capture this idea, one can define a *measure of dispersion* associated to the weight vector of the weighted arithmetic mean WAM_ω as the Shannon entropy of ω, see [20,21]:

$$H_n(\omega) = -\sum_{i=1}^{n} \omega_i \log_2 \omega_i.$$

Choquet integral $\mathcal{C}_v$	veto$(\mathcal{C}_v, i)$	favor$(\mathcal{C}_v, i)$
WAM$_\omega$	$\dfrac{1}{2} + \dfrac{n(\omega_i - 1/n)}{2(n-1)}$	$\dfrac{1}{2} + \dfrac{n(\omega_i - 1/n)}{2(n-1)}$
OWA$_\omega$	$\dfrac{1}{n-1} \displaystyle\sum_{j=1}^{n} (n-j)\,\omega_j$	$\dfrac{1}{n-1} \displaystyle\sum_{j=1}^{n} (j-1)\,\omega_j$
OS$_k$	$\dfrac{n-k}{n-1}$	$\dfrac{k-1}{n-1}$
min$_T$	$\begin{cases} 1 & \text{if } i \in T \\ \dfrac{nt-t-1}{(n-1)(t+1)} & \text{otherwise} \end{cases}$	$\begin{cases} \dfrac{n-t}{(n-1)t} & \text{if } i \in T \\ \dfrac{n-t-1}{(n-1)(t+1)} & \text{otherwise} \end{cases}$
max$_T$	$\begin{cases} \dfrac{n-t}{(n-1)t} & \text{if } i \in T \\ \dfrac{n-t-1}{(n-1)(t+1)} & \text{otherwise} \end{cases}$	$\begin{cases} 1 & \text{if } i \in T \\ \dfrac{nt-t-1}{(n-1)(t+1)} & \text{otherwise} \end{cases}$

Table 5. Veto and favor indices for various Choquet integrals

Such a function enables us to measure how much of the information in the arguments is really used. In a certain sense the more disperse the ω the more the information contained in the arguments is being used in the aggregation process.

Now, consider the ordered weighted averaging operator (OWA). For this aggregation operator, the measure of dispersion, which should not depend on a reordering of the arguments, should also be given by the Shannon entropy. In fact, Yager [25] proposed explicitly to use this concept as measure of dispersion for the OWA operators.

It is known that $H_n(\omega)$ is maximum only when ω corresponds to the weight vector of the arithmetic mean, see e.g. [24]:

$$H_n(\omega) = \log_2 n \quad \text{for } \omega = (1/n, \ldots, 1/n),$$

and minimum only when ω is a binary vector:

$$H_n(\omega) = 0 \quad \text{if } \omega_i = 1 \text{ for some } i \in N.$$

Thus, the measure of dispersion can be normalized into

$$\text{disp}(\omega) = \frac{1}{\log_2 n} H_n(\omega) = -\sum_{i=1}^{n} \omega_i \log_n \omega_i,$$

so that it ranges in $[0, 1]$.

The author [11, §6.2.4] proposed to define the entropy of a fuzzy measure $v \in \mathcal{F}_N$ as a measure of dispersion for the Choquet integral $\mathcal{C}_v$. This measure should identify with the Shannon entropy when the Choquet integral is either a WAM or an OWA.

On the one hand, comparing

$$\text{OWA}_\omega(x) = \sum_{i=1}^{n} x_{(i)} \, \omega_i$$

and

$$\mathcal{C}_v(x) = \sum_{i=1}^{n} x_{(i)} \left[v(A_{(i)}) - v(A_{(i+1)}) \right]$$

suggests proposing as measure of dispersion for $\mathcal{C}_v$ a sum over $i \in N$ of an average value of

$$[v(T \cup i) - v(T)] \log_n [v(T \cup i) - v(T)], \qquad T \subseteq N \setminus i,$$

that is, an expression of the form

$$\text{disp}(v) = - \sum_{i=1}^{n} \sum_{T \subseteq N \setminus i} p_t \left[v(T \cup i) - v(T) \right] \log_n [v(T \cup i) - v(T)],$$

where the coefficients p_t are non-negative and such that $\sum_{T \subseteq N \setminus i} p_t = 1$.

On the other hand, imposing the condition

$$\mathcal{C}_v = \text{OWA}_\omega \quad \Rightarrow \quad \text{disp}(v) = \text{disp}(\omega)$$

determines uniquely the coefficients p_t, so that the definition proposed is the following.

Definition 9. The entropy of a fuzzy measure $v \in \mathcal{F}_N$ is defined by

$$\text{disp}(v) := - \sum_{i=1}^{n} \sum_{T \subseteq N \setminus i} \frac{(n-t-1)! \, t!}{n!} \left[v(T \cup i) - v(T) \right] \log_n [v(T \cup i) - v(T)].$$

When the Choquet integral $\mathcal{C}_v$ is used as an aggregation operator, this entropy can be interpreted as the degree to which one uses all the information contained in the arguments $x = (x_1, \ldots, x_n)$ when calculating the aggregated value $\mathcal{C}_v(x)$.

Interestingly enough, its expression (which is of course non linear w.r.t. v) is very similar to that of the Shapley value (1). Notice also that this new definition has yet to be axiomatically characterized. However, to justify its use, one can show that it fulfills several properties required for an entropy [11], namely:

- $\operatorname{disp}(v)$ is *continuous* w.r.t. v.
- disp is *symmetric*, that is

$$\operatorname{disp}(\pi v) = \operatorname{disp}(v)$$

for any permutation π of N.

- We have

$$0 \leq \operatorname{disp}(v) \leq 1.$$

Moreover, $\operatorname{disp}(v)$ is maximum $(= 1)$ only when $\mathcal{C}_v$ is the arithmetic mean, and minimum $(= 0)$ only when v is a binary-valued fuzzy measure: $v(S) \in \{0,1\}$ for all $S \subseteq N$. Note that this latter case occurs if and only if $\mathcal{C}_v(x) \in \{x_1,\ldots,x_n\}$ (only one piece of information is used in the aggregation).

- We have

$$\mathcal{C}_v = \operatorname{WAM}_\omega \text{ or } \operatorname{OWA}_\omega \quad \Rightarrow \quad \operatorname{disp}(v) = \operatorname{disp}(\omega).$$

- Let $k \in N$ be a *null* element for v, that is, $v(T \cup k) = v(T)$ for all $T \subseteq N \setminus k$. Then

$$\operatorname{disp}(v) = \operatorname{disp}(v^{N \setminus k})$$

where $v^{N \setminus k}$ is the restriction of v to $N \setminus k$.

Fuzzy measure v	$\operatorname{disp}(v)$
$v_{\operatorname{WAM}_\omega}$	$-\sum_{i=1}^{n} \omega_i \log_n \omega_i$
$v_{\operatorname{OWA}_\omega}$	$-\sum_{i=1}^{n} \omega_i \log_n \omega_i$
v_{OS_k}	0
$v_{\min_T}$	0
$v_{\max_T}$	0

Table 6. Entropy of various fuzzy measures

Table 6 gives the entropy of fuzzy measures corresponding to particular Choquet integrals.

9 An illustrative example

In this final section we give an example, borrowed from Grabisch [6]. Let us consider the problem of evaluating students in a high school with respect to three subjects: mathematics (M), physics (P), and literature (L). Usually, this is done by a simple weighted arithmetic mean, whose weights are the coefficients of importance of the different subjects. Suppose that the school is more scientifically than literary oriented, so that weights could be for example 3, 3, and 2, respectively. Then the weighted arithmetic mean will give the following results for three students a, b, and c (marks are given on a scale from 0 to 20):

Student	M P L	Global evaluation (weighted arithmetic mean)
a	18 16 10	15.25
b	10 12 18	12.75
c	14 15 15	14.625

If the school wants to favor well equilibrated students without weak points then student c should be considered better than student a, who has a severe weakness in literature. Unfortunately, no weight vector $(\omega_M, \omega_P, \omega_L)$ satisfying $\omega_M = \omega_P > \omega_L$ is able to favor student c. Indeed, we have:

$$c \succ a \quad \Longleftrightarrow \quad \omega_L > \omega_M.$$

The reason of this problem is that too much importance is given to mathematics and physics, which present some overlap effect since, usually, students good at mathematics are also good at physics (and vice versa), so that the evaluation is overestimated (resp. underestimated) for students good (resp. bad) at mathematics and/or physics. This problem can be solved by using a suitable fuzzy measure v and the Choquet integral.

- Since scientific subjects are more important than literature, the following weights can be put on subjects taken individually: $v(M) = v(P) = 0.45$ and $v(L) = 0.3$. Note that the initial ratio of weights $(3, 3, 2)$ is kept unchanged.
- Since mathematics and physics overlap, the weights attributed to the pair $\{M, P\}$ should be less than the sum of the weights of mathematics and physics: $v(MP) = 0.5$.
- Since students equally good at scientific subjects and literature must be favored, the weight attributed to the pair $\{L, M\}$ should be greater than the sum of individual weights (the same for physics and literature): $v(ML) = v(PL) = 0.9$.
- $v(\emptyset) = 0$ and $v(MPL) = 1$ by definition.

The Möbius representation is then given by

$$a(\emptyset) = 0 \quad a(M) = 0.45 \quad a(MP) = -0.40 \quad a(MPL) = -0.10$$
$$a(P) = 0.45 \quad a(ML) = 0.15$$
$$a(L) = 0.30 \quad a(PL) = 0.15$$

Applying Choquet integral with the above fuzzy measure leads to the following new global evaluations:

Student	M	P	L	Global evaluation (Choquet integral)
a	18	16	10	13.9
b	10	12	18	13.6
c	14	15	15	14.6

The expected result is then obtained. Also remark that student b has still the lowest rank, as requested by the scientific tendency of this high school.

Now, let us turn to a deeper analysis of the orientation of the school or its director. From the fuzzy measure proposed, we obtain the following Shapley value and degrees of veto and favor:

	M	P	L
$veto(\mathcal{C}_v, i)$	0.362	0.362	0.525
$favor(\mathcal{C}_v, i)$	0.575	0.575	0.6
$\phi(v, i)$	0.292	0.292	0.417
$n * \phi(v, i)$	0.875	0.875	1.25

As we can see, it is convenient to scale the Shapley value by a factor n, so that an importance index greater than 1 indicates an attribute more important than the average. Moreover, looking at the veto and favor degrees, we observe that the school seems to favor slightly the students (disjunctive oriented). This is in accordance with the degree of orness

$$orness(\mathcal{C}_v) = 0.583.$$

We also have $E(\mathcal{C}_v) = 0.542$ and $\sigma(\mathcal{C}_v) = 0.180$, showing that the global evaluation is rather dispersed around its typical value 0.542.

Now, the interaction indices for the pairs of criteria are:

	P	L
M	-0.45	0.10
P		0.10

Moreover, the influence indices are:

	P	L
M	0.60	0.725
P		0.725

All these numerical values are also in accordance with the interpretation of the fuzzy measure.

Finally, the dispersion of the fuzzy measure is given by $\text{disp}(v) = 0.820$, which is rather satisfactory.

Remark that all these behavioral parameters have been obtained from a given fuzzy measure. In many practical situations, the fuzzy measure is not completely available. We might then fix its values from information on behavioral parameters, see [14].

References

1. Choquet G. (1953) Theory of capacities. Annales de l'Institut Fourier **5**, 131–295
2. Dubois D., Koning J.-L. (1991) Social choice axioms for fuzzy set aggregation. Fuzzy Sets and Systems **43**, 257–274
3. Dujmović J.J. (1974) Weighted conjunctive and disjunctive means and their application in system evaluation. Univ. Beograd. Publ. Elektrotechn. Fak., 147–158
4. Dujmović J.J. (1975) Extended continuous logic and the theory of complex criteria. Univ. Beograd. Publ. Elektrotechn. Fak., 197–216
5. Grabisch M. (1995) On equivalence classes of fuzzy connectives : the case of fuzzy integrals. IEEE Trans. Fuzzy Systems **3** (1), 96–109
6. Grabisch M. (1996) The application of fuzzy integrals in multicriteria decision making. European Journal of Operational Research **89**, 445-456
7. Grabisch M. (1997) Alternative representations of OWA operators. In: The Ordered Weighted Averaging Operators: Theory and Applications, R.R. Yager and J. Kacprzyk (eds). Kluwer Academic Publisher, 73–85
8. Grabisch M. (1997) k-order additive discrete fuzzy measures and their representation. Fuzzy Sets and Systems **92**, 167–189
9. Grabisch M., Marichal J.-L., Roubens M. (2000) Equivalent representations of set functions. Mathematics of Operations Research, to appear
10. Grabisch M., Roubens M. (1999) An axiomatic approach to the concept of interaction among players in cooperative games. Int. J. of Game Theory, to appear
11. Marichal J.-L. (1998) Aggregation operators for multicriteria decision aid. Ph.D. Thesis, University of Liège, Liège, Belgium
12. Marichal J.-L. (1999) Aggregation of interacting criteria by means of the discrete Choquet integral. Preprint 9910, GEMME, Faculty of Economics, University of Liège, Liège, Belgium
13. Marichal J.-L. (1999) The influence of variables on pseudo-Boolean functions with applications to game theory and multicriteria decision making. Preprint 9916, GEMME, Faculty of Economics, University of Liège, Liège, Belgium
14. Marichal J.-L., Roubens M. (1999) Determination of weights of interacting criteria from a reference set. European Journal of Operational Research, to appear
15. Murofushi T. (1992) A technique for reading fuzzy measures (I): the Shapley value with respect to a fuzzy measure. In: 2nd Fuzzy Workshop, Nagaoka, Japan, October 1992, 39–48. In Japanese

16. Murofushi T., Soneda S. (1993) Techniques for reading fuzzy measures (III): interaction index. In: 9th Fuzzy System Symposium, Sapporo, Japan, May 1993, 693–696. In Japanese

17. Murofushi T., Sugeno M. (1989) An interpretation of fuzzy measure and the Choquet integral as an integral with respect to a fuzzy measure. Fuzzy Sets and Systems **29**, 201–227

18. Murofushi T., Sugeno M. (1991) A theory of fuzzy measures. Representation, the Choquet integral and null sets. Journal of Mathematical Analysis and Applications 159/2, 532–549

19. Rota G.C. (1964) On the foundations of combinatorial theory I. Theory of Möbius functions. Zeitschrift für Wahrscheinlichkeitstheorie und Verwandte Gebiete **2**, 340–368

20. Shannon C.E. (1948) A mathematical theory of communication. Bell System Tech. J. **27**, 379–423, 623–656

21. Shannon C.E., Weaver W. (1949) A mathematical theory of communication. University of Illinois Press, Urbana

22. Shapley L.S. (1953) A value for n-person games. In: H.W. Kuhn and A.W. Tucker (eds). Contributions to the Theory of Games, Vol. II, Annals of Mathematics Studies, 28. Princeton University Press, Princeton, NJ, 307–317

23. Sugeno M. (1974) Theory of fuzzy integrals and its applications. Ph.D. Thesis, Tokyo Institute of Technology, Tokyo

24. Yager R.R. (1983) Entropy and specificity in a mathematical theory of evidence. Int. J. Gen. Systems **9**, 249–260

25. Yager R.R. (1988) On ordered weighted averaging aggregation operators in multicriteria decision making. IEEE Trans. on Systems, Man and Cybernetics **18**, 183–190

26. Yager R.R. (1996) Quantifier guided aggregation using OWA operators. Int. J. Intelligent Systems **11**, 49–73

To be Symmetric or Asymmetric?
A Dilemma in Decision Making

D81

Michel Grabisch and Christophe Labreuche

Thomson-CSF, Corporate Research Laboratory
Domaine de Corbeville, 91404 Orsay Cedex, France
E-mail: {grabisch,labreuche}@lcr.thomson-csf.com

Summary. The paper addresses the problem of dealing with real numbers for scores or utilities in decision making, that is, with numbers being positive or negative. The use of non-additive models, as the Choquet integral, entails the possibility of having (at least) two choices when defining the Choquet integral for real-valued integrand, which can be named, after Denneberg, symmetric or asymmetric. The problem is examined in the frameworks of multicriteria decision making and decision under risk and uncertainty.

1   Introduction

So far in multicriteria decision making, scores on criteria, considered most often as satisfaction degrees, i.e. membership degrees to the (fuzzy) set of satisfactory acts, have been positive real numbers in $[0, 1]$ (see e.g. [2]). However, some authors have advocated the use of larger sets to represent the satisfaction degrees, including negative numbers. This is in fact not uncommon in multiattribute utility theory [14], positive utilities representing *gains*, and negative utilities *losses*, although the terms "loss" and "gain" refer more to lotteries and similar devices common in decision under risk and uncertainty.

More in the spirit of multicriteria decision making, as psychologists do, we can define three types of scales for representing scores on criteria.

- the $[0, 1]$ scale, where 0 means the total absence of a property, and 1 the total presence, called *bounded unipolar* scale (and the corresponding criterion *bounded unipolar criterion*). It is suitable for representing the membership degree in fuzzy sets, the credibility, the satisfaction degree, etc.
- the set of positive real numbers $\mathbb{R}^+$. This means that it is always possible to find an act with a better utility. Such scales are called *unipolar*, and are convenient to represent priority, importance, etc.
- the set of real numbers $\mathbb{R}$. The value "0" has then a special role, and represents a kind of neutrality. In this type of scale, it is always possible to find (or imagine) a better act or a worse act than a given one. This type of scale is called *bipolar*, and is convenient to represent concepts which can be paired, such as attractivity/repulsion, etc.

In this paper, we focus on bipolar criteria, and the question arises, if there is some special treatment for the negative numbers. More specifically:

- On a mathematical point of view, how do usual methods generalize when negative numbers enter the picture?
- On a descriptive point of view, how react human decision makers when scores are negative, i.e. how do they evaluate acts which are less satisfactory than a given neutral level?

The first question may be of little interest when simple models are used, as the commonly used weighted average. Therefore, we focus in this paper on fuzzy integrals models, especially the Choquet integral, as it has been shown that these models are much more powerful and flexible to represent human behaviour [7,11].

It is commonly admitted by psychologists that the answer to the second question is that the behaviour is clearly different, we could say, symmetric. This entails that models used should reflect this symmetry.

In a second part, we will deal with decision under risk and uncertainty. In this area, Cumulative Prospect Theory (CPT) has been established [13,23] to deal with negative utilities. We will show underlying axioms in this theory, and compare them to their counterparts in multicriteria decision making.

2 Background

We give here basic definitions and results useful in the sequel. We consider a finite universal set $X = \{1, \dots, n\}$, which could be the (index) set of criteria, experts, states of the world, etc.

Definition 1. A *fuzzy measure* [21] or *capacity* [3] on X is a set function $\mu : \mathcal{P}(X) \longrightarrow [0,1]$ such that:

(i) $\mu(\emptyset) = 0$, $\mu(X) = 1$
(ii) $\mu(A) \leq \mu(B)$ whenever $A \subset B \subset X$.

For any fuzzy measure μ, the *conjugate fuzzy measure* of μ is defined by

$$\bar{\mu}(A) := \mu(X) - \mu(A^c), \quad \forall A \subset X, \tag{1}$$

where A^c is the complement set of A.

Some linear transformations of set functions are useful here, namely the Möbius transform, well-known in combinatorics [17], and the interaction transform [8].

Definition 2. Let μ be a fuzzy measure. The *Möbius transform* of μ is given by:

$$m^\mu(A) := \sum_{B \subset A} (-1)^{|A| - |B|} \mu(B), \quad \forall A \subset X.$$

The *interaction transform* is given by:

$$I^\mu(A) := \sum_{B \subset X \setminus A} \frac{(n - |B| - |A|)!|B|!}{(n - |A| + 1)!} \sum_{C \subset A} (-1)^{|A| - |C|} \mu(C \cup B), \forall A \subset X.$$

When possible, the superscripts μ will be omitted.

These transformations are invertible and can be composed (see [5,9] for a full presentation). For example, μ can be recovered from m^μ by:

$$\mu(A) = \sum_{B \subset A} m^\mu(B), \quad \forall A \subset X. \tag{2}$$

The interaction transform is a generalization of the Shapley value [20], and of the interaction index I_{ij} defined for a pair of elements i, j by Murofushi and Soneda [16]. The Shapley value of μ is the vector $\phi^\mu := [\phi_1^\mu \cdots \phi_n^\mu]$ defined by:

$$\phi_i^\mu := \sum_{K \subset X \setminus i} \frac{(n - |K| - 1)!|K|!}{n!} [\mu(K \cup \{i\}) - \mu(K)], \quad \forall i \in X. \tag{3}$$

The interaction index I_{ij} is defined by:

$$I_{ij}^\mu := \sum_{K \subset X \setminus \{i,j\}} \frac{(n - |K| - 2)!|K|!}{(n - 1)!} [\mu(K \cup \{i,j\}) - \mu(K \cup \{i\}) -$$

$$\mu(K \cup \{j\}) + \mu(K)], \quad \forall i, j \in X. \tag{4}$$

Clearly, $\phi_i^\mu = I^\mu(\{i\})$, and $I_{ij}^\mu = I^\mu(\{i,j\})$.

Since a model based on a fuzzy measure needs 2^n coefficients to be defined, simpler models can be envisaged [8], namely models based on k-additive measures.

Definition 3. A fuzzy measure is said to be a *k-additive measure* if $I(A) = 0$ for all coalitions of more than k criteria, and there exists at least one A of exactly k elements such that $I(A) \neq 0$.

An equivalent definition is obtained if I is replaced by m (the Möbius transform).

We introduce now integrals with respect to fuzzy measures. As we are in the finite case, we assimilate integrand functions (resp. positive integrand functions) with vectors in $\mathbb{R}^n$ (resp. $(\mathbb{R}^+)^n$).

Definition 4. Let μ be a fuzzy measure, and $x = (x_1, \ldots, x_n) \in (\mathbb{R}^+)^n$. The *Choquet integral* of x w.r.t μ is defined by:

$$C_\mu(x_1, \ldots, x_n) := \sum_{i=1}^n [x_{(i)} - x_{(i-1)}] \mu(X_{(i)}), \tag{5}$$

where $\cdot_{(i)}$ indicates a permutation on X so that $x_{(1)} \leq x_{(2)} \leq \cdots \leq x_{(n)}$, and $X_{(i)} := \{(i), \ldots, (n)\}$. Also $x_{(0)} := 0$.

The above definition is valid for positive integrands only. The question arises how to extend this definition to real-valued integrands, i.e. which may assume negative values. At least two solutions can be thought of:

$$C'_\mu(x) := C_\mu(x^+) - C_\mu(x^-), \quad \forall x \in \mathbb{R}^n$$
$$C''_\mu(x) := C_\mu(x^+) - C_{\bar\mu}(x^-), \quad \forall x \in \mathbb{R}^n$$

where x^+, x^- are respectively the positive and the negative parts of x, that is, $x^+ := (x_1^+, \ldots, x_n^+)$, $x^- := (x_1^-, \ldots, x_n^-)$, $x_i^+ := x_i \vee 0$, $x_i^- := -x_i \vee 0$.

These extensions are respectively named symmetric and asymmetric integrals by Denneberg [4]. The first one was in fact proposed by Šipoš [24], and the second one is the usual definition of the Choquet integral for real-valued functions. In the sequel, we will denote the Šipoš integral by $\check{S}_\mu$.

The properties of Choquet and Šipoš integrals have been studied in [10]. We give here some important results and properties. In the sequel, for any $a, b \in \mathbb{R}$, for any $A \subset X$, the notation (a_A, b_{A^c}) denotes a point x in $\mathbb{R}^n$ such that $x_i = a$ whenever $i \in A$ and $x_i = b$ otherwise.

Proposition 1. *Let $x \in \mathbb{R}^n$ and μ be a capacity, with Möbius transform m. The expressions of the Choquet and Šipoš integrals are given by:*

$$C_\mu(x) = x_{(1)} + \sum_{i=2}^{n}(x_{(i)} - x_{(i-1)})\mu(\{(i), \ldots, (n)\}) \tag{6}$$

$$\check{S}_\mu(x) = \sum_{i=1}^{p-1}(x_{(i)} - x_{(i+1)})\mu(\{(1), \ldots, (i)\}) + x_{(p)}\mu(\{(1), \ldots, (p)\})$$

$$+ x_{(p+1)}\mu(\{(p+1), \ldots, (n)\}) + \sum_{i=p+2}^{n}(x_{(i)} - x_{(i-1)})\mu(\{(i), \ldots, (n)\})$$

$$\tag{7}$$

$$C_\mu(x) = \sum_{A \subset X} m(A) \bigwedge_{i \in A} x_i \tag{8}$$

$$\check{S}_\mu(x) = \sum_{A \subset X} m(A) \left[\bigwedge_{i \in A} x_i^+ - \bigwedge_{i \in A} x_i^- \right]$$

$$= \sum_{A \subset X^+} m(A) \bigwedge_{i \in A} x_i + \sum_{A \subset X^-} m(A) \bigvee_{i \in A} x_i, \tag{9}$$

where $x_{(1)} \leq \cdots \leq x_{(p)} < 0 \leq x_{(p+1)} \leq \cdots \leq x_{(n)}$, $X^+ := \{i \in X | x_i \geq 0\}$ and $X^- = X \setminus X^+$.

Proposition 2. *Let $x \in \mathbb{R}^n$ and μ be a capacity. The Choquet and Šipoš integrals satisfy the following properties.*

(i) extension of the fuzzy measure

$$C_\mu(1_A, 0_{A^c}) = \check{S}_\mu(1_A, 0_{A^c}) = \mu(A), \forall A \subset X. \tag{10}$$

(ii) symmetry and asymmetry

$$\mathcal{C}_\mu(-x) = -\mathcal{C}_{\bar{\mu}}(x) \tag{11}$$

$$\check{S}_\mu(-x) = -\check{S}_\mu(x) \tag{12}$$

(iii) monotonicity

$$x_i \leq x_i', i = 1, \ldots, n \Rightarrow \mathcal{C}_\mu(x_1, \ldots, x_n) \leq \mathcal{C}_\mu(x_1', \ldots, x_n') \tag{13}$$

$$x_i \leq x_i', i = 1, \ldots, n \Rightarrow \check{S}_\mu(x_1, \ldots, x_n) \leq \check{S}_\mu(x_1', \ldots, x_n'). \tag{14}$$

(iv) invariance to positive affine transformations

$$\mathcal{C}_\mu(\alpha x_1 + \beta, \ldots, \alpha x_n + \beta) = \alpha \mathcal{C}_\mu(x_1, \ldots, x_n) + \beta, \quad \forall \alpha \geq 0, \forall \beta \in \mathbb{R}. \tag{15}$$

(v) homogeneity

$$\check{S}_\mu(\alpha x_1, \ldots, \alpha x_n) = \alpha \check{S}_\mu(x_1, \ldots, x_n), \forall \alpha \in \mathbb{R}. \tag{16}$$

Proposition 3. *[15, Theorem 6.1.1] Let us consider an aggregation operator $M_\mu : \mathbb{R}^n \longrightarrow \mathbb{R}$ defined with respect to a capacity μ. Then M_μ is the Choquet integral $\mathcal{C}_\mu$ for all capacities μ on X, if and only if M_μ satisfies the following properties:*

(i) M_μ is a linear function of μ, i.e. $M_\mu = \sum_{A \subset X} f_A \, \mu(A)$, where the f_A's are 2^n functions from $\mathbb{R}^n$ to $\mathbb{R}$.
(ii) M_μ is non decreasing in each place.
(iii) M_μ is invariant to positive affine transformations (see Proposition 2 (iv))
(iv) M_μ is an extension of μ (see Proposition 2 (i))

Proposition 4. *Let us consider an aggregation operator $M_\mu : \mathbb{R}^n \longrightarrow \mathbb{R}$ defined with respect to a capacity μ. Then M_μ is the Šipoš integral $\check{S}_\mu$ for all capacities μ on X, if and only if M_μ satisfies the following properties:*

(L) M_μ is a linear function of μ, i.e. $M_\mu = \sum_{A \subset X} f_A \, \mu(A)$, where the f_A's are 2^n functions from $\mathbb{R}^n$ to $\mathbb{R}$.
(In) M_μ is non decreasing in each place.
(H) M_μ is homogeneous (see Proposition 2 (v)).
(Sh) M_μ is invariant to positive shifts, i.e. $\forall x \in (\mathbb{R}^+)^n$, $\forall \alpha \geq 0$, $M_\mu(x + \alpha) = M_\mu(x) + \alpha$.
(Ind) M_μ satisfies independence between positive and negative parts, i.e. for any $a, b, c, d \in \mathbb{R}^n$, $a \geq 0, b \geq 0, c \leq 0, d \leq 0, \forall A \subset N$, we have

$$M_\mu(a_A, c_{A^c}) - M_\mu(a_A, d_{A^c}) = M_\mu(b_A, c_{A^c}) - M_\mu(b_A, d_{A^c})$$

(Ext) M_μ is an extension of μ.

The property (Ind) means that the difference $M_\mu(a_A, c_{A^c}) - M_\mu(a_A, d_{A^c})$ does not depend on a: positive scores and negative scores do not interact.

The above properties make clear the fundamental common points and discrepancies between the two integrals. The main difference lies in the treatment of negative vs. positive numbers. As remarked by Sugeno and Murofushi [22], if the scores a_i are on an interval scale, then the global score computed by the Choquet integral is also on an interval scale (i.e. relative position of the zero), and if the scores are on a ratio scale, then the global score computed by the Šipoš integral is on a ratio scale (absolute position of the zero). With the Choquet integral, the zero has no special meaning, hence formula (6) does not differentiate between negative and positive numbers. On the contrary, the Šipoš integral makes this difference, and the zero position acts as a mirror surface. Thus, the Šipoš integral makes the symmetry between positive and negative numbers, as observed by psychologists.

3   Decision with Multiple Criteria

We examine the use of Choquet and Šipoš integrals in multicriteria decision making. We present in a simplified way the framework, avoiding intricacies (see [10] for a complete construction). Let $N = \{1, \ldots, n\}$ be a set of criteria. Acts are denoted by points $x \in \mathbb{R}^n$, of which coordinates are the scores or utilities on each criterion for a given act (we suppose that utility scales have been built, and that commensurability issues have been solved, using suitable information from the decision maker).

Let us call any $A \subset N$ a *coalition* of criteria. We introduce the notion of importance of a coalition as follows.

Definition 5. Let $A \subset N$ be a coalition of criteria. The *importance* or *power* $\mu(A)$ of coalition A for a given decision maker is defined as the global evaluation of the fictitious act $(1_A, 0_{A^c})$, i.e. with $x_i = 1$ if $i \in A$ and 0 otherwise.

$$\mu(A) := u(1_A, 0_{A^c}), \quad \forall A \subset N,$$

where u denotes global utility.

Clearly, the importance of the empty coalition should be zero, and the importance of N should be maximum. Also, it is natural to require that the importance should be non decreasing when adding a new criterion in a coalition. In other words, we see that μ can be taken as a fuzzy measure.

An important consequence of this definition is that the global utility function u has to coincide with μ on all the vertices of $[0, 1]^n$, and so is an extension of μ on the whole unit hypercube. A study of the extension problem has been done in [10], based in pseudo-Boolean functions. It leads to the fact that the multilinear model, well-known in multiattribute utility theory [14], and the Choquet integral are natural extensions of the fuzzy measure, the former one lacking in fact useful properties, such as scale invariance, for multicriteria decision making. When the extension includes negative numbers, the Choquet integral splits into the usual Choquet integral and the Šipoš integral. In fact, this is not surprising looking at the characterization results of Choquet and Šipoš (Propositions 3 and 4), which contains the axiom of extension. This kind of link between the fuzzy measure and the global utility function has been brought into light by Marichal [15], and is the fundamental axiom in his result of characterization of Choquet integral.

Also, the previous results (see especially Proposition 2 (ii) and Propositions 3 and 4) show clearly the difference between Choquet and Šipoš integrals. The main fact is that the Choquet integral supposes an underlying interval scale (arbitrary zero), while the Šipoš integral supposes a ratio scale with a fixed zero. In multicriteria decision making using bipolar scales (that is, with positive and negative numbers), the meaning of the zero is that of a *neutral* satisfaction: the act is neither good nor bad on this criterion. It is commonly admitted that human decision makers have a different behaviour when faced to acts which are good or bad on a given criterion, which advocates the presence of a ratio scale instead of an interval scale.

The following example illustrates this.

Example 1. We consider a scientifically oriented school, and three subjects Maths, Physics and Literature. Let us suppose 2 students with the following marks:

Student	Maths	Physics	Literature
A	16	12	**
B	8	4	**

The following behaviour may be observed: since there is some redundancy between Maths and Physics in the sense that they require more or less the same kind of ability, a medium score in one of the two can be compensated by a good score in the other subject. Thus, we can give 15 or 16 to A (provided the literature is not too bad). But if both are bad as for B, due to the importance of scientific subjects, one should not be tolerant with such a student, and something like 4 or 5 should be given as global evaluation.

This example shows that tolerance is observed when scores are good, and intolerance when scores are bad, exhibiting a *symmetric* behaviour. Of course, the converse of this example may be built as well. We show in the sequel that the Šipoš integral can cope with this example, and not the Choquet integral. A clear explanation can be obtained by means of the interaction index and 2-additive measures.

The following can be shown [10].

Proposition 5. *Let $a \in \mathbb{R}^n$, and μ a 2-additive measure. Then*

$$\mathcal{C}_\mu(a) = \sum_{I_{ij}>0} (a_i \wedge a_j)I_{ij} + \sum_{I_{ij}<0} (a_i \vee a_j)|I_{ij}| + \sum_{i=1}^{n} a_i(\phi_i - \frac{1}{2}\sum_{j\neq i}|I_{ij}|)$$

$$\check{S}_\mu(a) = \sum_{i,j\in N^+, I_{ij}>0} (a_i \wedge a_j)I_{ij} + \sum_{i,j\in N^-, I_{ij}>0} (a_i \vee a_j)I_{ij}$$

$$+ \sum_{i,j\in N^+, I_{ij}<0} (a_i \vee a_j)|I_{ij}| + \sum_{i,j\in N^-, I_{ij}<0} (a_i \wedge a_j)|I_{ij}|$$

$$+ 2\sum_{i\in N^+} a_i \left[\sum_{j\in N^-, I_{ij}<0} |I_{ij}| \right] + 2\sum_{i\in N^-} a_i \left[\sum_{j\in N^+, I_{ij}<0} |I_{ij}| \right]$$

$$+ \sum_{i=1}^{n} a_i \left[\phi_i - \frac{1}{2}\sum_{j\neq i}|I_{ij}| \right].$$

with $N^+ = \{i \in N | a_i \geq 0\}$, and $N^- = N \setminus N^+$.

This leads to the following interpretation of the interactions in both integrals:

- a positive I_{ij} implies a conjunctive behavior between criteria i and j if the score for these two criteria is positive, and implies a disjunctive behavior if the score for the two criteria is negative. This implies that the decision maker changes his behavior when he considers positive or negative scores. By contrast, there is no change for the Choquet integral: positive interaction means a conjunctive behaviour.
- a negative I_{ij} implies a disjunctive behavior between criteria i and j if the score for these two criteria is positive, and implies a conjunctive behavior if the score for the two criteria is negative. Again, there is no change with the Choquet integral, which remains disjunctive.
- The Shapley indices appear in the linear part of the sum, in both integrals.
- for the Šipoš integral, there is no comparison of scores (by $\wedge$ or $\vee$) when one score is positive an the other negative. This is linked with property (Ind) in Proposition 4, and shows clearly the dichotomy of the scale.

We continue our preceding example by applying practically the Choquet and Šipoš integrals.

Example 2. (example 1 continued) we suppose as before that scientific subjects are more important, and that there is some redundancy between mathematics and physics. Moreover, we assume that literature has no interaction with scientific subjects. The following fuzzy measure could model this (fuzzy measure form and interaction form are given, $\mu(N) = 1$ assumed).

subset A	$\mu(A)$	subset A	$\mu(A)$
Maths	0.6	Maths, Physics	0.7
Physics	0.6	Maths, Literature	0.9
Literature	0.3	Physics, Literature	0.9

subset A	$I(A)$	subset A	$I(A)$
Maths	0.35	Maths, Physics	-0.5
Physics	0.35	Maths, Literature	0
Literature	0.3	Physics, Literature	0

Let us suppose the three students A, B, C, with following marks. We indicate in the table the result of global evaluation by the Choquet and Šipoš integrals, considering that the zero of the scale corresponds to 10 (i.e. the scale has been shifted of -10).

student	Maths	Physics	Literature	Choquet integral	Šipoš integral
A	16	12	10	13.8	13.8
B	8	4	10	8.2	6.2
C	6	6	10	7.2	7.2

Let us consider first A and B. As expected in example 1, the Choquet integral considers in both cases that Maths and Physics are disjunctive, while the Šipoš integral has a conjunctive behaviour with B (negative scores). Remark that both coincide for A since scores are positive, and since A and B have symmetric scores with respect to 10, we can verify the property $\check{S}_\mu(-a) = -\check{S}_\mu(a)$.

Student C illustrates the fact that for Choquet integral, B is preferred to C since B has at least a not too bad score in Maths, which compensates the very bad score in Physics, and for the Šipoš integral, C is better than B because the bad score in Physics cannot be compensated.

4 Decision under Uncertainty and Risk: Cumulative Prospect Theory

We turn to a different framework, which is decision under risk and uncertainty. We begin by decision under uncertainty.

Let $S = \{1, \ldots, n\}$, $n \geq 3$ be the set of states of nature. We consider acts as mappings $f : S \longrightarrow \mathbb{R}$, identifying the set of acts with $\mathbb{R}^n$. We denote for simplicity $f(i)$ by f_i, so that act f is denoted $(f_1, \ldots, f_n)$. Acts may take positive values (then we speak of *gains*) or negative values (*losses*), while the value 0 is considered as the *statu quo* (this is the standard vocabulary of prospect theory [13]). Every act can be divided between the "gain" part, denoted f^+, and the "loss" part, denoted f^-, so that $f = f^+ - f^-$ (in fact, the usual convention is $f = f^+ + f^-$, but we have to remain consistent with section 2).

The fundamental question in decision theory is to represent the preference relation $\succeq$ on the set of acts, given by the decision maker, by some functional $V : \mathbb{R}^n \longrightarrow \mathbb{R}$, i.e. $f \succeq g \Leftrightarrow V(f) \geq V(g)$. Such a V is called a *representing function*.

The most common model for V is *subjective expected utility* (SEU), which is of the form:

$$V(f) = \sum_{i=1}^{n} p_i \cdot U(f_i) \tag{17}$$

where $U : \mathbb{R} \longrightarrow \mathbb{R}$ is the *utility function*, considered here to be strictly increasing, continuous, and unique up to a positive linear transformation (i.e. it defines an interval scale). The quantities p_i, $i = 1, \ldots, n$ define a probability measure. The first axiomatization of this model was given by Savage [18].

A second model is the *Choquet expected utility* (CEU) model, which is:

$$V(f) = \sum_{i=1}^{n} \pi_i \cdot U(f_{(i)}) \tag{18}$$

with decision weights $\pi_i = \mu(\{(i), \ldots, (n)\}) - \mu(\{(i+1), \ldots, (n)\})$, and $f_{(1)} \leq \cdots \leq f_{(n)}$, as already used in section 2. μ is a fuzzy measure on S. CEU has been first axiomatized by Schmeidler [19].

The next model comes from in *Cumulative Prospect Theory* (CPT), as introduced by Tversky and Kahneman [23]. The representing function is defined as:

$$V(f) = \sum_{i=1}^{p} \pi_i^+ \cdot U(f_{(i)}) + \sum_{i=p+1}^{n} \pi_i^- \cdot U(f_{(i)}) \tag{19}$$

with $f_{(1)} \leq \cdots \leq f_{(p)} < 0 \leq f_{(p+1)} \leq \cdots \leq f_{(n)}$, and U is unique up to a multiplication by a positive number, $U(0) = 0$, and

$$\pi_i^+ = \mu^+(\{(i), \ldots, (n)\}) - \mu^+(\{(i+1), \ldots, (n)\}) \tag{20}$$

$$\pi_i^- = \mu^+(\{(1), \ldots, (i)\}) - \mu^+(\{(1), \ldots, (i-1)\}). \tag{21}$$

Assuming strict increasingness of U, easy computations can show that the CPT model coincide with the Choquet integral of the real-valued function $U \circ f$ (see (6)), while the CPT model is the Šipoš integral of this function (see (7)). Thus the two models coincide if $p = 1$, and moreover:

$$\mathrm{CPT}(f) = \mathrm{CPT}(f^+) - \mathrm{CPT}(f^-).$$

We introduce now an axiomatization of CPT found by Zank [25]. We need some definitions. First we define a particular class of utility functions.

Definition 6. A utility function $U : \mathbb{R} \longrightarrow \mathbb{R}$ is an *increasing linear/exponential* utility function for gains (resp. losses) if one of the following holds for all $x \geq 0$ (resp. $x \leq 0$):

(i) $U(x) = \alpha x$, with $\alpha > 0$

(ii) $U(x) = \alpha e^{\lambda x} + \tau$, with $\alpha\lambda > 0$, and $\tau \in \mathbb{R}$.

Note that the coefficients α, λ, τ may differ for gain and losses, and since we impose $U(0) = 0$, we have $\tau = -\alpha$.

Definition 7. The preference relation $\succeq$ satisfies *constant absolute risk aversion* for gains (resp. for losses) if:

$$(f_1, \ldots, f_n) \succeq (g_1, \ldots, g_n) \Leftrightarrow (f_1 + \epsilon, \ldots, f_n + \epsilon) \succeq (g_1 + \epsilon, \ldots, g_n + \epsilon)$$

whenever for all $i = 1, \ldots, n$, the outcomes $f_i, f_i + \epsilon, g_i, g_i + \epsilon$ are gains (resp. losses).

Remark that this property is similar to invariance for positive shifts (for the gain part), in Proposition 4.

We say that two acts f, g are *comonotonic* if there exists a permutation σ such that $f_{\sigma(1)} \leq \cdots \leq f_{\sigma(n)}$ and $g_{\sigma(1)} \leq \cdots \leq g_{\sigma(n)}$.

Definition 8. The preference relation satisfies *tail independence* if

$$(a_I, f_{I^c}) \succeq (a_I, g_{I^c}) \Leftrightarrow (b_I, f_{I^c}) \succeq (b_I, g_{I^c})$$

provided all acts are comonotonic and I is of the form $I = \{(1), \ldots, (m)\}$ or $I = \{(l), \ldots, (n)\}$.

Tail independence is a stronger version of comonotonic independence (or sure-thing principle) since it restricts the common part to be in the worst or best states. It can be shown that CPT implies tail independence.

Finally, as usual we say that $\succeq$ satisfies *monotonicity* if $f \succ g$ whenever $f_i \succeq g_i$ for all $i \in S$, and $f_j \succ g_j$ for some j. Also, $\succeq$ satisfies *continuity* if $\forall f \in \mathbb{R}^n$, $\{g | g \succeq f\}$ and $\{g | g \leq f\}$ are closed subsets of $\mathbb{R}^n$.

The following can be shown.

Proposition 6. *Assume $n \geq 3$. The following statements are equivalent.*

(i) CPT holds, with U being a continuous strictly increasing linear/exponential utility function, and positive decision weights π_i^+, π_i^-.

(ii) $\succeq$ is a weak order, satisfying monotonicity, continuity, tail independence, and constant absolute risk aversion for gains and losses.

Moreover, if (i) holds, μ is unique and U is a ratio scale (i.e. unique up to a multiplicative positive constant).

Note that the condition on decision weights to be positive is equivalent to the monotonicity of the fuzzy measure.

A similar result has been also shown by Zank [25] in the framework of decision under risk. Acts are now considered as lotteries with real-valued outcomes, named "gain", "losses", and "statu quo" when they are positive, negative, or zero respectively. A lottery is denoted $P := (p_1, x_1; \ldots; p_n, x_n)$, with the convention that $x_1 \leq \cdots \leq x_n$. The lottery can be splitted into the gain part P^+ and the loss part P^-, so that $P = P^+ - P^-$ (again, this is the convention opposite to the usual one).

Let $x_{(1)} \leq \cdots x_{(p)} < 0 \leq x_{(p+1)} \leq \cdots \leq x_{(n)}$. The representing function V of Cumulative Prospect Theory (CPT) is defined as:

$$V(P) = \sum_{i=1}^{p} \pi_i^+ \cdot U(x_{(i)}) + \sum_{i=p+1}^{n} \pi_i^+ \cdot U(x_{(i)}) \tag{22}$$

with $U(0) = 0$, and decision weights defined as:

$$\pi_i^+ = w^+(p_{(i)} + \cdots + p_{(n)}) - w^+(p_{(i+1)} + \cdots + p_{(n)}) \tag{23}$$

$$\pi_i^- = w^-(p_{(1)} + \cdots + p_{(i)}) - w^-(p_{(1)} + \cdots + p_{(i-1)}), \tag{24}$$

where w is a probability transformation, i.e. a strictly increasing function from $[0,1]$ to $[0,1]$, such that $w(0) = 0$ and $w(1) = 1$. Again, we recognize here (provided $w^+ \equiv w^-$) the Šipoš integral with capacity $w^+ \circ p$, with p being the probability measure induced by $p_1, \ldots, p_n$.

We introduce a special class of utility functions.

Definition 9. The utility function U is said to belong to the *positive power family for gains* if

$$U(x) = \sigma^+ x^\alpha, \quad \sigma^+ > 0, \alpha > 0, x \geq 0$$

and to the *positive power family for losses* if

$$U(x) = -\sigma^- |x|^\beta, \quad \sigma^- > 0, \beta > 0, x \leq 0.$$

We now introduce axioms that characterize CPT.

Definition 10. The preference relation satisfies *constant proportional risk aversion* if for all $\alpha > 0$,

$$(p_1, x_1; \ldots; p_n, x_n) \succeq (p_1, y_1; \ldots, ; p_n, y_n) \Leftrightarrow$$
$$(p_1, \alpha x_1; \ldots; p_n, \alpha x_n) \succeq (p_1, \alpha y_1; \ldots, ; p_n, \alpha y_n)$$

whenever all x_i's are gains or all x_i's are losses.

This property is similar to homogeneity (see Proposition 2 (v)). Given two lotteries $P = (p_1, x_1; \ldots; p_n, x_n)$ and $Q = (q_1, y_1; \ldots; q_m, y_m)$, the lottery mixture $\gamma P + (1 - \gamma)Q$, for any $\gamma \in [0,1]$ is defined as $(\gamma p_1, x_1; \ldots; \gamma p_n, x_n; (1 - \gamma)q_1, y_1; \ldots; (1 - \gamma)q_m, y_m)$ (up to a suitable reordering of the elements).

Definition 11. The preference relation satisfies *tail independence* if for all lotteries P, Q, C, C', for all $\gamma \in]0,1[$, we have:

$$\gamma P + (1 - \gamma)C \succeq \gamma Q + (1 - \gamma)C \Leftrightarrow \gamma P + (1 - \gamma)C' \succeq \gamma Q + (1 - \gamma)C'.$$

whenever outcomes in C, C' are all greater than those of P and Q, or all smaller.

As usual, we say that $\succeq$ satisfies *stochastic dominance* if $(p_1, x_1; \dots ; p_n, x_n) \succ$ $(p_1, y_1; \dots ; p_n, y_n)$ whenever $x_i \geq y_i$ for $i = 1, \dots, n$, and $x_j > y_j$ for some j. Moreover, $\succeq$ satisfies *simple continuity* if for any lottery $P = (p_1, x_1; \dots ; p_n, x_n)$, the sets $\{(y_1, \dots, y_n) | (p_1, y_1; \dots ; p_n, y_n) \succeq P\}$ and $\{(y_1, \dots, y_n) | (p_1, y_1; \dots ; p_n, y_n) \preceq P\}$ are closed sets.

The following can be shown.

Proposition 7. *The following statements are equivalent.*

(i) CPT holds, with positive power utility for gains and losses.

(ii) the preference relation $\succeq$ is a weak order, satisfying stochastic dominance, simple continuity, tail independence, and constant proportional risk aversion for gain and losses.

Moreover, if (i) holds, the probability transformations w^+, w^- are unique, and U defines a ratio scale.

5 Comments, Comparisons and Concluding Remarks

We give a tentative analysis of preceding results in this section.

The results presented in the framework of prospect theory have some links with the characterizations given in section 2, although the point of view is completely different: in prospect theory (and more generally in decision making), the basic material is the preference relation $\succeq$, and thus all axioms concern $\succeq$, while the axiomatization of section 2 is more in the spirit of an aggregation operator, and thus the basic material is the scores. Nevertheless, similarities exist and some have been already pointed out above:

- constant absolute risk aversion and constant proportional risk aversion correspond to invariance to positive shifts and homogeneity respectively.
- monotonicity and stochastic dominance correspond to non decreasingness.
- tail independence correspond to independence between positive and negative parts. More specifically, the tail independence property in decision under uncertainty says there is no reversal of preference when the constant part is changed, provided all acts are comonotonic, and the constant part is at the tail or head of $\{(1), \dots, (n)\}$. This is an ordinal condition. A strengthening of this condition, assuming that the preference intensity can be expressed on a difference scale, would be to impose that the difference of preferences should remain the same. Denoting by $d(f, g)$ the difference of preference between f and g, the tail independence condition becomes:

$$d((a_I, f_{I^c}), (a_I, g_{I^c})) = d((b_I, f_{I^c}), (b_I, g_{I^c}))$$

If the difference of preference $d(f, g)$ is modeled by $\check{S}_\mu(f) - \check{S}_\mu(g)$, we obtain formally the independence of positive and negative parts. Conditions on acts are different, but very similar: the tail or head condition for I means that the indices of the ordered values for a_I and f_I should be separated, a weaker condition than the separation in negative and positive parts.

On the other hand, the tail independence condition for decision under risk is very close to the previous one. In additive models of decision, the key axioms are the sure thing principle (Savage [18], decision under uncertainty) and the independence axiom (Anscombe and Aumann [1]), which correspond exactly to the two tail independence conditions where the comonotonic and the tail conditions have been removed. It has been proved by Fishburn and Wakker [6] that these two independence concepts are equivalent under the assumption that if two acts generate the same lottery, they are indifferent (implicit in our presentation), and also that the set of states of nature has no atom (i.e. every non singleton subset with a positive probability includes at least a subset with positive but strictly smaller probability). For a detailed analysis of the connection between these two independence concepts, as well as for an historical perspective of the notion of independence, see Fishburn and Wakker [6].

For the moment, we do not see any link between the results concerning the interaction index presented in section 3 and the axiomatization in cumulative prospect theory. Although the interaction index has been axiomatized by Grabisch and Roubens [12] in the framework of cooperative game theory, results linking the interaction index with behavioral properties in decision making are still lacking. This may be a future direction for research.

Now we come back the initial question:

To be or not to be symmetric ... ?

We hope that the paper has brought a clear answer to this. The Choquet integral (asymmetric side) deals with real numbers being on a difference scale, that is, the position of the zero is arbitrary, and there is no difference between positive and negative number. By contrast, the Šipoš integral (symmetric side) makes this distinction, and makes a symmetric processing of positive and negative numbers. The zero is a "true" zero, and the underlying scale is a ratio scale.

This can be seen clearly by looking:

- at the expression of $\mathcal{C}_\mu$ in terms of μ and m (see (6) and (8) and compare with corresponding formulas for $\check{\mathcal{S}}_\mu$)
- at the expression of $\mathcal{C}_\mu$ for 2-additive measures in terms of the interaction index (see Proposition 5 and comments below)
- at the axiomatizations in sections 2 and 4. For the Šipoš integral, an axiom separating the positive and negative numbers is needed (independence for positive and negative parts, and the tail independence).

Using a somewhat pictural comparison, we could say that the Choquet integral sees the zero level like a transparent glas surface, and the Šipoš integral sees it like a mirror surface.

Thus, clearly the choice lies in the semantic attached to the numbers, or more specifically to the fact that the universal set of these numbers is bipolar or unipolar. If you are in the bipolar case, like attractivity/repulsion or gain/loss, then *be symmetric*. If you are in the unipolar case, like membership degrees, importance, utility, *be asymmetric*.

References

1. F.J. Anscombe and R.J. Aumann. A definition of subjective probability. *The Annals of Mathematical Statistic*, 34:199–205, 1963.
2. S.J. Chen and C.L. Hwang. *Fuzzy Multiple Attribute Decision Making*. Springer-Verlag, 1992.
3. G. Choquet. Theory of capacities. *Annales de l'Institut Fourier*, 5:131–295, 1953.
4. D. Denneberg. *Non-Additive Measure and Integral*. Kluwer Academic, 1994.
5. D. Denneberg and M. Grabisch. Interaction transform of set functions over a finite set. *Information Sciences*, to appear.
6. P. Fishburn and P. Wakker. The invention of the independence condition for preferences. *Management Sciences*, 41(7):1130–1144, 1995.
7. M. Grabisch. The application of fuzzy integrals in multicriteria decision making. *European J. of Operational Research*, 89:445–456, 1996.
8. M. Grabisch. k-order additive discrete fuzzy measures and their representation. *Fuzzy Sets and Systems*, 92:167–189, 1997.
9. M. Grabisch. Fuzzy integral for classification and feature extraction. In M. Grabisch, T. Murofushi, and M. Sugeno, editors, *Fuzzy Measures and Integrals — Theory and Applications*. Physica Verlag, to appear.
10. M. Grabisch, Ch. Labreuche, and J.C. Vansnick. On the extension of pseudo-boolean functions for the aggregation of interacting bipolar criteria. *European J. of Operational Research*, submitted.
11. M. Grabisch and M. Roubens. Application of the choquet integral in multicriteria decision making. In M. Grabisch, T. Murofushi, and M. Sugeno, editors, *Fuzzy Measures and Integrals — Theory and Applications*. Physica Verlag, 2000.
12. M. Grabisch and M. Roubens. An axiomatic approach to the concept of interaction among players in cooperative games. *Int. Journal of Game Theory*, to appear.
13. D. Kahneman and A. Tversky. Prospect theory: an analysis of decision under risk. *Econometrica*, 47:263–291, 1979.
14. R.L. Keeney and H. Raiffa. *Decision with Multiple Objectives*. Wiley, New York, 1976.
15. J.L. Marichal. *Aggregation operators for multicriteria decision aid*. PhD thesis, University of Liège, 1998.
16. T. Murofushi and S. Soneda. Techniques for reading fuzzy measures (III): interaction index. In *9th Fuzzy System Symposium*, pages 693–696, Sapporo, Japan, May 1993. In Japanese.
17. G.C. Rota. On the foundations of combinatorial theory I. Theory of Möbius functions. *Zeitschrift für Wahrscheinlichkeitstheorie und Verwandte Gebiete*, 2:340–368, 1964.
18. L. J. Savage. *The Foundations of Statistics*. Dover, 2nd edition, 1972.

19. D. Schmeidler. Subjective probability and expected utility without additivity. *Econometrica*, 57(3):571–587, 1989.

20. L.S. Shapley. A value for *n*-person games. In H.W. Kuhn and A.W. Tucker, editors, *Contributions to the Theory of Games, Vol. II*, number 28 in Annals of Mathematics Studies, pages 307–317. Princeton University Press, 1953.

21. M. Sugeno. *Theory of fuzzy integrals and its applications*. PhD thesis, Tokyo Institute of Technology, 1974.

22. M. Sugeno and T. Murofushi. *Fuzzy measure theory*, volume 3 of *Course on fuzzy theory*. Nikkan Kōgyō, 1993. In Japanese.

23. A. Tversky and D. Kahneman. Advances in prospect theory: cumulative representation of uncertainty. *J. of Risk and Uncertainty*, 1992.

24. J. Šipoš. Integral with respect to a pre-measure. *Math. Slovaca*, 29:141–155, 1979.

25. H. Zank. *Risk and Uncertainty: Classical and Modern Models for Individual Decision Making*. PhD thesis, Universiteit Maastricht, 1999.

Monotone Functions on Finite Lattices: An Ordinal Approach to Capacities, Belief and Necessity Functions

D 00

D 8 0

Jean-Pierre Barthélemy

Ecole Nationale Supérieure des Télécommunications de Bretagne
BP 832
29285 Brest (Breizh), France
E-mail: JP.Barthelemy@enst-bretagne.fr

Summary. In this paper we investigate the theoretical possibility to extend Choquet monotonicity, Dempster-Shafer belief functions as well as necessity functions to arbitrary lattices. We show, in particular, that every finite lattice admits a belief function (while the existence of a probability measure on a lattice characterizes its distributivity). Thus belief functions appear as a good substitute to probabilities in the framework of a non-classical propositional calculus.

1 Introduction

The theory of expected utility as axiomatized by von Neumann and Morgenstern (1947) and Savage (1954) ends up, from Allais (1953), in numerous paradoxes. Attempts to escape from these paradoxes usually involve a weakening of the axioms of a probability measure. In that framework some models (see Schmeidler 1986, 1988; Tversky and Kahneman 1992) use Choquet's capacities (Choquet 1953), sometimes renamed as "non-additive measures".

The question of preference aggregation is central in multicriteria decision aid. Classical aggregation rules are, more or less, based on utilities (cf. Vincke 1989 for a review). When the data are intensities of preferences (the term "fuzzy preferences" is often used in this context) a lot of aggregation functions have been designed and studied (Fodor, Marichal and Roubens, 1996; Fodor and Roubens, 1995, cf. Fodor and Roubens, 1994, for a comprehensive study). In this context integral derived from Choquet's capacities (often renamed as "fuzzy measures") have been used as aggregation operators (Grabisch, 1996, Marichal, 1999a,b,c)

Belief functions introduced as "lower probabilities" (i.e. functions obtained as lower bound of probability measures, Dempster, 1967, 1968) and as "degrees of belief" (Shafer, 1976) appear both as special capacities and as a generalization of the Bayesian theory of subjective probability. Since Demster and Shafer pioneer's work a large amount of literature has been devoted to belief functions and related topics (like necessity functions, possibility functions, or more generally decomposable measures (on this last point cf. Fodor and Roubens, 1995; Dubois et al., 1996; Fodor et al., 1997).

The purpose of this paper is to investigate the theoretical possibility of extending the basic Dempster-Shafer theory to set of events who are not structured as Boolean algebras. There are two reasons for such a theoretical investigation: use of non-classical logics and applications to artificial intelligence.

1. Use of non classical logics. Since Zadeh's pioneer work (1965) a broad community is working at the "fuzzification" of notions arising from standard set theory (introduction of membership functions with values between 0 and 1, definitions of fuzzy measures, ...) and/or classical logics (for instance by replacing logical connectors by t-norms and t-conorms, cf. Fodor and Roubens, 1994). Goals for such fuzzifications is to account for uncertainty and approximate reasoning. An alternative way could be: use non-classical logics and try to manage with standard measurement as far as it is efficient. In that respect a reasonable probability theory apply as far the lattice induced by a propositional calculus is distributive. These extension covers intuitionistic logic and paraconsistent logic (the equality $p(x) + p(x^*) = 1$, where x^* is the negation of x, has to be replaced by $p(x) + p(x^*) \leq 1$ in the first case, and by $p(x) + p(x^*) \geq 1$ in the second). Since Poincaré's equalities are a necessary and sufficient condition for distributivity (lemma 4 in this paper), we have to find a convenient extension of probabilities in the general case. Belief functions that can be defined on any lattice (proposition 4 in this paper) appear as the natural candidate.

2. Artificial intelligence. Belief functions have numerous applications in Artificial Intelligence: expert systems, approximate reasoning, Bayesian networks etc. They appear also as a promising tool to evaluate knowledge extracted from data. In this last framework the objects under study are often structured as lattices. One of the most popular of them is surely the Birkhoff's Galois Lattice of a 0/1-array (cf. Barbut and Monjardet, 1971), which has been rediscovered many times under various names. A fundamental result is that any lattice is isomorphic to the Galois lattice of some 0/1-array. Since Dempster-Shafer theory a priori works only on Boolean lattice, its extension to any lattice deserve to be studied.

This paper is organized as follows: Section 1 provides a straightforward extension of Choquet's monotonicity theory, as developed, for finite Boolean algebras, in Chateauneuf, 1994 and Chateauneuf and Jaffray, 1989, 1994, to arbitrary lattices. It establishes some links between monotonicity and some structural properties of lattices. Section 2 is devoted to belief function themselves and Section 3 to necessity functions (called "consonant belief functions" by Shafer).

All the sets occurring in this paper are supposed to be finite. The reader is assumed to be familiar with basic terms of ordered sets and lattice theories like ordered set (poset) lower bound, upper bound, (semi) lattice, sublattice, (semi) lattice homomorphism, lattice isomorphism, etc. Throughout this text we shall use the following definitions and notations.

If X is a finite lattice, we denote by $x \wedge y$ (resp. $x \vee y$) the lower bound, or meet (resp. the upper bound, or join) of $x, y \in X$ and by $\underline{0}$ (resp. $\underline{1}$) the lowest (resp. the greatest) element of X. The elements $\underline{0}$ and $\underline{1}$ are called the *trivial elements* of X.

We say that $y \in X$ *covers* $x \in X$ whenever $x < y$ and $x \leq t < y$ implies $x = t$. The lattice X is *modular* whenever: x and y cover $x \wedge y$ implies that $x \vee y$ covers x and y, and $x \vee y$ covers x and y implies that x and y cover $x \wedge y$.

If Y is a subset of the lattice X, we denote, for $x \in X$, by $Y(x)$ the set $\{y \in Y \; : \; y \leq x\}$. We have:

$$x \leq y \text{ implies } Y(x) \subseteq Y(y) \text{ and } Y(x \wedge y) = Y(x) \cap Y(y), \; Y(x) \cup Y(y) \subseteq Y(x \vee y).$$

Notice that this last inclusion is not, in general, an equality.

A non-trivial element $s \in X$ is said to be *join-irreducible* if and only if s is not the upper bound of the set $X(s) \setminus \{s\}$. We denote by S the set of all join-irreducible elements of X.

A lattice is said to be distributive whenever

$$(x \vee y) \wedge z = (x \wedge z) \vee (y \wedge z)$$

(or equivalently: $(x \wedge y) \vee z = (x \vee z) \wedge (y \vee z)$). A distributive lattice is Boolean if and only if, for each $x \in X$, there exists $x^* \in X$ such that $x \wedge x^* = \underline{0}$ and $x \vee x^* = \underline{1}$. Every finite Boolean lattice is isomorphic to the lattice 2^U (ordered by inclusion) of all the subsets of a finite set U. Every distributive lattice X may be viewed as a sublattice of a Boolean lattice, since the equality $S(x) \cup S(y) = S(x \vee y)$ characterizes distributive lattices. This is a classical *representation theorem* (Birkhoff, 1967).

2 Monotonicity

2.1 k-monotone functions

Consider a finite lattice X and a real valued function f defined on X. Following Choquet (1953), we obtain the *difference functions* $\triangle_k f$, defined on X^{k+1} for each integer k, by the recursive formula:

$$\triangle_0 f = f,$$
$$\triangle_k f(x, y_1, \ldots, y_k) = \triangle_{k-1} f(x, y_1, \ldots, y_{k-1}) - \triangle_{k-1} f(x \wedge y_k, y_1, \ldots, y_{k-1}).$$

We have:

$$\triangle_0 f(x) = f(x),$$
$$\triangle_1 f(x, y) = f(x) - f(x \wedge y),$$
$$\triangle_2 f(x, y, z) = f(x) - f(x \wedge y) - f(x \wedge z) + f(x \wedge y \wedge z),$$
$$\triangle_3 f(x, y, z, t) = f(x) - f(x \wedge y) - f(x \wedge z) - f(x \wedge t) + f(x \wedge y \wedge z)$$
$$+ f(x \wedge y \wedge t) + f(x \wedge z \wedge t) - f(x \wedge y \wedge z \wedge t),$$

and more generally:

$$\triangle_k f(x, y_1, \ldots, y_k) = \sum_{J \subseteq K} (-1)^{|J|} f(x \wedge (\wedge_{j \in J} y_j)).$$

We say that f is *k-monotone* whenever

$$\triangle_k f \geq 0.$$

The proof of the following lemma is obvious.

Lemma 1. *f is 1-monotone if and only if $u \leq v$ implies $f(u) \leq f(v)$.*

Lemma 2. *A k-monotone function is also k'-monotone for $1 \leq k' \leq k$.*

Proof. The result follows recursively from the fact that

$$\triangle_{k-1} f(x, y_1, \ldots, y_{k-1}) = \triangle_k f(x, y_1, \ldots, y_{k-1}, \underline{0}) + \triangle_k f(\underline{0}, y_1, \ldots, y_{k-1}),$$

and $\triangle_k f(\underline{0}, y_1, \ldots, y_{k-1}) = 0$. □

The following example shows a function which is $(k-1)$-monotone, but not k-monotone, for every k. Let X be the lattice with $k+2$ elements including the greatest element $\underline{1}$, the least element $\underline{0}$, and k atoms (and coatoms, see Figure 1). Set $f(\underline{1}) = k - 1$, $f(\underline{0}) = 0$, and $f(a) = 1$, for each atom a. Then f is $(k-1)$-monotone, but not k-monotone.

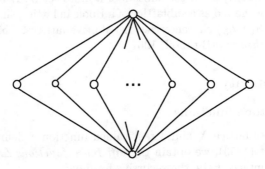

Figure 1.

Assume that f is 2-monotone and consider $u, v \in X$. If we set $x = u \vee v$, we get :

$$f(u \vee v) + f(u \wedge v) - f(u) - f(v) \geq 0.$$

Conversely, assume that f satisfies the above inequality and f is 1-monotone. Then, for $x, y, z \in X$, we have $0 \leq f(x) - f(x \wedge y) \vee (x \wedge z))$ by 1-monotonicity, and by 2-monotonicity:

$$f((x \wedge y) \vee (x \wedge z)) \geq f([[(x \wedge y) \vee (x \wedge z)] \wedge y) + f([[(x \wedge y) \vee (x \wedge z)] \wedge z)$$
$$- f([[(x \wedge y) \vee (x \wedge z)] \wedge (y \wedge z)).$$

However, in any lattice we have that $[(x \wedge y) \vee (x \wedge z)] \wedge y = x \wedge y$ and $[(x \wedge y) \vee (x \wedge z)] \wedge (y \wedge z) = x \wedge y \wedge z$. Thus, $f((x \wedge y) \vee (x \wedge z)) \geq f(x \wedge y) + f(x \wedge z) - f(x \wedge y \wedge z)$ and $f(x) - f(x \wedge y) - f(x \wedge z) + f(x \wedge y \wedge z) \geq 0$. Hence f is 2-monotone. It follows that f is 2-monotone if and only if it is 1-monotone and, for each x, y we have $f(x) + f(y) \leq f(x \vee y) + f(x \wedge y)$.

More generally, we say that f is *weakly k-monotone* whenever for each $x* = (x_1, \ldots, x_k) \in X^k$ we have

$$f\left(\vee_{1 \leq i \leq k} x_i\right) \geq \sum_{J \subseteq K, J \neq \emptyset} (-1)^{|J|+1} f\left(\wedge_{j \in J} x_j\right). \tag{1}$$

We remark that this definition applies from $k = 2$, and that if f is weakly k-monotone, then it is also weakly k'-monotone for $2 \leq k' \leq k$.

Lemma 3. *A k-monotone function is weakly k-monotone.*

Proof. Consider $(y_1, \ldots, y_k) \in X^k$. By k-monotonicity we get:

$$f\left(\vee_{1 \leq i \leq k} y_i\right) \geq \sum_{J \subseteq K, J \neq \emptyset} (-1)^{|J|} f\left(\vee_{1 \leq i \leq k} y_i\right) \wedge f\left(\wedge_{j \in J} y_j\right) \geq 0;$$

that is to say,

$$f\left(\vee_{1 \leq i \leq k} y_i\right) + \sum_{J \subseteq K, J \neq \emptyset} (-1)^{|J|} f\left(\wedge_{j \in J} y_j\right) \geq 0,$$

whence the result follows. $\square$

Proposition 1. *Let f be a real valued function defined on the lattice X and let $k \geq 2$ be an integer. Then the following two assertions are equivalent:*
(i) f is k-monotone,
(ii) f is 1-monotone and weakly k-monotone.

Proof. (i) implies (ii) comes from Lemma 3 and 2. To get (ii) implies (i), consider $(x, y_1, \ldots, y_k) \in X^{k+1}$. By 1-monotonicity we get

$$0 \leq f(x) - f\left(\vee_{1 \leq i \leq k} (x \wedge y_i)\right).$$

By k-weak-monotonicity we get

$$f\left(\vee_{1 \leq i \leq k} (x \wedge y_i)\right) \geq \sum_{J \subseteq K, J \neq \emptyset} (-1)^{|J|+1} f\left(\wedge_{j \in J} (x \wedge y_j)\right).$$

Hence the result follows. $\square$

The function f is weakly 2-monotone if and only if for $x, y \in X$ we have

$$f(x) + f(y) \leq f(x \vee y) + f(x \wedge y).$$

f is weakly 3-monotone if and only if for $x, y, z \in X$ we have

$$f(x) + f(y) + f(z) \leq f(x \vee y \vee z) + f(x \wedge y) + f(x \vee z) + f(y \wedge z) - f(x \wedge y \wedge z).$$

A 2-monotone function on X is also called a *convex function*. A 1-monotone function is simply called a *monotone* function.

2.2 Metric properties of k-monotonicity

Let f be a real valued function defined on the lattice X. Define the real valued function d_f on $X \times X$ by

$$d_f(x,y) = f(y) - f(x) \text{ for } x \leq y,$$

and

$$d_f(x,y) = d_f(x \wedge y, x) + d_f(x \wedge y, y)$$

in the general case.'

Clearly, d_f satisfies $d_f(x,x) = 0$ for each $x \in X$, and $d_f(x,y) = d_f(y,x)$ for all $x,y \in X$. Moreover, f is 1-monotone if and only if $d_f(x,y) \geq 0$, for any $x,y \in X$.

It is well known that f is 2-monotone if and only if d_f fulfills the triangle inequality $d_f(x,z) \leq d_f(x,y) + d_f(y,z)$, for all $x,y,z \in X$. Thus, in this case d_f satisfies the axioms of a distance function. Moreover, this metric is nothing else than the shortest path metric on the neighbourhood graph of X, with respect to the lengths $|f(y) - f(x)|$ on the edges xy. In particular, there exists always a shortest path between x and y that passes through $x \wedge y$ (for a review of many such results and references, see Monjardet, 1981).

Proposition 2. *The function f is 3-monotone if and only if d_f satisfies*

$$2d_f(x \vee y \vee z, x \wedge y \wedge z)) \geq d_f(x,y) + d_f(y,z) + d_f(x,z).$$

Proof. Assume that d_f fulfills the inequality in the proposition. Then, setting $z = x$, we get $2f(x \vee y) - 2f(x \wedge y) \geq 2(f(x) + f(y) - 2f(x \wedge y))$. Hence, $f(x) + f(y) \leq f(x \wedge y) + f(x \vee y)$, and f is 2-monotone. Thus we have to prove that a 2-monotone function f is 3-monotone iff d_f satisfies $2d_f(x \vee y \vee z, x \wedge y \wedge z)) \geq d_f(x,y) + d_f(y,z) + d_f(x,z)$. The function f is 3-monotone iff

$$f(x \vee y \vee z) \geq f(x) + f(y) + f(z) - f(x \wedge y) - f(x \wedge z) - f(y \wedge z) + f(x \wedge y \wedge z).$$

The result comes from the equality $d_f(x,y) = f(x) + f(y) - 2f(x \wedge y)$. $\square$

2.3 ∞-monotone functions

A function f defined on the lattice X is said to be ∞-monotone if and only if it is k-monotone for each integer k.

Proposition 3. *Set $|X| = n$. Then a real valued function defined on X is ∞-monotone if and only if it is $(n-2)$-monotone.*

Proof. It is sufficient to prove that if f is $(n-2)$-monotone then it is $(n-1)$-monotone and n-monotone.

f *is* $(n-1)$-*monotone.* Consider $x^* = (x_1, \ldots, x_{n-1}) \in X^{n-1}$. If two components, or more, of x^* are equal, then the required formula holds by

$(n-2)$-monotonicity. If the components of x^* are pairwise distinct, then either $\underline{0}$ or $\underline{1}$ occurs in x^*.

Case 1: $x_1 = \underline{0}$. Then we have

$$f(\vee_{1 \leq i \leq n-1} x_i) = f(\vee_{2 \leq i \leq n-1} x_i) = \sum_{J \subseteq \{2,\ldots,k\}, J \neq \emptyset} (-1)^{|J|+1} f(\wedge_{j \in J} x_j).$$

But, if $1 \in J$, we have $\wedge_{j \in J} x_j = 0$. Hence the result follows.

Case 2: $x_1 = \underline{1}$. Let $K' = \{J \subseteq K \ : \ 1 \in J\}$, and $K" = \{J \subseteq K \ : \ 1 \notin J, \ J \neq \emptyset\}$. The mapping which associates $J \setminus \{1\}$ to J realizes a bijection from $K' \setminus \{1\}$ to $K"$ and, for $J \in K'$,

$$(-1)^{|J|+1} f(\wedge_{j \in J} x_j) = (-1)^{|J \setminus \{1\}|+2} f(\wedge_{j \in J \setminus \{1\}} x_j).$$

Hence

$$\sum_{J \subseteq K, J \neq \emptyset} (-1)^{|J|+1} f(\wedge_{j \in J} x_j) = f(1) = f(\vee_{1 \leq j \leq n-1} x_j).$$

f is n-monotone. Consider $x^* = (x_1, \ldots, x_n) \in X^n$. If two components of x^* are equal, then the inequality (3) holds by 1-monotonicity. If not, then $\underline{1}$ occurs in x^* and the result is obtained by the preceding argument. $\square$

For $k \geq 2$, we define a k-*valuation* as a k-monotone function such that inequality (1) degenerates into the following equality:

$$f(\vee_{1 \leq i \leq k} x_i) = \sum_{J \subseteq K, J \neq \emptyset} (-1)^{|J|+1} f(\wedge_{j \in J} x_j). \tag{2}$$

f is an ∞-*valuation* if and only if it is a k-valuation for each integer k. *Strict k-valuation* $(k \geq 2)$ is a k-valuation which is strictly 1-monotone. Only two cases can occur and they are characteristic of the structure of the lattice X:

1. The existence of a strict 2-valuation characterizes the modularity of X.
2. The existence of a strict k-valuation, with $k > 2$, characterizes the distributivity of X.

These results are well-known (cf. Birkhoff, 1967, who calls 3-valuations *distributive valuations*).

In this second case a 2-valuation is a k-valuation, for any $k \geq 2$, and may be computed like a probability measure. The equality (2) (called also Poincaré's equality, or inclusion/exclusion formula) are known for the rank function of a distributive lattice (Barbut and Monjardet, 1971). They can be easily generalized to any valuation defined on a distributive lattice. All these results can be summarized in the following lemma.

Lemma 4. *Let X be a lattice. Then*

(i) X is modular if and only if it admits a strict 2-valuation.

(ii) X is distributive if and only if it is modular and every strict 2-valuation on X is a 3-valuation.

(iii) X is distributive if and only if it admits a strict 3-valuation.

(iv) X is distributive if and only if it is modular and every strict 2-valuation on X is an ∞-valuation.

In view of Lemma 4 a question arises: does the existence of a k-valuation on a lattice X induce some structural properties for X? Proposition 4 shows that the answer is no.

Proposition 4. *Any lattice admits an ∞-monotone function.*

Proof. Denote by S the set of all join irreducible elements of the lattice X, and for $x \in X$, by $S(x)$ the set $\{t \in J : t \le x\}$. We know that in any lattice $x \mapsto S(x)$ is injective, $S(x \wedge y) = S(x) \cap S(y)$, and $S(x) \cup S(y) \subseteq S(x \vee y)$. For $x \in X$ let $f(x) = |S(x)|$. From Lemma 4 and since $|A| + |B| = |A \cap B| + |A \cup B|$, we get for $x_1, \dots, x_k \in X$ that

$$f(\vee_{1 \le i \le k} x_i) \ge |\cup_{1 \le i \le k} S(x_i)|$$
$$= \sum_{J \subseteq K, J \ne \emptyset} (-1)^{|J|+1} |(\cap_{j \in J} S(x_j)|$$
$$= \sum_{J \subseteq K, J \ne \emptyset} (-1)^{|J|+1} f(\wedge_{j \in J} x_j).$$

2.4 A representation property for distributive lattices

Choquet's monotonicity and Dempster-Shafer theory of belief concern algebras of events, i.e. in the finite case a power set 2^E with union as upper bound and intersection as lower bound. We shall show that this set theoretic approach is, in a way, the general approach when the lattice X is distributive.

Define a *topological representation* of a lattice X by an injective map ϕ from X to some power set 2^E such that $\phi(x \wedge y) = \phi(x) \cap \phi(y)$ and $\phi(x \vee y) = \phi(x) \cup \phi(y)$. It is well-known that a lattice admits a topological representation, if and only if it is distributive. (The map $x \mapsto S(x)$ of the proof of Proposition 4 is a canonical example of a topological representation of a distributive lattice.) The proof of the following Proposition is straightforward.

Proposition 5. *Let X be a distributive lattice, E a set, ϕ a topological representation of X into 2^E and f a real valued function defined on X. Then f is k-monotone if and only if f' is k-monotone with f' defined on $\phi(X)$ so that $f' \phi = f$.*

This (not surprising) result shows that finite point set topologies are sufficient to account for k-monotonicity on distributive lattice.

3   Belief functions

3.1   Basic considerations

A *capacity* on the lattice X is a 1-monotone function f on X such that $f(\underline{0}) = 0$ and $f(\underline{1}) = 1$. A *convex capacity* is a 2-monotone capacity. A *belief function* is an ∞-monotone capacity. A *probability* is both a capacity and an ∞-valuation.

We know from results given in Section 2 that

 (i) A lattice admits a probability if and only if it is distributive.
 (ii) Each lattice admits a belief function.
(iii) The belief functions on point-set topologies constitute the general case for belief functions on distributive lattices.

3.2   Belief functions and mass assignment

The notion of mass assignment leads to an alternative proof for the existence of a believe function on any lattice.

A *mass assignment* on the lattice X is a real valued function w on X such that $w(x) \geq 0$ for each $x \in X$, $w(\underline{0}) = 0$, and $\sum_{x \in X} w(x) = 1$. The element x of X is said to be a *focal* element of w if $w(x) > 0$. The set of all focal elements of w is called the *focus* of w and denoted by $\mathrm{Foc}(w)$.

Consider a mass assignment w on X and define the real valued function bel_w by

$$(B) \qquad \mathrm{bel}_w(x) = \sum_{t \leq x} w(x).$$

Shafer (1976) noticed that if X is the lattice of all the events of a given σ-algebra (ordered by inclusion), then bel_w is a belief function. We shall use this result as a lemma.

Lemma 5 (Shafer, 1976). *If X is a finite Boolean lattice then bel_w is a belief function.*

The above formula does not give *a priori* the general form of a belief function. However, by Möbius inversion (Rota, 1964) each belief function may be expressed as bel_w but the "weights" may be negative (this point has been intensively studied by Chateauneuf (1994,) Chateauneuf and Jaffray (1989, 1994).

Lemma 4 extends to any lattice.

Proposition 6. *For any lattice X and any mass assignment w on X, the function bel_w is a belief function.*

Proof. Let w be a mass assignment on X. To each $x \in X$, we associate the set $X(x) = \{t : t \leq x\}$. We know that $x \leq y$ implies $X(x) \subseteq X(y)$, $X(x) \cup X(y) \subseteq X(x \vee y)$ and $X(x) \cap X(y) = X(x \wedge y)$. Consider the Boolean lattice 2^X together with the following weight distribution: $w'(A) = w(x)$ whenever $A = X(x)$ for some $x \in X$, and $w'(A) = 0$ otherwise. Thus we get $\mathrm{bel}_w(x) = \mathrm{bel}_{w'}(X(x))$. For $(x_1, \ldots, x_k) \in X^k$, we have

$$
\begin{aligned}
\mathrm{bel}_w(x_1 \vee \ldots \vee x_k) &= \mathrm{bel}_{w'}(X(x_1 \vee \ldots \vee x_k)) \\
&\geq \mathrm{bel}_w(X(x_1) \cup \ldots \cup X(x_k)) \\
&\geq \sum_{J \subseteq K, J \neq \emptyset} (-1)^{|J|+1} \mathrm{bel}_{w'}(\cap_{j \in J} X(x_j)).
\end{aligned}
$$

But $\mathrm{bel}'_w(\cap_{j \in J} X(x_j)) = \mathrm{bel}_{w'}(X(\wedge_{j \in J} x_j)) = \mathrm{bel}_w(\wedge_{j \in J} x_j)$, whence the result follows. $\square$

Lemma 6. *If the weight distributions w and w' are such that $\mathrm{bel}_w = \mathrm{bel}_{w'}$, then $w = w'$.*

Proof. It is sufficient to consider, for two possible weight distributions w and w', an element minimal among the elements x that fulfills $w(x) \neq w'(x)$. $\square$

3.3 Invertible belief functions

We say that a belief function is *invertible* when there exists a mass assignment w such that $f = \mathrm{bel}_w$. By the preceding remark, the weight distribution associated with an invertible belief function is unique. If $f = \mathrm{bel}_w$, we shall say that f is *supported* by $\mathrm{Foc}(w)$.

The invertibility of the belief function f can be tested with the set of linear inequalities involving the Möbius function μ of the lattice X

$$
(I) \qquad \sum_{0 \leq x \leq t} f(x) \mu(x, t) \geq 0.
$$

3.4 Linear believes

Proposition 7. *Let X be a lattice. Then the following four assertions are equivalent:*

(i) X is linearly ordered,
(ii) Every capacity on X is an invertible belief function,
(iii) Every capacity on X is a belief function,
(iv) Every capacity on X is convex.

Proof. Assume that $X = \{x_1, \ldots, x_n\}$ is linearly ordered with $\underline{1} = x_1 \leq x_2 \leq \ldots \leq x_n = 0$. Let f be a capacity on X. Set $w(x_i) = f(x_i) - f(x_{i-1})$, for $2 \leq i \leq n$, and $w(x_0) = 0$. Then clearly w is a mass assignment, and

$f = \text{bel}_w$. Hence, (i) implies (ii) and we have just to show that (iv) implies (i). Assume that X is not linearly ordered. Then there exist two incomparable elements x and y of X. We have $x \wedge y \notin \{x, y\}$ and $x \vee y \notin \{x, y\}$. Define the function f on X by $f(t) = 0$ if $t \leq x$ or $t \leq y$, and $f(t) = 1$ otherwise. Clearly f is a capacity, but is not convex. □

4 Necessity functions

4.1 Basic results

Following the terminology introduced by Dubois and Prade (1985), we call a *necessity function* on the lattice X a real valued function f defined on X such that $f(\underline{0}) = 0$, $f(\underline{1}) = 1$, and

$$(N) \qquad f(x \wedge y) = \min(f(x), f(y)).$$

Equality (N) implies the monotonicity of f. Thus, a necessity function f is a capacity and $f(x \vee y) \geq \max(f(x), f(y))$. A capacity on a linearly ordered set is clearly a necessity function, whence a belief function. Proposition 7 generalizes this observation.

Recall that a *chain* of the ordered set X is a subset C of X linearly ordered by the induced order.

Proposition 8. *For a real valued function f defined on the lattice X such that $f(\underline{0}) = 0$ and $f(\underline{1}) = 1$, the following two assertions are equivalent:*

(i) f is an invertible belief function supported by a chain of X,
(ii) f is a necessity function.

Proof. (i) implies (ii). Assume that C is a chain of X and consider the sets $C(x) = \{t \in C : t \leq x\}$. Assertion (ii) will come from the following facts: for $x, y \in X$, $C(x \wedge y) = C(x) \cap C(y)$ and $C(x) \subseteq C(y)$, or $C(y) \subseteq C(x)$. Assume that $C(x) \subseteq C(y)$, then $\min(f(x), f(y)) = f(x)$ and $f(x \wedge y) = \sum_{t \in C(x \wedge y)} w(t) = \sum_{t \in C(x)} w(t) = f(x)$. (ii) implies (i) is an immediate consequence of the following lemma. □

Lemma 7. *Let M be a finite meet semilattice and let f be a non-negative real valued function defined on M satisfying equality (N). Then there exists a chain C of M and a non-negative real valued function g defined on C such that $f(x) = \sum_{t \in C, t \leq x} g(t)$.*

Proof. Denote by $\mu_1 < \mu_2 < \ldots < \mu_p$ the values taken by f. We shall prove the result by induction on p.

If $p = 1$, then f is a constant and we get the result with $C = \{\underline{0}\}$ and $g(\underline{0}) = \mu_1$.

Assume that $p > 1$ and consider the subset $M_2 = \{x \in M : f(x) \geq \mu_2\}$. From equality (5), M_2 is a meet semilattice and the function f_2 defined on M_2

by $f_2(x) = f(x) - \mu_1$ satisfies the condition (N). By induction, there exists a chain C' of M_2 and a non-negative function g' defined on C' such that, for each $x \in M_2$, $f(x) = \sum_{t \in C', t \leq x} g'(t)$. We get the result with $C = C' \cup \{0\}$ and the function g defined by $g(\underline{0}) = \mu_1$ and $g(t) = g'(t)$ otherwise. $\qquad \square$

Proposition 7 characterizes the meet semilattice homomorphisms of X into the real interval $[0, 1]$. It is worth-noticed that a necessity function will not, in general, satisfy the dual equality $f(x \vee y) = \max(f(x), f(y))$.

4.2 Boolean believes

A *Boolean capacity* on the lattice X is a capacity f such that $f(x) \in 0, 1$, for each $x \in X$. We denote by $B(X)$ the set of all Boolean capacities on X. For $f \in B(X)$ we denote by $X[f]$ the set $\{x \in X : f(x) = 1\}$. Obviously, $X[f]$ is a final subset of X, i.e., $x \in X[f]$ and $x \leq y$ implies $y \in X[f]$. Conversely, the characteristic function of a final subset of X is a Boolean capacity.

The set $B(X)$ can be ordered by $f \leq f'$ whenever $f(x) \leq f'(x)$ for each $x \in X$.

Clearly, $f \leq f'$ if and only if $X[f] \subseteq X[f']$. Thus, $B(X)$ is a distributive lattice isomorphic to the distributive lattice of all non trivial final subsets of X. In particular, if α and ω denote respectively the smallest and the greatest element of $B(X)$, we have $X[\alpha] = \{\underline{1}\}$ and $X[\omega] = X \setminus \{\underline{0}\}$.

Recall that a *filter* of a lattice X is a final subset Y of X such that $x, y \in Y$ implies $x \wedge y \in Y$. We shall show that only two cases can occur for a Boolean capacity:

1) $X[f]$ is not a filter and f is not 2-monotone.
2) $X[f]$ is a filter and f is a belief function.

Proposition 9. *Let f be a Boolean capacity on X. The following five assertions are equivalent:*

 (i) f *is 2-monotone,*
 (ii) $X[f]$ *is a filter,*
 (iii) f *is a necessity function,*
 (iv) f *is an invertible belief function,*
 (v) f *is a belief function.*

Proof. (i) implies (ii). If $x, y \in X[f]$ then $x \wedge y \in X[f]$ follows from the inequality $f(x) + f(y) \leq f(x \wedge y) + f(x \vee y)$.

(ii) implies (iii). Assume that $X[f]$ is a filter. Then for $x, y \in X$ we have $x \notin X[f]$ and $y \notin X[f]$ imply $x \wedge y \notin X[f]$; $x \notin X[f]$ and $y \in X[f]$ imply $x \wedge y \notin X[f]$; $x \in X[f]$ and $y \in X[f]$ imply $x \wedge y \in X[f]$. These assertions may be summarized into $f(x \wedge y) = \min(f(x), f(y))$.

(iii) implies (iv) is obvious as well as *(iv) implies (v)* and *(v) implies (i).* $\qquad \square$

References

1. Allais (1953), Le comportement de l'homme rationnel devant le risque: critique des postulats et axiomes de l'école américaine, *Econometrica* 21, 503-546.
2. M. Barbut and B. Monjardet (1971), *Ordre et classification, algèbre et combinatoire*, Paris: Hachette.
3. G. Birkhoff (1967), *Lattice Theory*, Providence: Math. Amer. Society (2nd edition).
4. A. Chateauneuf (1994), Combination of compatible belief functions and relation of specificity, in: *Advances in the Dempster-Shafer Theory of Evidence*, Wiley, 97-114.
5. A. Chateauneuf and J.-Y.Jaffray (1989), Some characterisations of the lower probabilities and other monotone capacities through the use of Möbius inversion, *Mathematical Social Sciences* 17, 263-283.
6. A. Chateauneuf and J.-Y. Jaffray (1994), Local Möbius transform of monotone capacities, in: Klimont and Weber (eds.) *Uncertainty measures*.
7. G. Choquet (1953), Théorie des capacités, *Annales de l'Institut Fourier* 5, 131-295.
8. A.P. Dempster (1967), Upper and lower probabilities induced by a multivalued mapping, *Ann. Math. Stat.* 38, 325-339.
9. A.P. Dempster (1976), A generalization of bayesian inference, *J. Roy. Stat. Soc. Ser. B* 30, 205-247.
10. D. Dubois, J.C. Fodor, H. Prade and M. Roubens (1996), Aggregation of decomposable measures with application to utility theory, *Theory and Decision* 41, 59-95.
11. D. Dubois and H. Prade (1985), *Théorie des possibilités*, Paris: Masson
12. J. C. Fodor, J.-L. Marichal and M. Roubens (1995), Characterization of the ordered weighted averaging operators, *IEEE Trans. Fuzzy Syst.* 3, 2, 236-240.
13. J.C. Fodor and M. Roubens (1994), *Fuzzy Preference Modelling And Multicriteria Decision Support*, Dorbrecht: Kluwer.
14. J.C. Fodor and M. Roubens (1995), Possibilistic mixtures and their applications to qualitative utility theory I : Aggregation of possibility measures, in: G. de Cooman, D. Ruan and E.E. Kerre (eds), *Foundations and Applications of Possibility Theory*, Singapore: World Scientific, 246-255.
15. J.C. Fodor, D. Dubois, H. Prade and M. Roubens (1997), Consensus for decomposable measures, in: J. Kacprzyk, M. Fedrizzi and H. Nurmi (eds.) *Consensus under Fuzziness*, Dordrechet: Kluwer, 191-210.
16. M. Grabisch (1995), Fuzzy integral in multicriteria decision making, *Fuzzy Sets and Systems* 69, 279-298.
17. M. Grabisch (1996), The application of fuzzy integrals in multicriteria decision making, *European J. of Operational Research* 89, 445-456.
18. J.-L. Marichal (1999a), On Sugeno integral as an aggregation function, *Fuzzy Sets and Systems*.
19. J.-L. Marichal (1999b), On Choquet and Sugeno integrals as aggregation functions,
20. J.-L. Marichal (1999c), Aggregation of interacting criteria by means of the discrete Choquet integral.
21. B. Monjardet (1981), Metric on partially ordered sets – A survey, *Discrete Math.* 35, 173-184.

22. G.C. Rota (1964), On the foundations of combinatorial theory I : Theory of Möbius functions, *Zeischrift für Wahrscheinlichkeit Theorie* 2, 4, 340-368.

23. L.J. Savage (1954), *The Foundations of Statistics*, New York: Wiley.

24. G. Shafer (1976), *A mathematical Theory of Evidence*, Princeton : Princeton University Press.

25. D. Schmeidler, 1986, Integral representation without additivity, *Proceedings of the American Mathematical Society* 97, 255-261.

26. Q. Schmeidler, 1989, Subjective probability and expected utility ithout additivity, *Econometrica* 57, 571-506.

27. A. Tversky and D. Kahneman, 1992, Advances in prospect theory: cumulative representation of uncertainty, *Journal of Risk and Uncertainty* 5, 297-323.

28. Ph. Vincke, 1989, *L'aide Multicritère à la Décision*, Bruxelles: Presses de l'Université Libre de Bruxelles.

29. J. Von Neumann and O. Morgenstern (1947), *Theory of Games and Economic Behavior*, Princeton: Princeton University Press.

30. L. Zadeh (1965), Fuzzy sets, *Information and Control* 7, 338-353.

Studies in Fuzziness and Soft Computing